gary
BURBANK
Voices in My Head

gary BURBANK
Voices in My Head

GREG HOARD

ORANGE FRAZER PRESS
Wilmington, Ohio

ISBN 978-1933197-517
Copyright © 2009 Greg Hoard

Additional copies of *Voices in my Head* may be ordered directly from:

Orange Frazer Press
P.O. Box 214
Wilmington, OH 45177

Telephone 1.800.852.9332 for price and shipping information.
Website: *www.orangefrazer.com*

Book design: *Jeff Fulwiler*
Editing, formatting, and text blocks: *John Baskin*
Production manager for text: *Chad Lambert*

Library of Congress Cataloging-in-Publication Data

Hoard, Greg, 1951-
  Voices in my head : the Gary Burbank story / by Greg Hoard.
      p. cm.
  Includes bibliographical references and index.
  ISBN 978-1-933197-51-7
  1. Burbank, Gary, 1941- 2. Radio broadcasters--United States--Biography.
I. Title.
  PN1991.4.B87H63 2009
  791.4402'8092--dc22
  [B]
                              2009015665

Once more for my wife, Cindy, whose encouragement
and trust is without end.
Time, now, for her and promises to be kept.

Table of contents

Foreword

Right up until the day he retired from WLW/Cincinnati, Gary Burbank was the most talented English-speaking radio personality in the world. (Somewhere there might have been a better jock in another language, so I need a little waffling room.) Burbank was the best of the best. The rest of us just sat back, admired him, and were proud to be in the same business.

Gary did more things brilliantly than any other radio person I know —and I know a heckuva lot of talented radio people.

With most celebrities, there's one good anecdote that perfectly launches an introduction to a biography. With Burbank, it would be the first time I ever heard him—No, wait. It should be when he was pulled over by the police while riding his motorcycle to work . . .

No, even more representative is how a comedy bit he created was ripped off through three incarnations and then was used as the opening scene in a hit movie that launched the career of . . .

Well, wait. I should make this more personal. The time he took something (ethically) that I wrote and turned it into a piece of comedy so brilliant that I didn't even realize it came from my own work.

Damn you, Gary Burbank. So many great stories.

When I was a DJ in a tiny market in Florida, my second year in the biz, my monthly issue of a magazine-on-vinyl-LP called *Programmer's Digest* arrived. Each issue featured audio samples of various radio people. This particular issue included a recording of Gary's last day at WAKY/Louisville.

Gary was ending a spectacular five-year run as the afternoon jock at WAKY. Now, when someone leaves a radio station to take another job elsewhere, traditionally the "left behind" station deals with the air talent's disappearance in this manner:

They act as though he never existed. *"Gary Burbank? Hmm . . . name doesn't sound familiar. But have you heard our new afternoon guy? He's great!"*

You can look it up up in *The Radio Book of Rules* under "What To Do When A Disc Jockey Leaves Your Station." Burbank, however, never got around to reading *The Radio Book of Rules*. On his last day at WAKY, an angry listener burst into the broadcast studio and shot Gary dead.

It was featured in *Programmer's Digest,* it was my introduction to the existence of Gary Burbank, and it made me realize not that there's something called "Theatre of the Mind" (I already knew that) or that it's possible to be creative and entertaining on radio (knew that, too), but that the ceiling of what is possible in radio is so much higher than I'd imagined.

Gary was so original that you can't say "Gary Burbank" and "radio" without including "original."

So original that occasionally he found himself accused of stealing a comedy piece that he himself created. For example, "The James Brown Car Alarm." A simple comedic idea that is fairly self explanatory: When the car alarm goes off, you hear James Brown's trademarked shriek. A funny little bit that popped into Gary's mind, out of his mouth, and into a radio microphone in Cincinnati.

A DJ in Toledo, Ohio, heard it and stole it. Not just for himself; he submitted it (as his own original creation) to the American Comedy Network—a syndicator of radio comedy. ACN unwittingly paid the thief for it, reproduced it, and provided the new version to its affiliates across the United States. One of those affiliates was a well-known Los Angeles disc jockey, who shrewdly (and ethically—he had paid for it) reproduced the entire piece with his own voice rather than the ACN announcer's voice.

Enter Bruce Willis. More specifically, the film that launched his movie career: *Blind Date.* To establish that the story took place in Los Angeles, the film opened with that well-known L.A. disc jockey doing the "James Brown Car Alarm" bit. Millions of moviegoers laughed heartily at that funny L.A. disc jockey, and Burbank no longer could do his own original creation without being accused of stealing it from the L.A. DJ.

Gary was a master of characters. ("Gilbert Gnarley" is a marvel.) Given the title of this book and Gary's creative influences being people such as Ernie Kovacs and Jonathan Winters, I guess now I'm expected to catalogue Burbank's many characters. But to me, even more impressive than Gary's characters is *his* character.

I've never heard anyone—not a listener, a co-worker, or a competitor—say a bad word about Gary Burbank. I've lost track of the number of times some radio jock has told me, "When I was just starting out, I called up Gary Burbank and he invited me to come by the station and he took the time to talk to me, had me sit in on the show. He was just so . . . so real."

His own character remained intact throughout all his years as a star. Maybe that's one of the things that enabled him to create and inhabit so many other fictional characters.

I'd never say this to his face—fortunately, he's kind of dumb and isn't likely to read this—but Gary is the nicest, most generous, most decent comedy genius I've ever known. "Character" is the one-word definition of Gary Burbank.

Yeah, sure, I'm proud to say we're friends. But even more so, I'm proud to have worked in the same business as this guy.

—Dan O'Day, Los Angeles author of *Personality Radio*,
radio talent coach, and former major-market radio personality

Acknowledgments

So much is owed to so many but, of course, the thanks must start with Gary Burbank, who answered my every call and allowed me to walk around in his life without putting up a single boundary. The phrase is cast about so often that it loses heft, but this book is about a truly good man.

Thanks, too, to Carol, Gary's wife, for putting up with the endless phone calls, messages, and visits to the house that weren't always convenient.

Special appreciation must be offered to Chad Lambert, who spent hours and hours transcribing tapes, searching through files and making phone calls on my behalf. Without his help, I would have never made it through. Many thanks go to Chad for his knowledge, accuracy, and expediency. He pointed out paths I would never have found.

To my daughter, Megan Christine Hoard, thanks for your wit, your research, and your innate sense for a good story and when a story goes too far or not far enough, and for constantly reminding me that one good adjective is better than three weak ones. God bless you, child.

Thanks to my publisher, Marcy Hawley, for her patience and her persistent smile when, in fact, she had ample reason for neither.

vOices in mY heaD
xvi

Prologue

Last call

An hour before, he careened around a radio studio in a flagrant display of the innate spirit that has fascinated, entertained—and bewildered—friends, family, and fans for years. Gassed up on Mountain Dew and nicotine gum, he shifted from once voice to another, from "pro-nouncer and creator of round, pear-shaped tones," as he puts it, to his protagonists: Howlin' Blind Muddy Slim, Gilbert Gnarley, Deuteronomy Skaggs, and Earl Pitts, Uhmerikan—just a few of those who crowd his mind and jostle about the studio.

He was live. He was on tape. He played guitar. He sang. He fenced with callers, joked with friends and co-workers in the studio. He opened another Mountain Dew, popped some more Nicorette. It was the last hour of his three-hour show, an afternoon of deft orchestration with ample space provided for callers like Jerry from Hamilton, who was waiting on a new set of teeth and shared his dental dilemma over the airwaves.

All of it was a zany, inventive hybrid of satire, parody, and improv. Gary Burbank and The BBC, The Broadbank Burbcasting Corporation being a frenzied throwback to the days of Ernie Kovacs and Jonathan Winters, when the evolving new medium of television was first beginning to supplant radio's internal imagery. Burbank, however took the madcap ad lib and improv of Kovacs and Winters backwards, layering their off-the-wall ingenuity onto the older medium. It was still radio, but radio that few had ever heard before. (Kovacs, for instance, said he worked on the "incongruity of sight against sound;" Burbank did him one better: he worked on the incongruity of sound against sound.)

Five days a week for twenty-seven years, Burbank turned it up and on for Cincinnati's 50,000-watt WLW radio station, the last stop on a career that began in Lake Providence, Louisiana, and took him from Jackson,

Mississippi to Memphis, Detroit, Louisville, New Orleans, and Tampa. Along the way there was both monetary and professional reward. Twice he received Billboard and Marconi Awards for Large Market Radio Personality of the Year. But now in his mid-60s, he had decided it was time to do the things he had been longing to do.

So there he was—Gary Burbank, "World-Wide Frivovalist and International Juke Artist"—tending his flowers. Armed with a garden hose and an old-fashioned, long-necked, five-gallon watering can, Burbank moved diligently from one bed to another, one hanging basket to the next.

His home, tucked away on a heavily wooded hillside near Alexandria, Kentucky, abounds with flowers and hummingbird feeders, which draw dozens of the tiny creatures so close and so seemingly tame that, occasionally, the whir of their wings thrills the ear like a sweet whisper.

He seemed perfectly out of place. For every artist, regardless of his art and eccentricities, needs a retreat. His home in Kentucky, a low-slung tribute to Frank Lloyd Wright, is one. He has another on the Rainbow River in North Central Florida where he sips Gentleman Jack over the rocks with old friends: Dave "Jesse James" Warnock, whom he has known since his radio days in Jackson; Lon Wadsworth, who wins Ernest Hemingway look-alike contests in Key West; and Mark Anderson, a gentlemanly Cuban, who—thanks to recent developments in international law and payments from Fidel Castro's government—finds himself suddenly and fabulously wealthy.

"Trouble is, he's nuts," says Burbank. "He used to work and then party. Now he doesn't have to work and he parties all the time, and he expects everybody to party with him. Besides that, he's always jumping up and doing these wild Latino dances when you least expect it. He scares me."

Burbank hopes to have another home soon, maybe out west, maybe in the mountains. "Some little old shack or something where I can just throw down for a few days if I want to," he says. After all the years of work, he thinks about what he wants to do. "When this is all done," he says, "I'm gonna load up the truck and go back to Memphis and Mississippi, drive all over the country and see old friends I've only been able to talk to over the phone . . . I'm a busy kinda guy but sometimes it's not good. Things get lost.

"I'm not gonna retire and sit in a rocking chair out front and smoke Pall Malls and drink coffee all day like Dad did. I'm gonna stay busy, but I'm gonna do the things I want to do: play my music, read, play golf, ride my motorcycle out west, sit and look at the mountains, go to Alaska. Go to the Caribbean. Get lost on some island. Fish all day."

Then, he stops and smiles, before turning his attention back to the flowers. "I want to stay drunk for three days. I can only stay drunk for two days now cause I got to be at work on Monday. You know, do whatever I damned well please.

Slight and surprisingly spry for a man in his mid-60s, Burbank wound up the hose, stored the watering can in the pool house, and returned with a bottle of beer in each hand. He's built like a second baseman, on the short side but sturdy; he moves like a welterweight, smooth and sneaky fast. If trouble arises, he's the little guy to watch out for. As a young man, he was never afraid to take it outside with anybody, but, he admitted, "there were times the decision was genuinely regrettable."

He was born William Eugene Purser, Jr., July 29, 1941, at the John Gaston Charity Hospital in Memphis and raised in Southwestern Tennessee and the Mississippi Delta, where he learned at an early age that no matter what you had or didn't have, honesty and civility were free and expected unless, of course, you were crossed. Unfairly cross a Southerner and civility was generally replaced by something hard upside the head: iron skillets, ashtrays, shovel handles, big old sticks, and the occasional bullet.

When his mother, Dorothy, tired of his William Purser's philandering, she sent Billy's biological father packing by hitting him squarely in the forehead with a large, glass ashtray. "She left him with something to remember us by," Burbank said, "a big, old scar. Laid his forehead flat open. Mother was an All-City pitcher in softball. I'm not sure my father was aware of that."

Every life experience—from the supper tables, cotton fields, and general stores in The Delta to the streets and clubs of Memphis—fueled and guided his humor, a frenetic blend of satire, irony, and wit. Through most of his career he stood in a space somewhere along with Robin Williams, but chicken fried; Jonathan Winters with a side order of gravy; and Brother Dave Gardner and a good red wine. Contrast and irony— that was the key.

He was hip and he was grounded, cool yet country, cosmopolitan, metropolitan, but never far removed from meat and potatoes.

"For my money," says Hall of Fame radio broadcaster Marty Brennaman, "he is one of the funniest men in America. But he has another great skill: when there is a crisis, whether its of a national nature like 9/11 or the riots in Cincinnati (in 2001), there is no one on the radio better than Burbank and no one I want to listen to more. He's a comedic genius. That's a fact, but in those circumstances, he's the voice of civility, intuition, and understanding.

"When the story or the subject is greater and more important than the Gary Burbank Show, he instinctively knows when to get out of the way. A lot of people in his position don't have that ability. It always has to be about them. Gary's not like that. He is one smart SOB and he's funny as hell."

Burbank has been offered jobs in New York and Los Angeles, but he always declined. "I've always been a lifestyle guy," he says. "I was just more comfortable in the south and the Midwest. Besides, one of the few times I was in New York my bag with all my clothes in it was stolen at a train station. I figured if you lived there, that kinda thing happened every day . . ."

People would say, 'He's a big duck in a little pond,' but he never looked at it that way. "People in this business waste a lot of energy worrying about image, and how where they are determines how important they are. 'Hey, I work in New York so I'm automatically better than the guy in Kansas City.' Is an apple pie made in New York better than one made in Tunica, Mississippi? Depends on the damned cook.

"All I wanted to do was put on the best show I could every day. We worked really hard at that. And, for the most part—up until the past few years—it was fun and I was happy here."

The sun had descended behind the tall oaks and maples that surround his home and a soft breeze was rolling in from the west when Burbank determined it was time for a return trip to the refrigerator.

"Ten, maybe, fifteen years ago everything began to change in radio," he said, setting two more beers on the table. "It was like one morning I wake up and—bam!—the world of AM radio was totally different. It was like, 'Where the hell am I?' How did this happen?' We go from telling jokes and playing a few records, having some fun to . . . what?"

The thought seemed to give him uncomfortable pause. He reached for another piece of nicotine gum. "I'm not sure," he said, finally. "I'm not sure I fit anymore. When it comes to comedy, I'm not smash-mouth. I hold to my principles of having that twist and irony. What have we got now? Angry, middle-aged, white guys spewing conservative ideology and if you are not with them, then forget it—you're wrong. There's no room for debate or discourse or nuance. Today's radio is more—what's the right word— truculent? Abrasive?

"Put it this way. If no one is bleeding at the end of a joke today, what's funny? You got to fool somebody or make a fool of somebody. It's not in my nature. If I'm going to fool somebody, I will do it as Gilbert Gnarley and I will be the fool, and the person I'm talking to is going to be laughing along with everyone else."

There was no bitterness in his voice, only the resolve that he had heard enough; that it was time to leave the party. "It's just that the way I think doesn't seem to be mainstream anymore, and in radio you have to be mainstream. That's one reason I'm leaving."

Not long ago he was named one of the most influential talk show hosts in the country. He was shocked by the news. "My first reaction was: 'I'm not a talk show host, I'm an entertainer,'" he said. "Then I started thinking: *I'm a freaking dinosaur. I'm a leftover. I'm a throwback to Ernie Kovacs . . . people like that*. I like to make people laugh, but I like to make them think, too. In all good comedy there is room for thought."

With the angry tide of talk radio mounting, Burbank felt increasingly out of place. Going to the studio became a chore. "Everyday," he said, "I felt like I was on a road trip. I didn't feel like I was playing in front of the home crowd because the home crowd had become this hardcore inner-circle. I would look around, and no one was laughing at my stuff any more. I knew—I hoped—people were laughing at home and in their cars, but the people I worked with weren't laughing. They were laughing at the stick-in-the-eye stuff. Doing anything, saying anything—whether it's right or true, whether they believe it or not—just to light up the switchboard, anything to evoke a response: 'Yeah! They love me. Yeah! They hate me. Isn't it great!' That's all that matters.

"That's where radio stands and I don't fit. I don't want to sound bitter because I am not bitter. I just don't like what I see right now. The thing is, when it comes to my kind of comedy, the pendulum has begun to swing the other way. Watch television and comics these days. Ten years ago you had Sam Kennison screaming obscenities. People were laughing like crazy, and there was rarely anything clever about what he said.

"Now look what's going on: Jon Stewart and *The Daily Show*, *The Colbert Report*. Even though *South Park* seems crass, look at the satire involved . . . those people are very clever. The people watching this stuff are the 30-year-olds. Their 45-year-old big brothers and sisters are still into this smash-mouth, sophomoric crap. This younger generation is more intelligent about their humor. Maybe it will come all the way around—I hope."

The irony was that after announcing his retirement in March of 2007, he felt rejuvenated. He wasn't sure why. Maybe it was a product of finality, he thought. "Maybe," he said, "I just didn't give a crap about pleasing those people anymore or feeling like I had to please them." The edge returned. He was loose and slippery. Old friends and listeners began to call. "One guy called me and said, 'Damn, now that you are quitting, you're funnier than you ever were.' I don't know that it's true, but it feels like it and it feels good."

Darkness had fallen. Burbank had not bothered to turn a light on, but you could hear the smile on his face. Whippoorwills and crickets sang in the woods. He said nothing for a moment, then he sighed. "Sure is peaceful out here," he said. "We love to get out on the river. We fish a little, drink a little, tell some stories—lots of lies—and just float. Sometimes someone will ask me if I'm embellishing. I say, 'Of course, I'm embellishing. That's what I do. I'm a professional embellisher! Why would I change now?'"

He wondered what it would be like after his last show December 21st; wondered what it would be like to wake up in the morning and not rush to the studio. "Mostly," he said, "I wonder what it will be like to wake up and realize that I don't have to be funny.

"You get to be my age and you start asking yourself, 'How much longer will I live?' And, you start thinking about what you need to do." He's faced enough health problems that he recognizes his mortality and he has certainly availed himself of the many indulgences life has offered. "Oh, man," he said, "I'm lucky I've lived this long. This book should be titled: *I Ought to Be in Jail*."

At that point, the notebook was put away and the tape recorder turned off. We sat in the darkness sipping beer and talking about baseball and mutual friends, music, and comedy. We talked about his characters and where they came from, and one by one, they began to creep into the conversation, Burbank sitting in the darkness floating from Earl Pitts—who was based on his stepfather Raymond Woods—to Deuteronomy Skaggs, a product of countless evangelical ministers he came to know in Memphis and Mississippi. We laughed until our faces hurt.

Going back to the days when he would sit at the supper table spinning yarns for his mother and his stepfather, Gary Burbank has loved a good audience.

"Yeah, it's all their fault," he said. "They indulged me. They enabled me. But what else could they do? Hell, that was the only thing I was any good at. Most of my life I have been cuttin' up and telling jokes. I wonder, when it's all done, if I'm gonna think, *Have I wasted my life?* I don't think so. I hope not.

"You think?"

Part I
Growing up funny

Chapter one

Miss Dot, an eyeful

She got married early, divorced, then tried again. Which was followed by another *divorce*. Whatever she was looking for seemed not to be in sight. In the meantime, though, she had plenty to do: there was Billy and Glenna.

People were drawn to Dot Wells. There was something about

her bearing: graceful, unhurried, as if nature had given her more purchase on the moment than was afforded most other folks.

She was a striking woman with penetrating brown eyes and hair the color of a pine cone. She was playful in spirit, at odds here and there with the doctrines of her Southern Baptist upbringing, a matter of no small note to her parents, Marshall and Kitty Wells. Dot wore jeans when she could and shorts when the days turned hot and close in Memphis, and it was a mystery to no one who knew her that she was proud of her looks.

Kitty Robertson Wells, the matriarch of the family, worried about her third child. She was a smart girl, good at about anything she tried. She was witty and funny and sometimes Kitty hid behind a neatly folded handkerchief her amusement at what Dot said or did. Other times, though, she fretted that Dot's tongue—so quick in response—danced too closely to the profane, if not in word, surely in thought.

If Marshall Wells, a sturdy, gentle man who sang lullabies to his children at bedtime, had concerns about his daughter, he didn't express them. Of course, Marshall, a chrome-fitter who had moved his family from Halls, Tennessee, to Memphis to find better work, didn't say much about anything. And while he dutifully escorted his wife to church on Sunday and prayer meeting on Wednesday, he, like Dot, strained against the whole of Southern Baptist teachings.

In the evenings, he liked to sit in his chair in the front room and smoke Kent cigarettes. He sang cowboy songs, deep, slow and gentle: "Yellow Rose of Texas," "Abilene," "Do Not Forsake Me."

Once in a while, around Christmas—much to Kitty's dismay— he would pick up a bottle and add a slug or two to the eggnog, but only on Christmas and with the complete awareness that he would suffer Kitty's scorn.

After William Purser, you'd have thought Dot would have seen Junior Askins coming. She didn't though. He wasn't a terrible guy, just not husband material. And one more goodbye guy. And for Dot, that was it.

When the men started giggling in the kitchen and the language turned off-color, Kitty was apt to do more than put her foot down. Everybody knew that. In fact, Kitty's ire was probably more dreaded, immediately at least, than the preacher's warnings about the evil of drink and its inevitable path to oblivion. The fires of hell were distant, ethereal, like God's will. Kitty, white hair pulled up in a bun, apron around her waist and wooden spoon in hand, was right there in the house, quietly whistling "Rock of Ages."

Kitty held stern rule in the Wells's home at 868 Rayner Street, and all the kids—Ginny, Ed, Dot, and Ann—abided by her word. But Memphis was a big, roaring, rattling city filled with a reckless spirit. New worlds—and some old ones—were right around the corner. The churches were filled on Sundays, but the nighttime held every temptation known to man. Following a higher calling in Memphis, birthplace of "the Blues" and all the cultural, racial, and social experiences that gave it life, was the exception rather than the rule.

Kitty Wells may have been devout in her faith and beliefs, but not blindly so. At heart, she was a realist, a quality she shared with Marshall. They worked hard to provide for their children. They spoke to them of cautions and risks, knowing all the while they couldn't shield them forever. The children would grow up and make their own decisions. Meanwhile, Marshall worked and hoped, and Kitty prayed.

In her late teens, Dot was an eyeful. That was when she met and married William Eugene Purser, a handsome ex-policeman who bounced from one job to another. Speculation was that while Dot thought she loved the man, her primary motivation was to get out of her parents' house and on with her own life.

William and Dot Purser had two children: William Eugene, Jr., and two years later, Glenna Ruth. Billy was spunky and rambunctious. Glenna was sweet. Their biological father turned out to be a rounder. After one tryst or another, Dot's temper flared and she demonstrated the arm that made her All-City in softball, chucking a heavy, glass ashtray with deadly accuracy, catching William Purser squarely in the forehead. That was the end of that marriage.

Years later, during happier times, Dot informed her children that William Purser had never corrected his straying ways. He was married, she told them, thirteen different times. "Apparently," she said, a glint in her eye, "he didn't believe in one-night stands."

She and the kids moved back to Rayner Street for a while, but it wasn't long before Dot met Junior Askins, which led to another ill-fated marriage. Askins worked, but he didn't like it, preferring to lay out at every opportunity and with every possible excuse. Even so, things seemed normal, at least for a time.

On the day Billy was to start first grade, Dot combed his hair and steered him into a freshly pressed shirt, new britches, and a dandy set of suspenders, which—because Billy was so slight—she had to rig with safety pins.

Askins offered to usher Billy to school, rowing him across the Wolf River to Leroy Pope Elementary School on Mud Island. Other children either lived on the island or used the ferry. The teachers were so taken with Billy's appearance that they immediately placed him in the advanced class. Surely, a young man so well turned out would be a credit to Leroy Pope Elementary.

All went well until Billy sensed a rumbling in his stomach. Soon, he was shuddering and sweating. He asked his teacher to be excused, but she was slow in response. When she finally relented, Billy made it to the restroom only to discover that his suspenders had been booby-trapped, secured to his britches in some maniacal manner that defied six-year-old fingers.

Dreamy Billy

Beginning at an early age, young Billy Purser had an eye for material. It didn't much matter where it came from, either. Just as long as it was some impossible kind of story. Most of them, though, came from Billy himself.

He was violently sick but couldn't get his pants down. Nature, in its customary way, was oblivious. The consequences—a virtual eruption—appalled him. First, he was scared, then he was embarrassed. He worried about soiling his new clothes. He was afraid his mother would be angry. Since he didn't know what to do, he huddled in the boys' room, afraid to leave.

An understanding janitor ultimately discovered Billy and, finding his teacher, explained Billy's plight. They helped Billy clean himself up, but a new problem loomed: what would he wear?

After a thorough search of Leroy Pope Elementary, someone found a pirate's costume left over from a play—a blowsy shirt and pants, belt with enormous buckle—everything but sword and eye-patch, which Billy desperately wanted.

The other kids giggled and gawked at the boy in the pirate suit and Billy played along as well as he could. When school was dismissed, Askins was there to row him back home. They presented quite a picture, Askins as crew on their tiny vessel, rowing into port the little buccaneer, who was perched in the bow as though he would momentarily take Memphis.

From that day forward, Billy had a great love for pirate suits and costumes of all kinds—except those requiring suspenders. And when he returned to school the next day, he found himself removed from the gifted class and placed with the regular kids. Years later, recalling his early time as a pirate, he thought the move had been, on their part, an accurate assessment.

Dot's life with Junior Askins soon lost what small humor it may have had. Little inclined toward work, Junior became even less so. Sometimes there wasn't enough food. He stayed out until all hours of the night and slept most of the day. He left the house mysteriously, offering no hint as to where he was going.

Kitty Wells had a notion things were not going well for Dot. There was talk that Askins had fallen in with thieves who were stealing from one store during the night, then selling their cache to other merchants during the day. In her heart, Kitty Wells knew nothing productive would come of the relationship between her daughter and Askins. In her estimation, there was nothing beyond his winning smile but trouble.

Having a notion things were not going well for Dot, she made an impromptu call on her and the kids. Billy rushed to his grandmother.

"Mamaw," he said, "I'm hungry."

"Lord, child, you don't want for nothing," Kitty said. "We'll get this taken care of."

That evening, Marshall came to the house.

"Get your things," he said to Dot. "You and the children are coming home."

Marshall was quiet but intense. He was not a man to argue with and Junior Askins didn't.

Marshall carried little Glenna all the way back to Rayner Street. Billy walked beside him, holding his hand. That night, and for nights to come, Kitty Wells whistled and hummed her hymns and cooked big dinners: pork chops and fried apples, meatloaf, mashed potatoes, crackling corn bread, brains and eggs, jowl bacon, beans and ham hock with green onions and fresh tomatoes, greens of all kinds—turnip, kale, spinach, collard—beets and berries; rice served with spoonfuls of sugar and cinnamon, cantaloupe, and pitcher after pitcher of iced sweet tea.

Billy and Glenna loved the biscuits and the gravy: red gravy, cream gravy, sausage gravy. When he was older, Billy was surprised to learn that gravy wasn't a beverage.

At night, after dinner, Marshall sat quietly, sipping coffee, saying nothing much at all, lighting one of his Kents, taking the first long pull and then allowing the cigarette to burn down to the filter.

Glenna and Billy sat and watched the burning cigarette and wondered when the ash would fall. They were fascinated by the growing ash. *When will it fall?* they wondered, enthralled by the smallest, most insignificant thing in the room.

For a time, Marshall and Kitty provided them security and stability. Dot provided love and comfort. At night, Dot sang the old lullabies, the ones Kitty had sung to her:

A tiny turned-up nose
His lips just like a rose.
So sweet from head to toes
That little boy of mine.

No one will ever know
Just what his coming has meant
Because I love him so
He is something heaven has sent.

Dot said Marshall made them up, but Glenna was never sure. She never heard them anywhere else, though. In what seemed to be a hundred years later, Glenna's own granddaughters would sing the same songs to their babies. She could not express how pleased she was by this.

Chapter Two

Raymond

When she first met him, he was a short order cook, just back from *The War*. He was lanky, with big ears, not much to look at. But he was smart and kind. But she had done her time with the good-looking ones. She was ready for a change.

From the time she was a little girl, Dot wondered about what

was beyond her front door, out beyond the neighborhood, down those roads that led to cities she had only read about: St. Louis, New Orleans, Little Rock, Dallas, even up north to, say, Chicago. She imagined herself living in one of those places, part of a life she could only imagine.

Surrounded by folks of a practical mind, Dot allowed herself to consider circumstances beyond her immediate reach. She browsed through books and magazines, picturing herself in fine dresses, riding in shiny cars. She sensed something destined just for her.

The world was big, she understood, and in it anything might be possible.

She liked walking barefoot, dust surrounding her toes, forming a natural cushion. She liked walking in high heels, the click of their sound and the feel of her stockings. She liked putting the stockings on and smoothing them out, watching herself in the mirror, the dark seam perfectly aligned up the curve of her calf.

As she grew older, she sometimes looked at herself in the mirror and smiled at her dreams. At such moments, she longed for all the contradictions: risk and adventure, comfort and security—everything at once, both known and unknown. Sometimes she thought about the

story she had heard from her grandparents, Modica Date and Amerika Wells. The first time they crossed the river to Arkansas her grandma stood in the stern of the boat and waved goodbye, and when she started to cry and someone asked what was wrong, she said, "I'm waving goodbye to America, only country I have ever known." The story always made Dot smile, but it made her sad, too.

Raymond could have won an Abraham Lincoln look-alike contest, but his substance went far beyond his looks. It didn't take Dot long to see that. He was kind and smart, he liked music, and there was an added bonus: he loved Billy and Glenna, too.

Sometimes she cursed herself for her frivolous dreams. After two failed marriages and forced to rely once again on her parents, she began to lose hope. The past few years had not been easy. If her sense of trust had not been broken, it was surely dented. After William Purser and Junior Askins, she was smarter, and yes, a little harder.

She had taken work at the Ferry Morris Seed Company but only part time. Kitty and Marshall insisted the kids needed her more than they needed a little extra money. Work was steady for Marshall, and Kitty worked as a seamstress, doing alterations at Lowenstein's Department Store. Kitty assured Dot that things would work out fine, and Marshall nodded in agreement.

Kitty did worry, though. She didn't feel entirely right about being back living at home, and she worried about the kids. They needed a father and, so far, she had not made good choices: one rounder, one deadbeat and petty thief—probably headed for the state pen or, worse, Parchman Farm. How could her judgment have been so wrong—not once, but twice?

As bad as she was feeling about her life, however, she never let the children see that she was saddened. She made certain she had a smile on her face when she walked into the house. She played with Billy and Glenna, laughed with them and told them stories. Every night, she tucked them in and sang them to sleep.

When she was feeling particularly blue, she took long walks, just to think. Often, after work, she stopped at the Wil-A-Mar Café at the corner of Willet and LaMar, took a booth, ordered something to drink, and wondered what would become of her and the kids.

That's where he first saw her. She was a fine-looking woman, always alone. She caught his fancy even though he hadn't shared a word with her. He had seen her maybe three or four times, always in the same manner—having coffee, maybe mincing at a piece of pie—and he found himself wondering about her all the time. Was she married? Why did she seem so preoccupied? Could he muster the courage to go talk to her? Even if he did, would a woman like that have anything to do with a galoot like him? He had no idea, but he promised himself the next time he saw her, he was going to say something. That's all there was to it.

Raymond Woods was just back from the war. He had been a gunner's mate on the *U.S.S. New Jersey.* He had helped lay fire on Saipan, Tinian, Guam, Formosa, Leyte, Luzon, and Iwo Jima. He was there when Admiral William F. Halsey came aboard and the *New Jersey* was named the flagship of the Third Fleet.

When the war was over, he made his way home, riding the bus, catching a ride here and there, seeing mountains, deserts, big cities, little towns, watching the country turn from brown to green—making his way from California back to Water Valley, Mississippi. Raymond loved the little town and everyone in it—he probably knew each of them by name because few moved in and fewer moved away. He wondered if there was anything new in Water Valley and then he decided probably not, which was fine with him.

How many times, when exploding shells lit up the night, had he covered his ears and eyes, longing for the peace and quiet of Mississippi nights: frogs croaking, bats crying, katydids singing, the wind sighing through the elms and oaks after a hot day. God, how he dreamt of lemonade on the porch, dogs barking, and somebody coming down the dirt road from Paris playing a fiddle and singing "Possum Up a Gum Tree." Then, after a while, everybody would lay down the instruments and share a homegrown melon, laughing, talking, juice running down their chins, spitting seeds into the grass. (Watermelon was Water Valley's one claim to fame. It produced the sweetest watermelons in the world. That's what folks said, anyway, and experience left little room for doubt.)

He was drawn to the simplicity of Water Valley, but he was pulled in another direction, too. After the Navy, Raymond wanted more than home had to offer. He wanted to make a good living, and he didn't want to work cotton. Dragging those big, white sacks down one row after another broke many a young man before his time. It was one thing to own a plantation and quite another to sharecrop, as his family had done for years. Raymond hoped that his lot was somewhere between those extremes and surely—dear God—away from cotton.

He'd been home a while, helping around the place, when he'd gathered up his courage and told his folks that he was going to head up to Memphis and look for work. Pap Woods was a hard man, but he allowed that it wasn't every man's place to walk a field staring at a mule's ass from daylight to dark. He told Raymond to remember his way home. That's where they'd be if Raymond found out the city wasn't all it was cracked up to be.

Once in Memphis, it didn't take him long to find work as a short-order cook at the Wil-A-Mar and now, here he was, wiping his hands on his apron and asking a buddy to cover his orders for just a minute, all the while mustering up the nerve to walk up to the brown-haired woman sitting in the booth.

He walked up behind her and looked over her shoulder. She made no sign that she heard him. She was looking at a picture of a pretty little girl with curls, maybe 4 years old and wearing a Sunday dress.

"If you had a little boy that cute, I believe," he said, "I would ask you to marry me." At first, she was startled—almost as startled as he was that those were the first words out of his mouth. Dot Wells studied him for a moment, standing tall and awkward, a big, honest smile on his face.

"That's my little girl, Glenna Ruth, and this," she said, turning to the next picture, "is my little boy, Billy, my oldest. So I guess we're getting married."

Not only pretty but quick, too, he thought. He stole as much time as he could from the kitchen, explaining to her that he was home from the war and working at the cafe until he could find something better. She listened, thinking that this man was not much to look at—big nose, big ears, eyes kind of mournful except when he smiled. He reminded her of old pictures of Abraham Lincoln, lanky and tall. She thought, too, how she had learned that good looks didn't always count for much.

Then he said he had to get back to the kitchen or get fired, but he was wondering: could he call on her some time?

And she smiled and said yes.

Dot and Raymond kept regular company for a long while. After Purser and Askins, she wasn't about to make any hasty moves. Mostly, the two of them talked. Raymond told her about growing up in Mississippi, how he was trying to become a fireman. His words were slow and soft. They reminded her of a spring shower.

When Raymond came to call, he paid nearly as much attention to Billy and Glenna as he did to Dot. After a time, she came to believe in the sheer goodness of the man—thoughtful, funny, always telling her about things she didn't know or hadn't thought about. His favorite poet was Robert Service and he could quote entire stanzas from "The Cremation of Sam McGee:"

There are strange things done in the midnight sun
By the men who moil for gold;
The Arctic trails have their secret tales
That would make your blood run cold . . .

He loved that one the most, but the new poets—the Beats, they were called—had caught his attention, too. He had learned about them when he mustered out of the service and spent some time in California. Funny thing was, their poetry didn't rhyme, but he read them anyway.

Raymond asked Dot if she had read Aristotle or Plato. She only smiled. He liked to read what they had to say, too, even though he didn't always understand what they were talking about.

He told her about music from the Delta. He called it "the Blues." He said some people called it "Race Music" and he said it was the music of the future, the first tick toward a time that would be different from anything they had known.

He said—almost embarrassed by the confession—that he wrote songs himself, but wasn't sure they were any good. He didn't foresee getting rich writing songs for Robert Johnson or Hank Williams or Frankie Lane. He didn't imagine that he would replace William Handy as a songwriter:

> *Cornstalk fiddle*
> *Shoestring bow*
> *Broke in the middle*
> *Jumped up Joe...*

She laughed, telling him her daddy, Marshall, wrote songs, little ditties, and some had even made the radio. See, he said, something else in common.

Before bed, Glenna and Billy sat and listened to them talk. Billy wondered why his teachers weren't as entertaining. Glenna liked the sound of his voice.

After a time, Dot decided on Raymond Woods. Homely? Lord, yes, but he was as steady and deep as her first two husbands had been shifty and shallow.

In the summer of 1948, Raymond Woods and Dot Wells were married. Billy was 7. Glenna was 5. It wasn't long before they were calling him "Dad." He was the only father they really knew. Even as children, they knew Raymond had given their mother something she had lost. Something had come back to her, something that had been missing. She had a light in her eyes again.

Raymond had brought their mother home, and Billy and Glenna loved him for that. They loved him for who he was, too—always there with a cup of coffee, black with sugar; a pack of Pall Malls within ready reach, always there with a story, yet never too busy to listen to theirs.

He liked stories. He liked history. Stories and pictures, he told Billy and Glenna, were how we learn: captured memory, funny, sad, tall, all of it true to some degree, telling us who we are and where we've been. He didn't say it just so, but that's what they learned from him.

"He was a gunner's mate," Billy would say, years later. "A sharecropper, a short-order cook, but foremost a Mississippi renaissance man. He introduced us to stuff we would never have known. There was always something in our home—creativity, humor, a search for new things. That's what he brought to us."

Raymond rubbed off on everyone. Billy's stories became more elaborate. Glenna excelled at school and decided she could do anything she put her mind to. Dot, always drawn to art, started sketching, first in pencil and then charcoal. True to his word, Raymond became a fireman, passed all the tests, and they moved to a better neighborhood. Glenna and Billy had always shared a room, but Raymond said they were getting older so he gathered friends, hammer, nails and lumber, and added a room to the house. The children would have separate rooms. They would have as much as he and Dot could provide. Raymond loved the kids, felt fortunate to have them.

He liked sweet tea on sweltering days. He had no use for booze. He didn't gamble, didn't philander, but he had an inveterate passion for Pall Malls. At Fire Station 16, he became noted for his cooking—his signature spaghetti and chili—and the good luck Billy brought to the crew. Billy visited several times a month and not once was there a fire run. Soon, it became a standing joke. "You got to bring the boy down more often," the fireman said to Raymond. "He always makes sure we get the night off."

The boys at the firehouse thought Billy was a good luck charm: there were never any fire runs when he was around. Billy loved the atmosphere of the station, too. The specter of dramatic conflagration, well, he'd save that for his adult career.

young firebrand

Raymond would smile, flop a fireman's hat on Billy, and say that next time things got busy, he'd call home and make sure Billy came down. Billy loved it there, the men letting him climb around on the trucks, trying on the boots.

Mostly he liked that he could make them laugh, and when he did, one or another of them would rock back in his chair, slap his thigh, laughing and

saying, "The boy ain't shy, Raymond. You got a talker on your hands."

Raymond was proud of Billy, whose mouth ran like a motorboat, spirited talk and stories of all kind in its wake.

The fact was that Billy just liked being around Raymond. When he arose in the morning, Raymond was already up, having his coffee, listening to the radio. He drank from a heavy stoneware mug, smoking and singing along:

Better get your britches on, Sleepy-Eyed-John
Better tie your shoes, Sleepy-Eyed-John
Better get to heaven 'fore the Devil gets to you.

Raymond listened to the black stations in Memphis, WDIA and WLOK, and Billy listened with him. He remembered Raymond listening to one of the stations late at night, the announcer saying, "I got de blues after midnight," and Raymond, tall and angular, swaying in time with the music. Even though he was a child, he could tell Raymond was moved by the music, and the scene was imprinted indelibly on Billy's memory.

In his mind's eye, forever, he saw Raymond pull out the old record player, set it up on the kitchen table, and put his Robert Johnson records on. Robert Johnson was an incredible blues man, and when the music started, Raymond put on his sunglasses, placed his Pall Mall in a cigarette holder, and rode along with the music, tapping his foot to the beat.

Sometimes Dot looked in, her two boys sitting at the table, listening to Robert Johnson, Raymond in his shades, and she'd give them her great, sardonic smile and say, "Raymond, you are a sight." Raymond acknowledged her with the beat, his head moving in her direction.

So while other kids listened to "How Much is that Doggie in the Window?" Raymond was introducing Billy to Robert Johnson, Big Mama Thornton, Blind Lemon Jefferson, and telling him the legendary stories about Gertrude "Ma" Rainey and Johnny Shines.

Their home, like many in Memphis, then a segregated city, was filled with eclectic influence. The drawn lines were often crossed. Dot and Raymond kept their doors and windows open, which allowed the children to see and hear a world in change. They'd been born into a world of racism and simple attitudes. But they weren't about to stay there.

Chapter three

The Woods family

> Mississippi was another world. If the mosquitoes could carry off livestock, why, *Billy* might throw a saddle on one and fly to the gulf. Another world? He was in a new universe every time he stepped off the porch.

Supper was over and Dot was clearing the dishes. Raymond

eased back in his chair, thumbs in his belt. Glenna leaned on an elbow, fiddling with the food left on her plate. Billy was at it again, spinning a yarn about his backyard adventures: guns blasting, swords flashing, bad men, wild animals that led to hasty retreats or harrowing battles.

I grabbed him around the neck. He fought hard, but he couldn't handle me . . .

Fists flew and blood ran. Other times, he turned to caned poles, buck knives, and gigantic fish.

Darn near broke my pole in half. Biggest fish you ever saw . . .

Dot turned from the sink, threw a dish towel over her shoulder, and fixed her eyes on Billy. He knew that look, and the little smile that accompanied it.

"Son," she said. "All of that can't possibly be true, now can it?"

He smiled, too, saying nothing.

"Didn't think so," Dot said. "But, son, you surely did tell it well."

Theirs was a special relationship. She had Billy on a tether, which he needed, but her tether was sufficiently long enough that he had interludes when he forgot about it being there, even if she didn't.

Raymond sipped his coffee, rocked back in his chair, and announced that he had some news. Outside, cars moved down the street as music from their radios slid through the windows of the house on the early evening breeze.

Raymond said he had some time off from the firehouse coming up and they were all going on a trip. They were going to pack up the car and head back home to Mississippi, to the home place near Water Valley. The folks, he said, needed some help getting the cotton in. It was a way to make a little extra money, and besides that, he said, it would be good for everybody to get out in the country and breathe some fresh air.

Billy had the first question.

Yes, Raymond said, the kids were expected to work in the fields, just like the adults.

Billy peered around the table. This didn't sound good, but no one seemed to share his sense of foreboding. Raymond was happy to be going back home. His mother was clearly in agreement, and Glenna was just happy to be doing something different.

Billy had never been more than a few blocks away from home. He loved Raymond, but Raymond was talking about things Billy couldn't comprehend: picking cotton, going back to Mississippi. He didn't even know where Miss'sippi was—that's how Raymond said it. Miss'sippi. Billy thought Mississippi was a river. Now, he was learning it was a place.

Raymond talked about how hot it got in Mississippi. How could it be any hotter than a Memphis afternoon? He said work could be fun. But Billy didn't see how the two words fit together: work and fun. Once again, he searched the eyes around the table. Sure enough, they were all in agreement. He had no idea what to expect. All he knew was what Raymond said. They were going to see Papa Woods, Uncle Winford, and Aunt Irene.

They'd have fun, Raymond said. It wouldn't all be work. He told them about Papa, a thin, stern man who had no use for sloth or foolishness. When he was little, Raymond said, Papa would beat the stew out of him and his brothers if they didn't mind him. But, he said, smiling again, he does have some tales. "He'll tell you all about the biggest mosquitoes you ever heard of. Miss'sippi mosquitoes are so big they sometimes carry off the livestock."

A few days later, they packed up, threw their bags in the 1949 Ford and set off for Water Valley. Dot made a jug of sweet tea for the trip and filled a brown bag with sandwiches. This made Raymond chuckle. They were only going down the road about sixty miles and, he said, the family might take a turn with her wearing shorts.

"Then turn they will," she said. "I'll wear what I choose to wear."

To him, Dot was forever a pleasure.

Highway 51 rolled south out of Memphis on a straight shot, eventually yielding to the soft folds of the green, undulating countryside of northern Mississippi. They left late in the day, when the heat had begun to diminish. They passed Hernando and the Arkabutla Reservoir, fed by the Cold Water River. They traveled past Como and Sardis and saw the signs for Oxford.

"Home of the University," Raymond said, "and where William Faulkner lives, a famous author. Smart man. Hard to understand, though."

Billy and Glenna paid half attention, his words washing past like Highway 51, a kind of whir

Billy had no idea what to expect from Papa Woods. He was older than anything Billy had ever seen, and he was as straight and stern as a fence post. Before long, though, he'd discovered the barn, the animals, and, yes, good-looking Margie Lee.

The Patriarch

mixed with the music on the radio: the blues and gospel. The kids caught bits and pieces from the disc jockey, an excited man, his voice running deep, yet light, like a man with big money and small worries, talking about soap to buy and this and that, and then playing another song. Raymond tapped along with the rhythm on the steering wheel.

Billy and Glenna stared out the car windows, unable to turn their attention from the approaching darkness and the deepening woods that seemed to creep closer to the road. The farther the Ford traveled south, the more mysterious Mississippi seemed.

They passed the Tallahatchie River and near Enid Lake took a smaller road and turned east. That road led to another, lined by trees with long limbs like witch fingers reaching down and down, the moon hanging back filmy clear, casting shadows that set Billy's imagination on the run.

Highways had gone to blacktop, blacktop to gravel, and gravel to narrow rust roads. The woods, lit by the moonlight and the high beams of the Ford, crept ever closer. Raymond said they didn't have far to go.

Cousin Margie Lee Pruitt was the kids' summer guide. She wasn't intimidated by the grown folks, and she knew every secret of the place, including where to find cold pop. She couldn't keep Billy out of trouble, though. Nobody could do that.

Outside the car, everything seemed to sway about, long kudzu vines, shifting in the breeze, swelling, then fading.

Papa Woods's house stood on a rise just off a dirt road. Since his wife's death, he shared the house with his daughter Irene, Raymond's baby sister, and her husband, Winford Pruitt. There was a barn in back, sheds and a smokehouse. Across the road, the cotton fields stretched out like a long, green, white-capped river. You would have to throw a rock a lot of times to get past those fields, Billy thought.

There were workhorses, hogs, cows, and an ornery rooster. Dogs milled about, sniffing and scratching, marking the old Allis-Chalmers parked out by the barn. Some of the dogs had names, others didn't. Those without names had just showed up, attracted by chicken bones and scraps tossed out back. What slop didn't go to the hogs went to the dogs, and they fought over food and the pecking order. Often, they made a run at the chickens, and Papa Woods—a sun-weathered man who looked older than anything they had ever seen—raised holy hell.

The house was simple. It was a clapboard, shotgun house with a peaked tin roof and a gallery out front big enough to accommodate family and friends. It was spare and neat and something about it appealed to Billy. Everything was clean, the linoleum floors, the wood tables and chairs, as if they had been washed and rubbed smooth.

Out back was a clothesline where bed sheets and overalls—fresh off the washboard—baked in the sun. When there was a breeze, the curtains licked out the windows carrying the smell of whatever Aunt Irene was making on the wood stove.

She seemed to permanently inhabit the kitchen, surrounded by her granite pots and iron skillets, always cooking, especially when there was cotton to be picked and crops to harvest. She wore print dresses and big aprons. She was friendly but rigid, too. Nothing like Dot.

It didn't take long for Billy and Glenna to settle in. Billy loved being around the animals, though the rooster—red-brown with long black tail-feathers—always seemed to be staring at him, stalking him. Everywhere he went, the rooster seemed to be there, too, making its herky-jerky chicken motions. He didn't like the rooster, and the rooster seemed to mirror perfectly Billy's own dislike.

Billy liked the barn, the way it smelled. He loved the rich, mellow smell of the drying manure. It's what he would always remember about Mississippi, the smell of manure mixing with the lilacs and magnolias, the smell of vegetation exploding everywhere. He and Glenna learned how to pinch the backs off honeysuckle blossoms, pulling the stems through backwards for one brief taste of nectar. They spent hours around the honeysuckle bushes, competing with the bees.

Glenna was impressed most by the absence of any bathroom. There was only an outhouse, its boards worn smooth by daily use, and a sack of lime nearby. Instructed by necessity, she was surprised to find herself adapting.

Bath night required an entirely new mindset, as well. The modesties of Memphis had little place in Mississippi. On Saturday nights, Aunt Irene and Dot hauled out the Number Three washtub, filled it with water from the well, then heated just enough water on the stove to knock off the chill. One by one, in the middle of the kitchen, they took turns in the tub: little ones first, then the men, and later, when everyone else was in bed, the women refilled the tub and started afresh. The routine and its realities made Billy

appreciate his youth. The best thing about being a kid, he thought, was that you got to get in early before the water got cold and started looking like pond water.

Aunt Irene and Uncle Winford had four children: Mary Francis, Margie Lee, Ethel Fay, and the baby, a little boy saddled with mental and physical disabilities. Mary Francis was just old enough that she didn't want to play with Billy and Glenna. She stayed close to the house, helping her mother tend to the cooking and her little brother.

Margie Lee was long-legged, good-looking, tan, and clever. In addition, she had a smile that could stop an avalanche. Billy was immediately taken with Margie Lee, who made subsequent trips to Water Valley seem far more inviting. She became their guide. She knew which dogs would nip, advised them to stay away from the rooster, and urged them not to believe everything grown folks said. Yes, the mosquitoes were big and sometimes thick like a gray cloud. But, no, they wouldn't carry you away. That's just tales, she said.

It was an eventful sojourn in a strange, new land. The three of them—Billy, Margie Lee, and Glenna—were inseparable all summer. And then there were his major adventures—being attacked by a million wasps and a killer chicken.

The three musketeers

They went to bed with the sun, but the three of them—Billy, Glenna, and Margie Lee—lay in the featherbed talking. Billy and Glenna told her what they could about Memphis and city life. She listened intently, then said, "Know what we should do tomorrow? Walk down to the store and get a cold pop."

The store was a half a mile down the road, and tiny. There were two gas pumps out front, each bearing a picture of a red, winged horse, Pegasus ascending. Three plank steps led up to the porch where there was usually a collection of men sitting on benches and chairs, all of them dressed like Papa Woods: straw hats and bib-overalls washed and worn until they were the color of the sky and soft as clouds. They talked without looking at one another, whittling, chewing, and spitting until a newcomer made his way up the steps, then everything stopped.

"Who you young 'ins?" one of them asked. When they were satisfied as to the children's place in the immediate universe—part of the Woods and Pruitt families, just down the road—the whittling and spitting continued. They all seemed to have dogs and were forever talking about whose dog was best. Occasionally, the debate reached a contentious pitch and someone might say, "Well, let's just see."

Then two of the dogs would be sicced on one another. There would be a skirmish of dogs in the dirt, until one of them yelped and ran away, at which time the victor's owner sat back proudly and said, "See, told ya." Thus the great issues of the day were decided, and the whittling and chewing resumed.

The screen door clattered, and even a child's step brought creaks and groans from the sagging wooden floor that yawed this way and that. It was a tiny store, shelves stacked with bolted cloth, sugar, flour, salt, coffee, and behind the counter, chewing tobacco, canned tobacco, cigarettes, cigars and candy.

In the back was a large, red cooler. The raised white letters on the front—Coca-Cola—had long ago faded away. For Glenna, Margie Lee, and Billy it was a treasure chest. There were doors on top and the drinks sat on the bottom of the chest, immersed in water so cold it made the bones in your forearm ache. Billy quickly learned that if you wanted a lot to drink, you went for a Royal Crown or a Double-Cola (twice the amount for the small nickel), and if you wanted a wallop—Margie Lee taught him this—you went for the little Coke.

They seldom tarried at the store. Aunt Irene fretted when they were too far away or gone too long. Besides, there was too much to explore, and for all Raymond's talk about the hard work in Mississippi, the kids were mostly left alone to play.

But in short order, Papa, Irene, and Winford learned what Raymond and Dot had told them: Billy was dangerous with tools of all kinds and accident-prone, as well. Even at play, Billy was at risk. The boy tugged at their hearts—always in motion, bright, good-looking, forever talking—but they found him a caution. Later, when he recalled that summer, he thought they embraced him because they thought he wasn't quite right—daydreaming and telling stories. He couldn't do anything they thought a boy his age should do.

Past that, he was always finding trouble. If anything bad happened, it happened to Billy. If he wasn't in the middle of it, he was nearby. One day, while playing in the woods, Margie Lee found a length of rope. She began to run, taking high, long strides to clear the undergrowth, Billy and Glenna giving chase.

Back in Memphis, on paved streets, Billy was one of the fastest kids around, but this was different. Vines and weeds reached out for his ankles. There were clods of dirt everywhere, and here and there, a camouflaged hole. Every time he got close to grabbing the rope, he found himself splayed out on the ground, much to the delight of Margie Lee. Not one to give up—and charmed by Margie Lee—Billy bounced up and renewed the chase. The last thing he wanted to do was appear defeated in the eyes of this tantalizing, olive-skinned girl.

Somehow, Margie Lee stirred up a nest of red wasps, but rather than swarm their antagonist, they attacked Billy, who suddenly ran into a wall of them. He swatted and screamed, which further infuriated his attackers. Papa said Billy could have been heard all the way to the Delta. He counted seventeen different stings, and spit tobacco juice on each one. Sure enough, they didn't hurt as badly. It was when he first learned about the medicinal effects of tobacco, and an advocate ever since, he would say.

Margie Lee and Glenna explained what had happened, while Billy, in full character despite the pain, added elements of embellishment. Must have been a thousand of them.

His folks gave him that familiar look. It was the same look he got when he was caught shooting a BB gun at the cows. Papa grabbed him and told him if he kept it up, it would sour the milk. After that, when he could, he shot at the hogs. They didn't seem to mind.

Papa, Winford, and Irene suggested that what the boy needed was work—maybe that would straighten him out. They'd give him a sack and send him to the fields. Raymond agreed. Dot just smiled. She knew better.

Shortly after dawn, with full stomachs from Irene's kitchen—bacon, eggs, fried potatoes, gravy, biscuits, jam, honey, and whole milk—the family made their way to the cotton fields. Winford and Papa were workers, leading the way. Raymond wasn't far behind, just a little out of practice. Dot tried it, then went back to the house. The fields weren't for her.

Margie Lee hustled about. Glenna did her best. Billy was mostly distracted, studying the clouds, wondering when the work would be done.

He fiddled. He dawdled. At day's end, everyone weighed their yield. Billy's sack was lightest and last. Eight cents! Little Glenna produced two dollars.

The next day, Billy was given a new job. He would fetch water to the fields: fill the buckets from the well, wash out the dippers, and carry them down to the workers. Papa and Winford offered one instruction. Just don't spill too much on the way. To Billy, this seemed a far better task than picking cotton. He could find some shade along the way. He didn't have to keep up, just haul the water. But given his disposition and imagination, Billy could turn a quarter-mile walk into an odyssey, and he did. Somewhere along the way from the field to the well, he drifted off, thinking about Don Winslow, USN, one of his favorite comic strips, and Don Winslow fighting to save the world from those who menaced the American way: The Scorpion, The Crocodile, and Dr. Q.

Chores forgotten, Billy was off in his imagination when he encountered once again his Mississippi nemesis, the arrogant, omnipresent Rhode Island Red. The rooster eyed him malevolently. After all the taunting and near confrontations, Billy, who had been emboldened by Don Winslow turning back world destruction, would now deal with the rooster.

Chickenfight at the OK Corral.

No more would this spawn of satan extract his unholy tribute from the entire barnyard.

This mysterious country of Papa Woods and Raymond influenced him in ways even he didn't understand. It was there, though, in both voice and outlook. Billy took everything in, then filed it away somewhere. He never forgot where he'd been.

The chicken took up his post near the porch. Billy dropped the buckets and pulled out his Barlow knife, a gift from Raymond. He bared the blade, rushed the porch, and launched himself fearlessly at his feathered tormentor.

The rooster squawked, flew a few feet off the ground, and disappeared, headed for the safety of the barn. While the fowl was not wounded, Billy was. The Barlow had folded back on his hand, leaving a small cut. The sight of blood reminded him, for some reason, of his chore. He rinsed out the dippers, filled the buckets, and inadvertently washed the blood from his hand into the drinking water.

When he reached the fields, Uncle Winford took a dipper and asked, "Why is this water pink?"

In a fit of inspiration, Billy said, "I put Kool-Aid in it."

There were two results from the Don Winslow caper: the rooster steered clear of everyone, even the hens, and while Billy wasn't free of chores, little was expected of him. Billy was just Billy, they shrugged, a boy apart.

The general consensus was that he was going through a stage. The hope was—that sooner or later—he would see the value of hard work. Dot suspected otherwise, and Glenna knew better.

Over the years and left to pursue matters of his own design, Billy cherished the frequent trips to Mississippi. He was forever learning something, it seemed, forever asking questions, not all of them well received.

He'd been out piddling around one day when he came across a frisky puppy. It followed Billy back to the farm, where they continued to roughhouse in the yard. Billy was showing the puppy to the other kids when Aunt Irene approached.

"Billy," she said, "you can't be playing with that dog!" He didn't understand. He knew she liked animals.

"Why?" he asked. "What's wrong?"

"Why? Because that's a nigger dog," she said.

He had never heard his mother or Raymond use that word. He knew what it meant, though. He had heard it in Memphis, but not from anyone he respected. He looked at his aunt and then at the pup.

"Aunt Irene," he said, "the dog is white."

"I know it's white, Billy," she said. "It belongs to the niggers down the road. You shouldn't be playing with it."

Again he studied his aunt, then turned his eyes back to the playful puppy.

"Aunt Irene," he said, "this white dog is a nigger dog and I can't play with it, but your dog is black and it's a white dog, so can I play with it?"

She didn't answer, just huffed her way back into the house. The moment was his first real recognition of racism, as well as the futility of it.

It was all around him. Blacks worked in different fields, picking the same

crops. They went to different schools, drank from different water fountains, and used separate dippers at the wells. They had their own churches, but they sang the same hymns. Back in Memphis, the black kids played the same games the white kids did but on different ball fields and playgrounds that were separated, even if by nothing more than fencing.

But there were times and a place in Water Valley when whites and blacks came together. Years ago, Papa had built a berm house in the side of a hill beyond the barn. When the sky turned yellow and gray, the family retreated to the safety of the storm house, surrounded by earth. They sat on crates and stools, riding out the bad weather by the light of coal oil lamps, sometimes singing hymns, sometimes telling stories.

On occasion, when a storm was truly bad, there would be a knock on the door. The blacks wanted to be safe from the storm, and Papa and Uncle Winford always let them in. The blacks didn't say much, but they sang with the Pruitts and the Woodses, and when the storm passed, they each went their own way, separate once again.

No one seemed to think a thing about it, except Billy. He wondered why the blacks sang so much better than the whites.

Chapter four

Elvis and them

The trials of adolescence
had only begun.
How could Billy and his
friends possibly transport
their *overheated* selves
safely to the other side?
Pray to St. Donna, patron
saint of nekkidness.

They met at church. Soon they were an inseparable gang:

Billy Purser, David Welch, Tommy and
Bennie Vance, and Glynn Bishop, all of
them straining toward adolescence and away
from the unforgiving doctrine of Beverly
Hills Baptist Church. There, they sat under
the torrent of hellfire and damnation and
wondered about Proxidee Jacket's daughter,
Donna, who lived across town.

Donna Jacket was the loveliest thing
any of them had ever seen. The merest
glimpse of her enflamed each of them with
an exquisite ache. In her presence, they
found themselves sweating. She meanwhile,
cool as river moss, was wearing a *sweater*.

The minister talked about *Jeeee-zus!*

They wondered about Donna *nek-kid!*

Sin?

What was it, really?

There must be a loophole there somewhere, a gray area, some escape clause.

How could something as tantalizing as the thought or—*Hallelujah!*—the reality of Donna Jacket without clothing be bad? Nekkid, they thought, *had* to be good. It wasn't, they were told. It was *bad*. But Donna without her clothes, they thought, would be perfectly saintly. Saint Donna, patron saint of nekkidness.

They tried—at least in church—not to think about her. But they could think of little else. It was an ethical tug of war, Jesus on one end and Donna Jacket on the other. They all knew who was going to win.

Sorry, Jesus.

To make matters worse, there was Sylvia Nichols in the next pew, and she wasn't far behind Donna Jacket. *Why, Lord*, David Welch thought, *is there an unfair share of hot chicks in our church? Why do they come to church? My church?*

They had all heard the joke:

Why is it that Southern Baptists don't have sex standing up?

Because it might lead to dancing.

They loved dancing. They wondered what would happen if anybody found out they snuck down to the Methodist Church on Sunday nights because the Methodists actually *had* dances. (And, by the way, what eventually happened to *them?* The boys pictured a pit of fire, dancing Methodists writhing eternally to a satanic beat, doubly punished for dabbling in both R&B *and* dancing.)

In the matter of worldly experience, Billy held a superior knowledge. He had actually seen a woman's breast, and the others implored him to tell the story at every opportunity: how he was at the Memphian Theater for a matinee, how he was walking to the concession stand for popcorn when a young women flounced out her breast to nurse her baby. How he made so many trips up and down the aisle—each time slower—until the usher finally collared him and told him to take a seat or leave. How when he told the usher what he was doing, the usher instantly decided to accompany Billy back to his seat.

C'mon, Billy. Tell it again!

And he did, embellishing the story each time along with the young lady's anatomy, which grew with the telling until she could have nursed an entire orphanage.

The minister pounded the pulpit while the boys wondered about the spiritual costs. What would, say, just a glimpse of Donna Jacket or Sylvia Nichols naked actually cost? Perhaps merely blindness, as opposed to eternal damnation? They would take their chances. They were breathlessly and unwittingly aligned with St. Augustine, who said, "Give me chastity and continence, but not quite yet."

They were, after all, just *boys*.

Besides the unfair share of hot chicks at Beverly Hills Baptist, their only true interest in church was the recessional. They just wanted to burst through the church doors and out into their lives, which seemed suspended amidst the incomprehensible liturgy. There were more pressing pursuits, and since none of them was prone toward scholastic achievement, there was always baseball.

Billy was slick with the glove, a line drive hitter— soft liners. Tommy, the oldest and the biggest, hit the long ball. Bennie emulated his brother. When he connected, his power was dazzling, which was fortunate since Bennie had little interest in running and even less proficiency at it. David was an enthusiastic outfielder whose uncommon wit often led to conflict. Playing baseball or kick-the-can, David's interjected sarcasms were routinely misunderstood, followed by trouble. That's where Glynn Bishop—too cool to play ball—came in.

Glynn didn't attend Beverly Hills Baptist on a regular basis. He lived near the church and showed up for ice cream socials or pie sales, that kind of thing. It was as if the church was a kind of minor club to which he belonged, and so he would check in from time to time. He was totally unfettered by the church, or anything else for that matter. The word was that Glynn walked out of school in first grade. He had tried it, found it wanting, and just left.

No one was quite sure about his parents or what they did. They just knew Glynn was a good guy to have on your side. He wasn't much taller than Billy, but he was thick and broad with fists like a pair of eight-pound shots. That wasn't what made Glynn so daunting, however. It was the look in his eyes—menacing, vacant, without fear. The other boys had the occasional tussle; Glynn had *fights*, at least once a week, and he won them all.

Somewhere along the way, Glynn had fashioned crude tattoos on his fingers, just below his knuckles. On one hand, the word "love," on the other "hate." The toughest boys in Memphis, even the treacherous Tiller brothers who dabbled in drink, smoke, and petty crime, gave Glynn Bishop wide berth.

Glynn was comfortable in the shadows of Beverly Hills Baptist with Billy, David, and the Vance boys, or down at Smith's Sundries, where he'd earned the respect of those who weren't so innocent: Charles "Dago" Tiller and his younger brother Tom, Danny Kipps, Buddy Gilbert, Crossett Stamper, Tom Coburn, Eddie "Three Gun" Braddock, and a guy known only as "Pug," who had a bald parakeet, as well as a squirrel that had once attacked the cops.

While Billy, David, and the Vance boys busied themselves with baseball and basketball and the pursuit of girls, Braddock's bunch were generally trying to scrape up a buck and a half.

A buck and a half meant that one was flush. Fifty cents for gas, fifty cents for two packs of cigarettes, and fifty cents for two quarts of beer. Braddock and the others would usually head up to Buddy Gilbert's house near Orange Mound, mostly a black part of town, call down to Jack's Place, and shortly a black delivery guy on a bicycle showed up with the beer in a brown paper bag. "No never mind how old you is," he said.

That was a world Billy's crowd didn't know, although Glynn Bishop filled them in. They didn't drink, didn't smoke, and had little opportunity for trouble. First of all, their parents would have killed them. Beyond that, there was no time. They were always in church: Sunday morning and night, Wednesdays for prayer meeting, Thursdays for visitation, and Fridays for choir. For any possible straying, there were only three days left.

In their small amount of idle time, they might meander around town, maybe stopping at the Rexall Drug Store for a soda, maybe have a look-see over at Little Beretta's where the tougher crowd congregated, but always on Saturdays they went to the Park Theater or The LaMarr, for the serials and the cowboy pictures. The matinees took up the whole afternoon, from two o'clock until six, plenty of time to stroll up and down the aisles to see what they could see, but none of them was ever so lucky as Billy.

They were stuck fast in an odd territory, somewhere between Hopalong Cassidy and James Dean, Maggie "The Cat" Pollitt and Our Miss Brooks. *Would any of it ever make sense?*

Often the boys gathered at Billy's house. Dot might fix them a pitcher of lemonade and the boys lingered, telling stories about their latest escapades. Dot sat with them, asking questions here and there. They viewed Dot as a second mother, mostly because she could be trusted, unlike the other moms. They could tell Dot things they wouldn't dream of uttering in their own home, such as their attraction to Sylvia and Donna.

Raymond joked with the boys and teased them, but he never talked down to them or made them feel foolish. He always seemed glad to see them, and they liked going there because not only were they welcome, they were accepted.

Billy was ahead of the schoolyard curve: after all, he'd actually seen a woman's breast. Then he introduced Luis Aparicio to air conditioning. Finally, he cemented his teenage reputation by spending an afternoon with Elvis. What was left?

Many adventures were launched from Billy's front porch, the boys setting off with no destination in mind. David would be talking, joking; Tommy, always serious, with his determined stride; Benny, strikingly good looking, bringing up the rear; and Billy, lost in one reverie or another.

His reveries always had the same result: someday a big, black Cadillac would roll up in front of the house. A guy would get out and say, "C'mon kid. I'm gonna make you a star."

He talked about it all the time. His friends laughed at him and punched him in the arm. Nothing could dissuade him. And why not? Not much else interested him. Tools confounded him and he didn't like school. Besides, there were dreams all around. Elvis Presley had lived in the same housing project where Billy's own family had lived: Lauderdale Courts. Elvis had practiced guitar right there in the laundry room when no one was around and learned to sing in church, just as Billy had.

There were all those other guys, too. Johnny Cash lived on his paper route—though he didn't subscribe to *The Commercial Appeal*. (Odd, though, how the lights were always on at his house.) Jerry Lee Lewis rode his Harley Davidson motorcycle around town. And how many times had they walked into a restaurant or a diner and saw Carl Perkins having a sandwich?

Anything could happen and there was no one, Billy's friends admitted, who seemed to stumble into more good fortune than he did. Nobody else had been lucky enough to get a job as batboy with the Chicks, or made friends with Luis Aparicio, who would one day soon become the great shortstop, Luis Aparicio.

His aunt Ann knew someone, Billy said. That's how he got the job. One day, during batting practice, he was shagging flies, running down grounders, and the ball kept slipping through his glove. Aparicio was sitting in the dugout watching. He motioned Billy over, took a look at his mitt, and pointed out the broken strings.

Aparicio didn't speak English well, but he tightened and restrung Billy's glove. When he was finished he said, "Should be good now. Better. Try again."

It was better.

A few weeks later, he was downtown, visiting his Mamaw at Lowenstein's. He looked across the street and there was Aparicio, waiting on the corner for a bus or a cab. It was a hot day. He crossed the street and told Aparicio they should go to the drug store. They went to Rexall's and ordered a soda. Aparicio was astonished by the air conditioning. After that, Aparicio said he was always looking for those signs with the polar bear, just like the one at Rexall's. Billy told everyone he introduced Aparicio to air conditioning.

Then there was the day Billy and David Welch were downtown hitchhiking and a panel truck passed by.

"That was Elvis Presley," Billy said. "I swear."

"You're crazy," said David.

Then the truck stopped and began backing up. The passenger door opened and, big as a billboard, was Elvis Aaron Presley himself.

"Jump in boys," Elvis said. "Where you fellas headin'?"

Since they had begun hitchhiking with no firm destination in mind, they figured they were already there. So they rode around with Elvis for a hour or so, just talking. They were surprised to find that he seemed almost like an older one of *them*.

He explained that there had been some kind of party at Graceland, and he was hauling off the remains of it. It must have been *some* party, the boys thought. There was a sudden, illuminated glimpse of a world they could only barely imagine, where people gave parties so animated the furniture didn't survive. And Elvis couldn't go out the front gate because of all the people who wanted to talk to him and get his autograph. But apparently there was a back way out of Graceland, and he could leave in the old panel truck and no one paid any attention.

He saw some girls on the sidewalk, and he slowed down and said, "Hello, girls, how ya'll doin'?"

They were so shocked, they walked into each other. Elvis just laughed. So did Billy and David. It might have been the greatest afternoon of their lives.

For David, it was an unforgettable memory. But for Billy, it was another reason to believe in his dreams. The Vance boys never believed the story and Glynn Bishop didn't really care, one way or another. Dot didn't know whether to believe them or not and Raymond was more than skeptical.

It's true! We met Elvis. Rode around town forever . . . .

Dot and Raymond looked from one to the other, David and Billy bouncing around the room, describing every moment, the truck and Elvis's escape route from Graceland, dropping off junk. Could this elaborate tale possibly be true? Not likely, but how did the boys get so excited?

That night, late, Dot and Raymond wondered, just as they had in Mississippi: *What will become of our dreamer? Elvis in a panel truck, dropping off junk. Who could even imagine such a thing?*

High school, a half-life

It was a refrain that would follow him forever, it seemed: "What we gonna do with you, Billy?" No one knew. Least of all Billy. The *highlight* of high school seemed to be tagging Tom Tiller with a good left and joining the army.

Dot and Raymond hoped that in high school Billy would

find his way. Instead, he found music, an obsession that ultimately led to a death in the family. The deceased, Petey the parakeet, died prematurely of excitement or percussion, most likely the latter. And of course there was a story . . .

Petey was Dot's cherished pet. Housed in the living room, he sang and danced, innocently hopping from his swing to one side of his cage to the other. When the birds sang outside, Petey seemed to sing along. When Raymond played his radio, Petey pranced. The bird—blue and yellow with little black specks—was a perfect live-in, little trouble, though perhaps a bit eccentric. Any time he heard R&B, which was often, he ruffled up around the neck, roused himself, and did a little bird dance. Like everyone else in the house, Petey liked music.

One day, Billy had the radio on—just the two of them in the living room—listening to WDIA or WHBQ's "Red, Hot and Blue," hosted by Dewey Phillips. The music rocked the room and Billy was particularly moved by the backbeat, the drums just behind the music, setting up the horns and the lead.

He ran to the kitchen, searching through the pantry, grabbing pots and pans and wooden spoons, and assembled a make-shift drum kit: pie pans, skillets, and boilers. Then he went to work trying to follow along with Willie Mae "Big Mama" Thornton and Little Willie John—whoever Dewey was playing next.

There was only one problem. He had no pot that could replicate the sound of a snare drum, he had the ting and ding, but the rattle of the snare was missing. Without it, the show playing out in his mind—the filled house, the adoring fans—it just wouldn't work. He began to look around the house. Lampshades didn't work. The cheese grater was close, but not close enough. And then he tapped Petey's cage with a wooden spoon.

Perfect! It had both the whap *and* the rattle.

Billy started to play, keeping pace as best he could, plinging the pie pan cymbals and carrying the bass with the boilers, all the while trying to keep two-four time on Petey's cage. Petey seemed to like it, dancing faster and faster, as excited as Billy, jumping from his swing to this side of the cage and the next, hanging upside down and then—when the song was done . . .

Petey? Petey, you alright?

The bird lay on his back, toes curled up, eyes wide open, dead as a doornail—another casualty of the music business, one of many who succumbed to the drive and energy of R&B. Billy wanted to believe Petey died happily, but he was both mortified and scared to death of what his mother would say.

He didn't try to hide the dead bird. When his mother came home he confessed, told her about the drums and the music and Petey's final dance. She didn't get angry. She didn't scold him. As sad as she was, she could see his own hurt.

"Mom," he said, "I loved that bird as much as you did."

He never forgot the look in her eyes: concern, sadness, curiosity.

Why would this boy do such a silly thing?

Petey wasn't the only casualty of Billy's tomfoolery. He lost things, left his chores half-done. Things turned up broken all the time, such as the night Dot, Raymond, and Glenna came back to the house to find Billy's bedroom door smashed in and the cuckoo clock dangling awkwardly from the wall like a broken limb, the cuckoo bird making odd, broken calls.

"What on earth happened here?" Dot demanded.

A coffee table was askew. It looked like furniture had been overturned and hastily returned to order.

"Well," Billy said, "first I locked myself in my room and had to break down the door to get out."

Cuck . . .

"But," Raymond noted, "your door was broken in from the outside."

"Hmm," Billy said.

"And what about the clock?"

Cooooooo . . .

"Well," Billy said, "I was playing baseball and pretended the clock was second base. I made the throw, a good one, too, just a little too hard..."

"And you expect us to believe that?" Dot said. "Go on with you. Go to bed!"

He couldn't tell his parents—thank goodness they hadn't noticed the tear in his shirt—what really happened, because if he had, it would have meant real trouble for Harry and Harold, his friends from school who were probably going to be in enough difficulty when they showed up at home all soused and beat up.

"And you are gonna pay for that clock and fix the door!"

Cuck-o-o . . .

"What are we gonna do with you, Billy?"

Cu . . .

Harold and Harry were out fooling around that night and decided to get a couple of quarts of Falstaff. The more they drank, the more the topic turned to folks who were just getting too full of themselves—like Billy Purser and those guys he hung around with, wearing their matching satin jackets, combing their hair in ducktails, smart-mouthing around. Probably making fun of them, Harold and Harry, behind their very backs.

Billy once hung out with them, too, but now he hardly gave them the time of day, as if they weren't good enough. When the second quart of Falstaff had disappeared, they decided, muddily, that Billy Purser needed a little comeuppance. They gave brief thought to possible retaliation from Glynn Bishop, but fortified by Falstaff, they dismissed him.

When they showed up at Billy's house and announced they were there to kick his ass, he just stood on the porch, smiling, clearly thinking he was a tough little hombre.

"Better get on home before you get in trouble," he said. "I ain't gonna fight you 'cause you're both drunk."

Then he walked back into the house. From inside, they heard a door slam and the sound of a lock.

"See," one of them said, "he's scared."

They decided to go after Billy, slamming into his bedroom door, breaking the lock and hinges.

Billy, angry now, pushed one of them over a coffee table and bounced a hard rubber ball off the head of another. The ball ricocheted and hit the cuckoo clock. A few punches and shoves later, Harry and Harold found themselves outside on the ground, still drunk and more than a little embarrassed.

Billy had acquired justice but also a problem: what would he tell his parents? If he told them the truth, they would call Harold and Harry's folks and that would not be good for Harold and Harry.

Best make something up. As with scoundrels and thieves, there was still honor among boys in the neighborhood.

In time, Billy made good on the damaged door and the clock, with his wages as after-school bagboy at Hogue & Knott's grocery store. The grocery was another job that didn't quite work out. He put milk on top of bread and eggs underneath soup cans, and once he filled a bag so thoroughly with small jars of baby food that it split under the pressure and he spent the rest of the afternoon cleaning up a slippery conglomeration of split peas, apricots, applesauce, and broken glass.

He made a mess of the cleanup, but his apologies to the offended mother were effusive and sincere. He was, by far, the friendliest bagger at Hogue & Knott's, but he was also the most inefficient. Patrons loved to talk to him but did everything to avoid his line. His ineptitude as a bagger was of such magnitude that managers began sending him on errands just to get him out of the store.

One night when Billy came home, bedraggled and spent, Raymond asked how his day had gone at work. (He had long since abandoned asking Billy about school.)

"Well," Billy said, "they had me running all over town and I didn't do any good. I'll probably have to do it again tomorrow night."

"Running all over town?" Raymond asked. "For what?"

"We were all out of sack-stretchers and they needed some real bad."

"Sack-stretchers?"

"Yeah. They sent me to the hardware store and they were all out. At the hardware store, they sent me to drug store, and they were out. They sent me to another place and everywhere I went they sent me someplace else. There is not one sack-stretcher in the city. I don't know what to do."

"Lord, son. Don't you know when you are being put on? You were on a snipe hunt."

"No, I was looking for a sack-stretcher."

"Son, they are all in on it except you. There is no such thing as a sack-stretcher. How would you stretch a sack?"

"Well, if it was a gunnysack, you would get it wet."

"Daggone, boy, do you use gunnysacks at the store? No! You use paper sacks. You can't stretch paper sacks."

Raymond, like Dot, couldn't keep from laughing. "You got to embrace the child," they said, "even if something is just flat missing."

At Messick High, Billy rarely missed a day of school, but his stellar attendance was driven not by intellectual curiosity but rather his zest for social interaction.

He didn't like English, didn't like history, and as for the health class, who needed to be told to brush your teeth? Even the music class bored him because the music of the class wasn't his music. The music in school was too structured, had no feeling. Had the instructor ever heard the banjo and fiddle players who came down the road ever so often in Mississippi? Obviously not. Billy was an eight-to-the-bar kid moving through his days in waltz time.

The studious kids gathered at a small grocery store across the street from Messick High. Billy's crowd, the "cool" kids, chose nearby Smith's Sundries, where the parking lot was always full, the jukebox jumped, and there was so much cigarette smoke you became addicted by merely walking onto the premises and taking a deep breath.

The boys wore blue jeans and "peggers," slacks gathered tightly around the ankle, and ducktails, artfully shaped with just the right amount of Brylcream or Royal Pomade. The girls wore poodle skirts and bobby socks; their hair pulled back in ponytails tied with brightly colored scarves. They sipped Coke through a straw, stood in clusters around the jukebox and the soda fountain waiting for one of the boys—or the boy—to approach. Some of them smoked and did so with an elegance that stirred every male in the room.

You know what they say about girls who smoke?
They do it!

From Smith's Sundries—this smoky, hormonal haze—sprang aspiration, intention, hope, lust, schemes, and grand design. It was here that Billy decided to take up smoking, not because the other kids were doing it, but because he needed a final prop to complete his image. He had the hair, the strut, the clothes, and with a Marlboro dangling from his lips, the picture was finished.

Smoking, like drinking, was frowned upon in the Southern Baptist Church, but Billy was already questioning the practices of his church. So were David and Glynn, as well as Tommy and Bennie (although slightly more reluctantly since their mother, Betty, was secretary of Beverly Hills Baptist).

Being at church four days a week for years, they had become friends with Robert, the janitor. Robert talked with the boys about baseball and music. He knew their families, where they lived.

"How's life treatin' you fine boys?" he'd say whenever he saw them.

They thought the world of Robert, though they had never heard his last name. In the 1950s, young white boys were often acquainted with blacks, most of whom did menial jobs here and there but seldom knew their sire names: just Robert or Mizz Jessie. It was merely a part of the times when not everyone possessed an equal share of the goodness found in the good old days.

One day they were all sitting around at church talking with Robert.

"Robert, how long you been working here?" someone asked.

"Oh, my, probably since 'fore you all is born."

"Every day?"

"Yes, mos' every day."

"Well, how come we never see you except when you are working? How come you never come to service?"

"Now, that wouldn't do, would it? Cain't be. T'ain't allowed. 'Sides, I got my own church. It's a colored church for colored people. This, why, this is a white church for white people."

"What do you mean, ain't allowed? They won't let you come to service?"

"Naw, sir. Jus' the way it is, boys. Yawl'll come to understand."

"Wait a minute, you can come clean and work, but you can't come to church or prayer meeting?"

"Why you boys talkin' and frettin' about a thing like this. It's no never-mind. We got our own schools; we got our own churches. Ought not be talking all this. Things just fine. Now go on with you. Stop all this nonsense about Robert going to your church. Cain't be. All there is to it."

But the boys weren't satisfied. Their affection for Robert was matched by their confusion over his exclusion from their pews, Robert being permitted into Beverly Hills as long as he was carrying a bucket, but not if he was carrying a bible.

They arranged a meeting with Brother Vernon A. Dutton, their minister. In his dimly lit office, Brother Dutton told the boys Robert was not allowed to come to their church because he was a black man and carried the mark of Cain, his people cursed by God because Cain had slain his brother, Abel. "Genesis, Chapter 4," he said.

The boys looked around at one another, blankly. They arrived looking for answers; they left more bewildered than before. They did notice how uncomfortable Brother Dutton had been with the whole topic, and how he delivered his explanation with something less than high conviction.

So Robert was banned from Beverly Hills Baptist for a 2,000-year-old grievance? Wasn't there a statute of limitations, or something? What did Robert have to do with Cain and Abel, anyway?

Life at the sundry shop made more sense. The music made sense. Elvis seemed to have something they were all looking for. If nothing else, then unceasing motion, which was always the province of the young.

Just after Billy turned 16 and aided by his mother, he scrounged together

$300 and bought a black 1949 V-8 Ford. But it wasn't just any Ford. It was a sleek machine. Someone had customized the car, adding Buick holes to the fenders. Billy and Glynn waxed it every chance they had and raced it at every opportunity. They would head off to Colonial, Glynn riding shotgun, busting through a quarter mile, Billy jamming through the "three-on-the-tree" until the transmission groaned, spit its gears, and died. It seemed as if Glynn and Billy were running to the junkyard every week, picking up a new transmission and switching it out.

They went to the clubs: Beretta's and Little Beretta's, and The Casino at the Fairgrounds where Billy lost his two front teeth in a fight over a girl. They swiped hubcaps and siphoned gas, but they didn't drink and, consequently, they got by with more than their share of the same misdeeds that landed others in jail. Clarity of mind—sobriety—they decided, was a great equalizer.

Sometimes they went downtown for Junior Achievement, but Billy always snuck out, never quite taken with the idea of a business career. The boys always found him at the same place, lingering outside Keegan's Technical Institute on Union where there was a radio school with an outside loudspeaker. He'd be staring through the window, watching, listening, as if he was trying to absorb it all through the pane of glass.

Often they went cruising, Billy wheeling up to Robert's church or another black church, cutting the V-8, all of them rolling down the windows and listening to the music, voices filled with joy and sorrow and hope.

They never tried to go inside, though they thought they might be welcomed. That's just the way it was.

Billy thought about the musicians who came down the road in Mississippi, the banjo and fiddle players, the black people who used to come to the storm house in bad weather, and the boys who lived beyond the fence behind Glynn Bishop's house, black boys who played the same games they did but never dared climb the fence.

But while they thought about it and talked about it, they were never consumed by anything for long. Too much was going on.

Billy did, indeed, put together a band: Billy and The Red Hots, a group founded on the considerable skills of B.B. Cunningham, a guitarist and classmate, and a small tribute to Billy's favorite radio personality, Daddy-O-Dewey Phillips, the first man to play an Elvis Presley record on the radio.

In July of 1954, Sam Phillips of Sun Records dropped off a 45 he thought Dewey would like.

The A side was "That's All Right." The flipside was "Blue Moon of Kentucky." Phillips, a fast-talking hillbilly hepcat who coined the phrase "rockabilly," played the record over and over, followed by a one-on-one interview with the painfully shy Presley.

While Billy Purser and The Red Hots offered homage to Phillips, Billy's act was an unconcealed imitation of Presley—without the talent. He went to Lansky Brothers' on Beale Street—where Elvis shopped—and bought an emerald green jacket for $15. He paired the jacket with black pants with pink stitching, another purchase from Lansky's, and took the stage as the lead man of The Red Hots. They played at cantinas and middle school dances, and once in awhile the boys came by to listen.

The boys shared one quality. They were uncommonly kind to one another.

The band sure did sound good tonight, one might say. Or: *Billy, well, you sure did shake it like Elvis.*

Midway through his sophomore year, Billy had given up on homework altogether and wasn't involved in after-school activities. His lasting mark on Messick High was an ironic act of heroism. At 5-foot-9 and 140 pounds, he won a fight that went down in the Messick annals as "the greatest in Messick High School history."

Joe Butler was a shy little guy, a studious kid who gravitated between the smarter kids and the cool ones, who barely noticed him. Joe was just the type of person Tom Tiller (whose brother, Dago, was considered one of the orneriest men in Tennessee) preyed upon, pushing him around in the halls, knocking him up against lockers, slapping him in the back of the head, punching him in the stomach. Tiller was forever picking on weaker, smaller kids, adding cowardly victories to his burgeoning reputation as a tough guy.

Billy liked Joe and befriended him. In turn, Joe tried to help Billy with his studies. One day, Billy caught Tiller picking on Butler. Billy told Tiller he was tired of his nonsense.

"And what is Billy Purser gonna do about it?" Tiller sneered.

"Let's just meet behind the sundry shop after school," Billy said, "and I'll show you what I am going to do about it."

Word spread through the school faster than stolen copies of an upcoming exam. Purser, most said, didn't have a chance.

Only David Welch, his best friend, followed Billy to the sundry shop, and when they got there, there may have been a hundred people already waiting.

Fed by torrents of resentment, the fight began quickly. But whereas most fights ended quickly, at first blood or a loose tooth, this one went on. Billy went down, then Tiller. Back and forth they went, slugging, punching, wrestling. The longer they fought, the more intense the fight became.

Ultimately, there was the turning moment: Billy tagged Tiller with a right and a left, and he went down and stayed down. In the silence, David handed Billy his jacket and they went home. After half a century had passed, there were those who said they could still point out the ditch where Billy put Tom Tiller in his place.

And so Billy had made his name, but his time at Messick was short. School held nothing for him. By the time he was in the eleventh grade, the gang had fallen apart. Tommy Vance and David Welch had graduated. Welch and Glynn Bishop had enlisted in the army. Bennie Vance was still in school, but without his brother around, he and Billy spent less and less time together.

Billy was lost at school. He knew it and so did his teachers. One afternoon, he was drifting through history class, a music magazine tucked inside his textbook.

"Billy," the teacher said, "who were the Lake Dwellers? Billy, are you with us?"

Roused from his reverie, Billy pondered the question. He had not read the assignment. He was reading about Billy Lee Riley.

"Uh, fish, I guess," he said.

"What?"

"You asked who were the Lake Dwellers. I said, 'Fish.'"

"That's it. Go to the office, right now!"

"I can't."

"What? Why not?"

"They said they don't want to see me down there anymore."

"Right now!"

He went to the office for the last time and drove home to tell his mother what he was going to do. They went into the kitchen where they always talked. He loved his mother with a depth that couldn't be plumbed and he knew he was about to inflict a hurt that he couldn't help.

"Mom," he said, "I quit school. I'm going to join the army."

For the longest while, she didn't speak. Then she cried. Billy asked her if she would help him. He needed her signature to enlist. With no small amount of resignation, she assured him that she would. First, though, they had to tell Raymond.

"Well," Raymond said, stubbing out a Pall Mall, "they'll straighten his ass out."

Chapter six

You're in the army now

When Billy turned out to be an expert *marksman*, it looked as if he might be a soldier. The only thing he couldn't do was put a decent shine on his shoes. Maybe the army would be the answer. Then Billy forgot the question. It always seemed to happen that way.

The sergeant was a handsome man with a toothy smile, and his

chest flapped discordantly with ribbons and medals. Billy admired his shirt and pants, nattily pressed with creases like an axe blade. He looked good, even with that G.I. haircut. Other men kept coming into the room, without as many stripes or medals, but their smiles were just as big.

Staff Sergeant Long loved the U.S. Army, and he kept telling Billy how wonderful life was going to be once he signed the papers. Yessir, life was going to change. Everything would be great.

I would buy a car from this man, Billy thought.

The army, the sergeant said, offered every opportunity in the world, and around the world.

Billy kept looking at his shoes. They looked like black mirrors. He had never seen a shoeshine like that.

"We need good men like you," one of the officers said.

Men?

No one had ever called him a man. People had told him to be a man, but no one—ever—had called him, Billy Purser, a man.

"So," Sergeant Long said, "are you ready to be a soldier in the United States Army? The army can train you to be anything you want to be. What would you like to do, son?"

Billy thought about Dewey Phillips and Rufus Thomas and Jack Parnell, then said, "I want to be in radio. I want to be a radio personality. A DJ!"

Sergeant Long leaned back in his chair, offering Billy yet another smile that would soften cement.

"Why, we got radio," he said. "The army can teach you everything you need to know about radio."

Billy didn't know snake oil from motor oil, and he wasn't that far removed from scouring Memphis for a sack-stretcher.

"All you do," said Sergeant Long, is enlist in regular army and when you get to basic training tell 'em you want to go into radio. They'll take care of everything."

That was it. The army was the answer. He was sick of school, and the army was his way out. All he had to do was have his mother sign his enlistment papers, saying it was okay for a 17-year-old to join up.

When he told Dot and Raymond how nice the officers were and how they would see that he was trained in radio, Raymond shook his head.

"I don't know if it will be just like that, Billy," he said.

But nothing could suppress Billy's excitement. He could not go back to school, and Sergeant Long said he could finish high school in the army.

"So," he asked, "will you sign for me?"

"Are you sure this is what you want to do?" Dot asked. Billy said he had never been more certain about anything.

Three days later—May 13, 1959—he was on a bus headed for Fort Jackson, South Carolina, and basic training. Most of the boys on the bus looked the same: ducktails, T-shirts, jeans, and jackets. Some had been in trouble with the law. Others were at loose ends. Some had enlisted. Some

had been drafted. They didn't talk much, but when they did the topic was how they wanted to get away from the oppressive discipline of parents and teachers, how the job at the gas station was going nowhere. Once in a while, they talked about music and sports and girls. They did not talk about soldiering; there was nothing about soldiering.

Billy, one of the younger boys on the bus, talked to no one. He had never been more than seventy miles out of Memphis, except for the time when he and Glenna boarded a Greyhound with Mamaw Wells and went to Corpus Christi, Texas, to see a relative. He remembered joking with his grandmother at a rest stop, picking up a napkin and saying, in his best Mississippi drawl, "Hey, Mamaw, what are these for?"

Determined to make a go of his career in the army, he remembered how he did nonsensical things, just to get a rise from his parents and grandparents, his teachers, his bosses—everyone, it seemed, even friends.

Time to get your shit together, he thought. *Be a good soldier. Make Mom and Dad proud. I'm tired of everybody seeing me as an idiot.*

It was a long ride, ten or twelve hours, most of the boys smoking, looking out the windows, none of them knowing exactly what was ahead.

When they finally arrived at Fort Jackson, not far from Columbia, South Carolina, the terrain changed. "Here we are, men," said an escort officer. "It's time to become soldiers."

One by one, they stepped out, each carrying a few things from home, as well as a share of anxiety, guarded closely by a measure of cockiness. *Nothing at Fort Jackson I ain't seen before*, their stances seemed to say. They assembled casually, grinning, and then a voice rained down, part locomotive, part bull's bellow. It belonged to Sergeant Britt, their drill instructor.

"Well, well, well, what the hell do we have here? What a bunch of pukes. Never in my career have I seen a worse bunch get off the bus. *Never!* And I'm supposed to make you soldiers. And you *will* be soldiers or I will kick your ass from here to Fort Dix, damned if I won't."

At that point, Billy felt it necessary to intercede. "Uh, sir. Over here."

"What? WHAT? Who's talking?"

"Yessir, here."

"Well, I can't believe my ears. Are you speaking to me, maggot?"

"Uh, yessir. I am not here to be a soldier. I'm here to learn about radio, to be a DJ."

"Say what? Radio? Who's laughing? Shut the fuck up, pukes. Let's hear what the little man has to say. Now what is it, son?"

"I am here to learn about radio. I want to be a radio personality, a DJ. They told me I would learn about radio in the army."

"Is that right? You don't say. What is your name, boy?"

"William Eugene Purser, Memphis, Tennessee."

"Well, William Eugene Purser, Memphis, Tennessee, who wants to learn about radio, let's see what we can do. Here's a rake. Pretend it's your goddang microphone and get your ass under that barracks, on your hands and knees, and give me some damn straight radio waves, nice and straight so I can see 'em in the middle of the night, and I'll see your ass in the morning."

"Uh . . ."

"Straight clean lines! And the next punk-puke who laughs is gonna be right there with him!"

Billy raked well into the night, his thoughts going back and forth. What a terrible mistake he had made. But now that he was here, he had to make the most of it, even if it meant making straight lines in the dirt. Long after, when everything was quiet except the sound of his rake, the sergeant came back.

"Get some sack time, radio boy," he said.

"Yessir," he said, dashing off into the dark.

The next morning, he was poked, probed, prodded, inoculated, shorn, and uniformed. Odd, he thought, how different they had all looked just the day before, riding in on the bus, and how similar they looked now, assembled and ready for drill. He was determined—like no time before—to be a good soldier, driven by a feeling he couldn't quite grasp.

In the coming weeks, Billy proved a crack recruit. He qualified as an Expert Marksman on his first day on the rifle range, a direct result of afternoons in Mississippi spent plunking water snakes in the head with Uncle Winford's .22.

He took the lead on forced, seventeen-mile marches through the sand, humping his field pack with a smile on his face. He survived the fact that he looked exactly like another grunt, some guy named McGahee, who had managed to piss off half the people on the base and owed the other half money. During a combat mile run, a brassy lieutenant trudged by saying, "Better pick it up."

I'll kick his ass, he thought. He passed the lieutenant and finished yards ahead of the breathless lieutenant. Billy was named acting platoon leader, then promoted to squad leader.

He got drunk for the first time in his life, went into town, sat down at the bar and, urged on by a waitress—his friends called her a "bar girl"—wrapped himself around a bottle of Old Crow. He sat, looking in a mirror on the wall, and watched himself get drunk. He bought the girl drinks, his mind growing blurry, and he thought, *So this is what it's like being drunk.* And: *I think this girl likes me.*

His friends pointed out that she wasn't drinking anything but lemonade, that it was her job to push drinks on guys.

"No," he said, "she likes me. I'm gonna get laid. Sure, she likes me. I know she does." But just the same, he slurred, "I'll test her drink."

They were sitting, talking, knees touching, her hands on his arms and legs, when Billy reached over and took a sip of her drink

With no hint of an uprising and in mid-sentence, his stomach revolted on the Old Crow and lemonade, and he spewed an arching fountain of vomit that drenched both the waitress and the bar.

His friends howled with laughter. "Good grouping, Purser. Just like on the rifle range. Expert marksmanship."

They liked Purser. They found him funny, if a bit green, and they vowed to get him out on the town more often.

Everything seemed to be working out as it should—except for that drunk thing. Billy didn't quite understand the allure of drink. The next day he was hardly the sharpest tool in the box and nothing could remove the bilious, sweet taste in his mouth, but he managed to muddle through. All day he thought about nothing but his bunk. Otherwise, he was earning notice from his sergeants and making friends.

He even liked the food, especially the chipped beef on toast, which was roundly criticized by everyone else in B-Company (and universally referred to as "shit on a shingle"). Billy's major concern was getting a proper shine on his shoes. It was always his downfall at inspection. "Boy," the sergeant said, time after time, "you can get a better shine on those shoes."

No matter what he tried—water, spit, cloths, brushes, paying somebody to help him—he couldn't achieve that high buff, which stood as the single flaw on his short service record. He thought, as basic training moved toward conclusion, that everything was good.

He couldn't wait to get home and strut around in his uniform, show

everyone that he had finally found his place, that he had made it in the army, that he was on a run, that he wasn't lost, wasn't a total screw-up. He was still homesick but he was happy.

On the morning B Company was released from basic with a two-week leave ahead of it, the men were called to assembly in the yard. They were fit and trim, a smart-looking, unified bunch. For the most part, their independence had been quelled. They were soldiers, headed to stations from California to Key West, and Billy stood proudly among them.

Buses rolled in to take the troops to Columbia, where they would make their way back home. The C.O. barked out names. He wanted the bus boarded in an orderly fashion and quickly. He went on and on. Somehow, Billy never heard his name. Everyone was on the buses except him, and he was standing alone in the yard and wondering what the hell was wrong.

"Goddammit!" the C.O. began. "I should have known it would be you, Purser, you piece of shit. Can you get anything straight? Get your shit squared away. Get on the bus so they can get the hell outta here. Move it, you dumbass!"

Billy was bewildered, infuriated, embarrassed. He had worked hard trying to please his superiors and now this. Had his name been called and he didn't hear it? Here he was, once again, at a familiar juncture—the butt of criticism. Maybe he wasn't meant to be a soldier. As the bus headed toward Columbia, he thought: *Finding your place in life sure as hell ain't easy.*

The C.O.'s words echoed through his mind: "I should have known it would be you that screwed everything up. You piece of shit."

He tried to put the thought away, but he couldn't shake it. He was still brooding over it when he arrived at the Greyhound bus station in Columbia. Across the street, he noticed other soldiers milling about a vendor's stand. He elbowed his way into the group, and spread out on tables and in boxes was every military decoration imaginable: ribbons, medals, braid, scarves in blue and red and yellow. The vendor urged the boys to step up.

"Want to go home looking good, don't you? Impress the girls. I got everything you need. Easy boys. One at a time. I'm here all day."

Minutes later, Billy was in the men's room of the bus station arranging his new appointments. He stepped back, straightened his jacket, adjusted his cap just so, and sized himself up in the mirror. *There*, he thought. In the new glory of his uniform, the words of his C.O. began to fade.

When the bus hit Memphis, Billy went to the firehouse. He wanted to see Raymond to tell him how things had gone. Only problem was, he wasn't exactly sure how things had gone. Raymond's friends made a huge fuss.

"Look at you."

"My Lord!"

"Hey, Billy's here. No fire runs today."

"Did you win the war? Look at all these medals."

Raymond eyed his boy up and down. He had a blue scarf around his neck, braid on his shoulder, medals across his chest—both sides. Billy was a walking military Christmas tree. The only thing missing was a Sousa march.

"Hi, Dad," Billy said.

"Good to see you, son," Raymond said. "What the hell is all that stuff?"

Billy wasn't sure, although someone pointed out that he had a Silver Star, which was awarded for gallantry in action. Billy didn't know. He just thought it was pretty.

"So how was it?" Raymond said. "Like they said it would be?"

"Not really," Billy said.

"Thought not. Learn anything about radio?"

"No, not yet. That comes at Fort Gordon."

"Well, welcome home, son. Seen your mother and sister yet? No? Better be off with you. They're missing you. Mamaw Wells, too."

In the coming days, he spent hours at the kitchen table talking with his mother, getting lost in that sardonic smile he loved so much. He went to Mamaw Wells's where he ate brains and eggs and crackling cornbread. He sat with Grandpa Wells watching Hopalong Cassidy on television, the Kent cigarette burning down to the filter just as it always had.

He looked up Glynn Bishop, already back from the service. They went to the Casino and all the other spots they used to hit, drank a little, danced a little, and right before Billy was to leave for Fort Gordon, Glynn dug out his uniform and they posed for a photograph like old war buddies, like the photographs they had seen from World War II and Korea.

While he was home, Billy spent as much time as he could with Joyce Arnold. When he left for the service they promised they would write all the time, but their correspondence had dwindled. She seemed somewhat distant, but nonetheless they renewed their promise. Yes, they were in love; distance could not separate them. Yes, they would write more frequently.

Promise?

Promise!

Soon it was time for Billy to leave for Fort Gordon.

"So," Raymond said, "this is where you'll learn about radio?"

"Yep, going into Signal," Billy said.

"Signal?"

"Yep, that's where I'll learn about radio."

"Well, son, it might not be just like that. Might want to clean that uniform off a little, too, before you head back. No need in drawing unnecessary attention."

"Yessir."

Somewhere along the way, he tired of the bus ride and decided to hitchhike. He was on a strip of highway hanging out his thumb, wishing he had saved some of his braid and a few of the medals when a convertible pulled up: three girls, two of them immensely good-looking.

"Where you headed?"

"Fort Gordon, Georgia."

"Oh, yeah, then off to war?"

"There is no war."

"Good, 'cause you sure are cute. We'll give you a ride a ways."

They had the radio turned up loud: "Sixteen Candles" by The Crests. The girls loved The Crests and Fabian and Paul Anka. He liked the girls. He didn't like the music.

"Ever heard of Billy Lee Reilly or Jerry Lee Lewis?"

"You mean that rockabilly crap?"

He was thinking he might get lucky, and then he knew he wouldn't. *That rockabilly crap?* He wondered if he would ever get lucky.

Later, back on a bus and glad to be surrounded by its monotonous comforting hum, he wondered who the hell was Paul Anka? Who was Fabian? The girls called it "Top 40, the best."

Hardly, he thought.

Someone asked him where he was going.

"Fort Gordon, Georgia," he said.

"And what are you going to do?"

"Signal Corps," he said, politely.

The fact was, he didn't have a clue.

Chapter seven

Billy and the Cold War

The paintbrush was a better weapon than the M-1. He could kill entire weeks with it. It was *the music* that staved off the unholy boredom of the army, though. Music saved him. And it was where he first found himself.

Of this he was certain: Somebody was confused.

Apparently, the army had decided radio had something to do with climbing telephone poles and the heavy work of setting those creosoted behemoths, attaching crossbars, and stringing wire. It was, in fact, a high-wire act, with the actor himself swaying uncertainly atop a fifty-footer.

The army's radio was arduous, sweat-soaking work and had nothing to do with music, humor, or a resonant voice. "Get your butt up that pole" passed for innovative patter, and music was the sound of a squeaking hand drill, going slowly nowhere in wood so hard the termites around Fort Gordon required dentures.

The only humor was when some grunt's spikes kicked out of the pole, and he came sliding down, landing in Georgia's red dust and arising—if fortunate—rolled like a chicken leg dredged for the fryer. That was always good for laughs.

As for the resonant voices, they all belonged to the sergeants: *C'mon, meat! I gotta tell you twice? Climb that pole. Bolt down that crossbar and secure the wires. Move it!*

This was the army's way, however, and Billy had been around long enough to know there was no reward in bucking the army way. He had given up on being a good solider back in the yard at Fort Jackson. His plan was to keep his head down, do enough to get by, and escape with an honorable discharge.

Being agile and light, though, he was a pretty good lineman, and few could match his speed getting up the poles. He gained a measure of expertise with the drills and wrenches, and even the sergeants thought he was pretty slick up there, leaning confidently back on his safety belt.

There was one continuing problem—getting down.

His agility in ascent was matched by his futility in descent.

Look out, Purser!
Make sure those gaffes are secure.
You're going too fast.
Good God, soldier. You okay?

He was never hurt seriously—no broken bones—but his sergeant said that Billy sustained more injuries individually than the entire company did collectively.

Doctors, cringing at his fate, pulled long, creosoted spurs from his arms and legs. "Son, I do believe this might hurt me as much as it does you," one doc said, preparing to pull a spur from Billy's groin.

Finally, Billy was beginning to understand that the army had no intention about guiding him toward his desired profession. There was not a soul who cared if he worked in radio, and he decided this state of affairs was his fault. Even Raymond had said, "I don't think it will be just like that." He didn't listen. He never listened.

Yet for his foibles, he became a popular guy in his unit. He was funny,

and he wasn't afraid to step outside with anyone who wanted to fight. He was pretty good, too. He whipped a lot of guys bigger and stronger than he was—to the surprise and delight of his brethren. (None of them knew that he had learned to box at the YMCA.)

But he smoked too much, drank too much, and heading back to Memphis—then to Germany and assignment to the Signal Corps—he worried about Joyce Arnold. Her letters were fewer and farther between and when she did write, she talked about—of all things—the weather, for God sakes! Billy was beginning to doubt the old aphorism about absence making the heart grow fonder.

How are you? I'm fine . . . It sure has been hot here. How's the weather there? Hope they are not working you too hard . . . Got to go . . .
Love, Joyce

Each day at mail call, he eagerly awaited a letter from Joyce, and when one did come, he raced to the barracks hoping for passages thick with blue prose and reminiscences of nights in the back of the Ford. Instead, he read: *It sure has been hot here . . .*

Absence, he thought, *makes the heart go yonder.*

Maybe he could make things right when he got home. At the bottom of his heart, he knew that he and Joyce would never get married. Still, he clung to the idea.

This time when he arrived back in Memphis there was no braid, no scarf, no medals. His uniform was spare.

"Glad to see you've smartened up," Raymond said.

His time at home was a blur. He spent some time with Raymond and Dot, Mamaw and Grandpa Wells. He went to The Casino and the Sundry Shop. He went down to Keegan's, standing on the street and listening to the boys training to be disc jockeys.

He listened to the radio: Dewey Phillips and DJGK. The black DJs on WDIA, especially Rufus Thomas. He turned the dial to WLAC in Nashville and listened to John R.

He was never quite sure why radio had such a hold on him. Everything about the stations and DJs he liked was fast, clipped, funny, fresh, and seldom serious. There was no room for anything laborious in radio. Maybe that was what he liked most. Radio didn't sound like work. It sounded like

nothing more than people laughing, talking, and enjoying themselves.

At night, he and Joyce drove out in the country, the radio down low, making out to the tunes of Bob Whites and Whippoorwills. They steamed up the windows but to Billy's dismay, they remained on familiar ground. Finally, on one of his last nights home, he played every adolescent soldier's trump card.

"You know," he said, "I might not be coming back."

"What do you mean?"

"I might die over there."

"Die? How would you die? There is no war."

"No, but there is that whole East Berlin-West Berlin thing, that thing with the Russians. That could blow up at anytime. They've told us all to be ready."

"But you are going to be a DJ. You're not a real soldier."

"Yeah, but if trouble breaks out, the DJs will be the first ones they bomb."

"What?"

"Yeah. When the DJs go, it destroys morale. Yep, shipping out in just a few days."

Joyce Arnold was unmoved. Days later, Billy wasn't thinking about his futile tactics with Joyce. He was hanging his head over the railing, spilling the contents of his stomach into the rolling pitch of the Atlantic Ocean.

His first days and nights on board ran together. He was trying to sleep in swaying bunks stacked four deep, running to chow and then running up to the decks or the nearest latrine to expel everything in his stomach and some things that weren't. He was homesick and seasick, and just about the time he had decided death might be a vacation, word passed that lifted his spirits and settled his stomach: The ship's band needed a drummer.

He had never really played before. He had sat behind the drums back in the days of Billy Purser and The Red Hots, fiddling around with the sticks and the pedals, trying to get a handle on how anybody could make their hands and feet work independently, and always intrigued (God bless Petey the parakeet). So for the first time in his military career, he volunteered for something. It might just keep him out of anything that resembled work, he decided, which was his primary motivation as a full-fledged member of the United States Army bound for the 229th Signal Battalion in Böblingen, Germany, near Stuttgart.

His audition was just short of awful, but he got the job and it made the rest of the voyage passable. He ate more, slept better, and spent less time with his head over the railing. He struggled through a few shows on board, but by the time he was headed for Böblengin and Panzer Kaserne, he had found some minor agreement between the snare and the bass.

Between rehearsals and performances, which were few, Billy had managed to avoid some hard duty, but he missed Memphis. He missed Mississippi, too, the way it sounded at night; the smell of the oaks and sweet gums mixing with that of the pines and kudzu; how there was always the scent of smoke in the air, someone burning a stump, burning something; the smell of the earth itself.

Sometimes, in his mind, the sounds of the ship were drowned out by cows lowing in the distance, the slam of a screen door, people talking—way off somewhere, crickets singing. How comforting it all was—fireflies at night, heavy dew hanging low with the dawn, the smell of bacon frying and coffee brewing.

He'd never seen anything as beautiful as the Stuttgart region, even if he did miss biscuits and sausage gravy. Then he met Buddy Pearson. Buddy auditioned him, stuck him on drums in his Blues All-Stars, and almost overnight, Billy's life changed.

He couldn't wait to get back home. It would be awhile, of course. He pounded his pillow, tossed in his bunk, and tried to sleep.

Everything on the ship smelled like metal and oil.

In the fall of 1959, fresh off the ship, Billy was captivated by the countryside around Stuttgart: the green rolling hills, the graceful turns of the Neckar River, and the vineyards that seemed to hang on every hillside. The buildings were enormous and old. There were castles, sprawling and immense. There were vast museums and opera houses, and the homes were stacked three and four stories high with sharply slanted tile roofs. He felt as if he had stumbled onto a movie set. There was nothing like this in Memphis.

An early morning fog spiraled from the valleys through the shanks of the hills. It seemed magical except for the ride, bumpy and cold. He was in a transport truck with five other GIs headed for Panzer Kaserne in Böblingen, where the German army had maintained Panzer tank divisions.

Everything was so peaceful and beautiful that it was hard to grasp the reality that Stuttgart's heart, its industrial center—Old Stuttgarter—had been nearly destroyed by Allied air raids. During the course of the war, Stuttgart suffered more than fifty separate bombings that wiped out nearly 70 percent of the city's buildings and led to well over 4,000 civilian deaths. He had difficulty understanding the firestorms and the death, the Jews driven from their homes and transported to camps for extermination. It was all so antithetical to the postcard that was lying so peacefully before him.

He wanted to talk about it as they bounced along to Böblingen, but no one else seemed interested. They nodded. They dozed. They swore. Every day he spent in the army brought a stronger sense that he should be elsewhere. But where?

The driver, a grizzled sergeant, announced that he had missed chow and by damn, no matter what, he was stopping for breakfast. He didn't care if they were late; nobody cared.

They pulled into a roadhouse at 7:30 in the morning. Billy and the GIs were looking for eggs and bacon. The driver laughed.

"No such thing," he said. "Not off the base, boys." They had wurst and wiener schnitzel, strudel, washed down with oversized bottles of beer.

Billy wanted biscuits and sausage gravy. He nibbled at the sausage, drank some beer, and eyed the beer maids—especially the big blonde with the pleasing smile. How long had it been since he had received a letter from Joyce Arnold? He had no idea.

After breakfast, the driver was more talkative. He said the Marshall Plan had restored Germany, which was why you saw so few signs of the war, but a lot of folks here hadn't put the war away. There were places where the boys shouldn't wear their uniforms, he said. Civilian clothes made things easier.

Some of the Germans were angry about the Allied presence, the fact that Germany had lost the war and the country had been partitioned, and he thought that was understandable. A lot of people lost family, he said: husbands, sons, and brothers. The American uniform was a reminder of what had been lost.

He told them where to buy booze and cigarettes, where to find women, what bars were safe, and who to look out for on the base. He was a rolling orientation officer, reinforcing some of the things they had heard back at base in the States, telling them other things they hadn't been told, and then: "Last chance, fellas," he said, "let's duck in for a bracer and then we hit the base. Gonna be awhile 'fore you can wet your whistles again."

Billy thought that he had plenty of time to grow accustomed to things—nearly three years. Lord, it seemed like a lifetime, a sentence rather than service.

Amidst the beauty of the Stuttgart region, Panzer Kaserne was a conglomeration of unimaginative structures, all green and brown, gray and tan, dedicated to function rather than form. Every thing and every person inside the fences that enclosed it had a place and purpose, and there was no room for deviation unless, of course, the army decided there was.

Moments after arriving at Panzer Kaserne, Billy decided two changes had to be made: he would spend as much time as possible off the base, and he would find the easiest job on the base.

During roll call, he learned that the army had enough linemen. But it needed typists. Only an ill-fated paper wad incident involving his typing teacher, Mrs. Irons, had prevented a passing grade in high school, and so he immediately volunteered, even if he was only a few tottery steps beyond the hunt-and-peck stage.

Nevertheless, he believed he could fake it well enough to get by, thinking all the while how much better typing would be than climbing poles in falling temperatures. He also thought how true was his aim on the wastebasket, and how the unsuspecting Mrs. Irons had walked right into the spitwad. It was as if she had walked into a fastball. God, one more failing grade. Why couldn't he have been graded on his over-the-plate spitwad?

He envisioned his days in Teletype as getting up in the morning, typing all day, then mess and sack time: comfortable, easy. Once more, his judgment was faulty. Teletype did not excuse him from ditches that needed to be dug, holes that needed to be filled, everything that needed to be painted—there was always something that required a fresh coat of green—or driving trucks that had to be transported from one base to another for no apparent reason.

In addition to his obligations in Teletype, there were formations, inspections, drills, details, duties, and maneuvers that took him into the dead of night and a continental winter with which he was completely unfamiliar. No one made any of this clear when he signed up for Teletype. Or, once again, had he missed something? It seemed as though he was always missing something. The army, he thought, had a way of showing just a portion of its hand and was forever pulling some heretofore unsuspected thing from under the table.

Radio? DJ? Sure we got radio. And you end up climbing telephone poles.

Who can type? We need typists for Teletype. And you end up on a forced march through the woods, tree limbs slapping you in the face, freezing to death and sleeping on the ground.

He still could not shine his shoes well enough to suit the sergeants. He couldn't get his bunk right. His footlocker was never up to muster and someone was always yelling at him. He didn't really try to be inept. It just seemed as though he was, in spite of his best intentions. *But perhaps,* he thought ruefully, *I am merely getting excellent at being inept. I may be better at it than anyone in the unit.*

Between roll call and lights out, life at Panzer Kaserne was tedious, too regimented, and far too much work. Time away from the base was too short and infrequent. He became a goldbricker of premier proportion, a full-blown deadbeat, a master of the bug-out, avoiding work and responsibility at every turn.

He was an observant young man, alert to any practice that might help him escape work, and his work had become, in effect, avoiding work. Then one day while walking the yard, he had an epiphany.

What was it that took place every day? What was it that seemed so important to the army? Exactly! That everything was clean, spit-shined. For all that was so dull—green, brown, and tan—the army insisted, *demanded,* in fact, that everything was freshly painted and in those same bland colors.

All he needed was a paintbrush, a bucket, and some paint. He scrounged around the base and came up with a splayed, worn-out four-inch paintbrush he found in the motor pool. It was stiff and stained. Exactly right.

The next day, after chow, as his company was preparing for a field exercise, Billy lagged behind as the other GIs boarded trucks heading for the fields and forests beyond the gates. The winds howled and their gear rattled and creaked as they loaded up.

"Where's Purser?" a sergeant barked. "He's doing it again. Screwin' things up."

At that point, Billy walked into view and held up his paintbrush.

"Oh! Okay, Purser. Carry on. Didn't know you were on paint detail."

Billy smiled. He enjoyed few things more than ducking authority. It was his game and he was good at it. For weeks to come, he walked around the base with the paintbrush tucked into his fatigues, always at the ready. Any sign of maneuvers or undesirable work details, Billy brandished the brush. He had no paint and no bucket, but the brush proved enough to cover him.

The paintbrush became a cherished object. When it wasn't in use, and no one was around, he hid it in a grate in the wall and pushed a toolbox up against it, assuring that no one would locate it. He could have secured another brush, even bought one in town, but part of the pleasure was in the clandestine nature of his ploy.

At every opportunity, Billy made his way into town. He went to the GI bars on DI Square, where the night usually ended in a fierce brawl. Billy never ran from a fight, but he liked himself far too much to get scarred or seriously injured over what generally amounted to nothing. Consequently, he frequented places most GIs didn't: The Dolly Bar or Mom's Guest House, where he met Toney, a redhead with a pixie haircut who made him forget about Joyce Arnold and the letters that never arrived.

Toney taught him to speak some German. He helped her improve her English. She took him to The Eldorado Club, passing him off as an American but not a soldier. The German people believed GIs were always drunk and causing trouble, she said.

Toney took him to her home and introduced him to her 80-year-old neighbor, Frau Bressler, a widow who spoke broken English and had lost her son in the war. Frau Bressler reminded him of his grandmother, Mamaw Wells: the bun in her hair, the way she moved about the house, her soft-spoken demeanor.

They sat in her parlor for hours talking and sipping homemade schnapps. She said the Führer's insanity had cost her country too much, but when Billy asked her if she had ever said, "Heil, Hitler!" she turned away and dropped her head.

She was embarrassed and pained. "Please understand," she said, "there was no room for dissent or free expression." The slightest thought of

rebellion against The Reich could mean death. The SS was everywhere. No one could be trusted, not neighbors, not friends. It was a horrible time. After a point, many did anything they could to protect their lives and their families—sometimes unspeakable things. Her country was filled with guilt and sadness.

If there was anyone she hated worse than Hitler, it was Stalin and the Russians. Stalin, she said, was just as evil as Hitler, but he was convenient for the Allies. She feared the Russians and tried to make Billy understand why so many Germans resented the occupation and the wall separating East and West Berlin.

For one of the first times in his life, he found himself actually listening. He thought he understood her fears and her losses.

She kept her son's guitar, an old acoustic Hofner, on a stand in the parlor. Once in a while, Billy tried to play for her. He could manage his way through a few basic chords. She told him he had a nice voice.

Billy developed a taste for schnapps and wiener schnitzel, wurst, spaetzle, and sauerbraten, and promised himself that, someday, he would become an accomplished guitar player.

Perhaps it was Frau Bressler's influence, but Billy remembered another promise, one he made to his mother—that he would complete his high school education while he was in the army. The process was easier and more beneficial than he anticipated—time in class was better than time in the field. The instructor covered some English, a little history, touched on the basics of science, and was impressed that in less than six months, Billy had developed a working knowledge of the German language. He was even more impressed when Billy explained how some of the residents felt about the occupation and the war.

Billy finished the program with the highest grade in the class. For his achievement, he received his high school equivalency diploma and a carton of cigarettes. As he had recently sold his gas mask for cigarette money, it was an unexpected and appreciated bonus.

Boredom.

He blamed his increasing smoking habit on boredom. There were times when he almost wished something would happen in Berlin, something exciting, but short of war. He didn't want to hurt anybody, or see anyone hurt, and, above all, he didn't want to be engaged in anything that required a

gas mask. He had dreams about the sirens that signaled a general alert and he would awaken yelling, "Who's got an extra gas mask?"

His dreams were met with the notion that Private Billy Purser—a nice guy and popular enough—was not quite right and a magnet for trouble. Most days brought another example, but none better than his run-in with Top Sergeant Anderson, 6-foot-2 and 220 pounds of hardened war veteran muscle, the most feared man on the base.

At the five o'clock formation, Anderson was particularly displeased. He stormed up and down in front of the assembled troops, shouting commands and dictating how every soldier in his command would conduct himself from that point forward.

With each of Anderson's directives, the troops answered: Yes, sir. Yes, sergeant. Sergeant Anderson paced up and down, veins popping in his neck and forehead, pelting them with his spittle, everyone pinned under his gaze, which made them feel like freshly matted butterflies.

Billy found himself drifting away, not paying attention. Every time Anderson yelled, he responded as loud as he could, adding his voice to the chorus. Soon, he had no idea what Anderson was saying. He was just yelling, hoping it would be over and he would be free of the nonsense.

Finally, Anderson screamed, "Is there anyone here who wants to take me on, anyone who doesn't want to comply with my wishes, anyone who thinks he can beat my ass? If so, let's hear ya."

The entire troop was silent, except for one.

"Yes, sir! Yes, sergeant!" Billy yelled.

No one moved.

No one *breathed*.

Sergeant Anderson descended on Billy like a summer storm.

"Is that right, Private?" Anderson snarled, eyes flashing. "You think you can take the Top?"

"What? What? What did I say?"

"You said you think you can take me. Well, let's just us go see."

The sergeant grabbed Billy by the arm, dismissed the rest of the troops, and marched him behind a barracks. Billy was quaking. He had no idea what had taken place. He feared few, but he was no match for the Top. He was 5-foot-8 and 137 pounds. The Top was the size of an earth grader. While the sergeant rolled up his sleeves, Billy pleaded his case: he didn't know what he was doing, he wasn't paying attention, he never paid attention.

Finally, the sergeant softened. He almost smiled. "I like you, Purser," he said. "You are just such a screw-up. So, what are you gonna tell 'em when you get back to the barracks? That I backed down?"

Billy said nothing for a moment, then he smiled.

"Do you mind?" he said sheepishly.

The sergeant chuckled.

"Jesus," he said. "Go on Purser. Get yourself squared away. And pay attention. It's the only way to get through this man's army."

That, of course, seemed to be the problem.

During Billy's time at Panzer Kaserne, only one man truly commanded his attention—Buddy Pearson, a tall, slender, sophisticated black man from Illinois. Pearson held a special place on the base; he was the leader of a band that due to its popularity enjoyed an extreme privilege. While others were on work detail, Buddy Pearson and the Blues All-Stars practiced at the recreation hall or performed at officer's clubs, NCO Clubs, and other bases around Stuttgart. Given their skill and popularity, company commanders even signed off on performances in civilian bars in nearby towns.

Pearson looked a little like Sidney Poitier, and he didn't walk, he glided along like he was on skates. He was soft-spoken except when he sang and then his voice turned full but ragged around the edges with a poignant, bluesy appeal.

The Blues All-Stars were impressive enough that generals ordered command performances at prestigious parties. Had it not been for the presence of Elvis Presley in Friedberg, serving with the Third Armored Division, Buddy Pearson and the Blues All-Stars might have been recognized as the premier musical act in the European theater.

However, Buddy Pearson, a man who seemed to have never faced a predicament he couldn't resolve, had a problem. His drummer had rotated back to the States and the Blues All-Stars were on hiatus until they found a replacement. They had a well-paying gig coming up, and the need was urgent.

Pearson, wearing shades, sliding along, searched the base. Anybody know a drummer? Anybody know anyone who could play the drums, even a little? His search was notable, for few had seen him off-stage, in fatigues, or even in the light of day.

Eventually, days drawing down on the show, Pearson heard about a kid named Purser, just 18 or 19 years old, who had played drums on the troop ship. Buddy tracked Purser down and arranged an audition. He found the kid eager but barely competent. He seemed nervous. He smoked too much. Every sentence ended with a laugh. Pearson wasn't sure, but time was short, and the kid would have to do.

They practiced every day. Pearson got Billy freed from some of his duties. Otherwise, Billy turned to his own catalogue of escape plans: the paintbrush, toothache, stomachache, diarrhea, overall incompetence. He made every practice but not every beat. Buddy Pearson winced and wondered. His old drummer was accomplished, schooled in jazz, never missed a beat. This new kid was not schooled at all, filled too much, missed too much. Sometimes he was too fast; other times he was too slow.

He liked the kid's energy, though, so he told him to sit back some. "Just stay with us," he said. "Don't be crazy. Don't try to be good, be smooth. Think smooth. Just follow us along."

The Blues All-Stars were known for one thing; they had the Ray Charles act down. Close your eyes and Ray Charles Robinson was in the room. Pearson turned the piano inside out. Michael Vozelli was a wonder on tenor sax, and the bass man, a short, effeminate man the others called "Sweet and Low," approached the talents of Curtis Ohlson, Charles's longtime bassist.

The night they played, Billy was so nervous he didn't know where they were. He unloaded the drums, slipped into the suit that had belonged to his much larger predecessor, pushed up his sleeves, and when Buddy kicked it off with "Mess Around," Billy did his best to stay with the beat.

They came back with "I Got a Woman," and Billy went off, too loud and too quick, prompting Pearson, in mid-lyric, to look back over his shoulder and scowl. Noting the prompt, Billy cut it back. That night, Buddy Pearson and the Blues All-Stars were met with standing ovations.

It was two o'clock in the morning, they were packing up, and Billy had made it through the night. The club smelled of spilled liquor and cigarette smoke. He was spent and energized at the same time. He had to be up at five, but he didn't care. He didn't think he had ever been happier.

He was putting the cymbals in their cases, when Buddy Pearson strolled up with a Scotch in his hand.

"What d'ya think?" he said, quietly, swirling the glass and taking a sip.

"Thought it went well," Billy said.

"Not bad. Not good," Pearson said. "We got another gig in less than a week. If I can't find somebody better, you're back in."

Moments later, they were in a van headed back to the base. Billy was tired. He tried to sleep. Vozelli was out, snoring. Sweet and Low and a few of the other guys were passing around a little pipe. Sweet smoke filled the car. Buddy Pearson drove. He drank nothing. He didn't touch the pipe. He stared down the road, headed back to Panzer Kaserne.

After his first show with the Blues All-Stars, Billy went on the dodge. He spent every moment possible in the rec hall, practicing the songs still stuck in his head. From time to time, Pearson dropped by to listen, nodded his head and moved along. In a few days, Pearson scheduled a practice. He had not found another drummer. Billy was back in.

"For now," Pearson said.

During the practice session, Vozelli and the other band members commented on Billy's improvements. Pearson said nothing until the session was over and the other members had left the hall.

"Put your mind to it," he said, "and you might be a good drummer."

So Billy kept the sticks close. He tapped away on desktops, tables, and pillows, learning that soft surfaces increased his hand speed and strength. When he wasn't playing on something, he was seeing the drums and cymbals in his mind. During the next performance, there were no scowls from Pearson. There was a slight nod and when they were packing up, Buddy, Scotch in hand, strolled up to Billy.

"So?" he said, swirling the ice in his glass. "How do you think it went?"

"What did *you* think?" Billy said.

For a moment Pearson said nothing, then he gave Billy a slight smile. "Better," Pearson said. "Still got a ways to go."

He turned to walk away, then stopped and looked back at Billy.

"See you Monday afternoon at practice."

"I'm in?"

"You're in," Pearson said. "Unless you screw up."

"That won't happen, sir."

"It's Buddy," he said.

Billy laughed. It was that nervous laugh.

"Uh, yeah. Buddy!"

Billy became an accomplished self-taught drummer and, if possible, a worse soldier. He was excused, in part, for his incompetence because he was a member of Buddy Pearson's Blues All-Stars. The band played private parties and clubs where people cheered every song and every brawl, too. They played clubs where the patrons' only interest seemed to lie in starting a fight. The fights went on, but the music never stopped.

During one particularly violent fracas, the manager of the club raced to the bandstand pleading with Pearson to play something that would calm the crowd. Pearson turned to the band and called for "Peter Gunn," Henry Mancini's driving theme song from the hit television series. The tune only escalated the fight, and the All-Stars were forced to flee the stage to protect themselves and their instruments.

The band played three or four nights a week, and Billy took great pleasure when, during a set, Buddy Pearson paused and introduced the members of his band. "And on drums—Billy Purser, Memphis, Tennessee. Billy has that instinctual, southern rhythm, you see."

The recognition reinforced Billy's newest goal. After the army, he would go back to Memphis and spend the rest of his life as a musician. The life felt right: the clubs, the nightlife, the excitement. He even liked that dank smell that settled in at the end of the night when the music stopped and the last of the revelers were heading out the door into the night.

Playing in Buddy Pearson's band was the only thing that made the army bearable. He enjoyed every moment in the music. Finally, he had an identity and people he could relate to. Vozelli and Purser became friends. They talked about music and women and home. Billy told Vozelli how he missed things like jowl bacon and sweet tea. Vozelli's home was in Philadelphia. He took Billy into town and introduced him to pizza, told him about cheese steaks and the delis and diners up and down Broad Street in South Philly.

"Funny," Vozelli said, "must be an Italian thing. We got the delis, the diners and a couple doors down, funeral homes. An Italian thing or Catholic. We think about food and wine, work, family, and dying."

Back in Memphis, Billy said, everybody was Southern Baptist. "You could sell tickets to see a Catholic," he said. He told Vozelli about meeting Elvis and riding around town in an old beat-up truck. He tried to describe Memphis barbecue, how you could walk into Leonard's and sitting in front of a plate of ribs or pulled pork, you might see Jerry Lee Lewis or Clyde McPhatter.

Memphis was the center of the music world, he argued, but Vozelli said it was New York. Billy wondered if he had ever heard of Dewey Phillips, the man who brought rock 'n' roll to the world. Vozelli said, no, that would be Alan Freed, who started in Cleveland at WJW, moved to New York and WINS, and didn't play that hillbilly crap Billy was talking about.

Billy had never heard of Alan Freed and wondered about the intelligence and awareness of anyone in the music business who wouldn't play Elvis or Jerry Lee.

Vozelli and Billy argued and laughed. They came at the music from different regions and cultures, but they found something in the music that brought them together. Billy said it was just like back home. Blacks and whites were segregated, but they shared the music—like they did with Buddy and the band. Vozelli agreed that there was something to the idea, then started talking about genres. Billy said in Memphis there weren't any genres, just music—everywhere.

Billy had six months left on his hitch when Buddy Pearson and the Blues All-Stars played their last show. That night, they packed up slowly, drank more than usual, and laughed less. Days later, Buddy shipped out but not before praising Billy.

"Didn't think you would make it," he said, "but you became a damn good drummer. Enjoyed it, man."

For the next six months, Billy kept the paintbrush at the ready and spent as much time off the base and out of sight as he possibly could, a prospect made easier by his assignment to the notorious coal detail.

On the surface, this was a grimy detail assigned to the least industrious soldiers on the base. Every morning, those assigned to the job had to sweep out the trucks, make the short drive to Ludwigsburg, fill the trucks with coal, and drive back to the base to unload. It was a process that ostensibly required the entire day. But nothing was further from the truth.

The first day Billy showed up for the assignment, a veteran of the detail turned to him and said, "Where's your civvies?"

Billy didn't understand.

"Your civies, your street clothes—where are they? Look, this is the way it goes. The trucks are loaded before 10 or 11 o'clock. They just dump it in the trucks. Takes no time. Leaves the rest of the day wide open. So instead of coming straight back to the base, we park the trucks at this soccer field, change into our civvies, and go into town for a few beers. About three, we head for the trucks, change clothes, rub coal dust all over us, and drive back to the base. I'm tellin' ya, it's the best worst job in the army."

For the next six months, Billy was an enthusiastic member of the coal brigade, telling everyone how horrible the job was and how much he hated it, stumbling off the truck at day's end feigning mortal fatigue, a smile hidden behind the soot on his face.

In the spring of 1962, Private William Eugene Purser received an honorable discharge and mustered out at Fort Dix. He had no notable citations, just the single stripe on his shoulder. Near the train station, he spotted a clothing store. This time, homecoming would be shorn of decoration. He was going home as Billy, just Billy.

He went to the men's room at the train station, stripped off his uniform, put on his new clothes, and looked in the mirror. He liked what he saw. He picked his uniform off the floor, wadded it up, and threw it in a trashcan. He had all he needed from the army in his duffle bag: a couple of books, his drumsticks, and some cash.

He was going back to Memphis and there were three things he had to find right away: a job, a place to live, and a long-legged woman. It would be nice if she had a job and a place to live, he thought.

Always the dreamer.

Part II

Kick-starting a life

Chapter eight

The Little Black Book

She was gorgeous and she was in pharmaceuticals. The guys joked that Billy got a *good-looker* and a source to boot. The differenc was, he married her. And there was another difference She had a tin ear for the musicians' lifestyle.

Billy parked the car, killed the engine, and lit a cigarette.

He stared at the line of homes in various states of disrepair. It was the middle of the day and except for an occasional passerby on the sidewalk and children playing in the yards, it was quiet.

He sat for a while and smoked, looking at the houses, his left arm propped on the window frame of the car. On the passenger's seat beside him was a bulky brown case that was quickly assuming the ominous property of a weight manacled to his wrist, as if any moment he—and it—could be tossed into the Mississippi.

He took a last pull on the cigarette, glanced at his reflection in the rearview mirror, grabbed the case, and stepped out into the street. This was his "territory." That's what the man had called it, but from the looks of things, Billy believed he had gained ownership only because no one else saw any prospects in this godforsaken parcel of downtrodden Memphis.

He walked down the street eyeing each house for potential customers, practicing his pitch: *Good morning, sir/madam. My name is Billy Purser. I'm your Fuller Brush Man.*

Sometimes people answered the door, sometimes they didn't. Occasionally, someone opened the door, spotted the case, and slammed the door in his face. Coming home had not been what he expected. He had been home for weeks, living with Dot and Raymond and selling brushes and cleansers door to door was the best job he had been able to find. He could have applied at several of the plants around town, but as he had explained to Dot and Raymond, he just wanted something to tide him over until his music career took off.

Shortly after arriving in Memphis, Billy found out that Eddie Bond and The Stompers were looking for a new drummer. This was not just some slop-it-around garage band. In 1956, The Stompers had a hit, "Rockin Daddy," and signed with Mercury Records. They toured with Roy Orbison, Carl Perkins, Johnny Horton, and Johnny Cash.

Charlie Freeman, a studio guitarist at Stax Records, told Billy he had to be at his very best. Others had tried out and failed to impress Bond or John Huey, the steel-guitarist and leader of the band.

"No mistakes," Charlie said, "no mistakes."

Billy's audition was quick. Midway through the third song, lead singer Doyle Nelson stopped singing and looked at Huey, then Bond. For a moment, no one said anything. Billy thought he was through; that he had failed. Then Nelson turned to Huey and Bond.

"Hire him," Nelson said. "Ain't nobody gonna touch him."

They played five and six nights a week, and some afternoons. Their primary gig was as the house band at The Little Black Book, Bond's popular club on Highway 51, but they traveled some, too. Huey had three rules: *Be on time. Play well. Be mostly sober.*

The Stompers packed the club every night they played, but the pay was meager. Billy made $55 a week with the band, necessitating a side job, one that allowed him to sleep in and work when the notion struck him.

After a few weeks of peddling brushes and cleansers, he knew he needed to find another job. He spent hours describing the products to folks who gave him orders for one thing or another. At delivery, he was surprised to learn how many of his friendliest customers had either forgotten about the order, didn't have the money and wanted him to come back in a few days, or had just changed their mind.

Consequently, he was often stuck with the bill and had to pay the company. There was little doubt in his mind that this circumstance had given him status as the biggest investor in Fuller Brush products in all of Shelby County. Raymond sympathized with Billy's financial plight and together they hatched a plan to urge some of the delinquent customers into paying.

Raymond would put on his fireman's uniform—it bore great resemblance to those worn by Memphis policemen—and ride along the route with Billy while he tried to collect. If the customer was still unwilling to pay, Billy would simply point to the car and say, "I've been very patient and I don't want to involve the police, but if you look, there is a patrolman sitting in my car and he will arrest you."

Raymond, meanwhile, sat in the car, grim-faced and scowling, doing his best to look as threatening as possible.

The role pleased Raymond and the subterfuge worked well enough that Billy was almost financially even, at which time he quit Fuller Brush and traded one sample case for another.

He became an encyclopedia salesman.

There were distinct benefits to selling encyclopedias. The neighborhoods were more prosperous, the dogs kinder. Buoyed by the potential of his new position, Billy hit the streets armed with a new pitch: *Congratulations, sir/madam. You have been selected to receive a brand new set of encyclopedias.*

On the first call of his first day, a pleasant couple bought an entire set of books for their children, writing a check on the spot. But after that initial success, few doors were answered. Those that were then slammed in his face. People peered surreptitiously through blinds, then disappeared silently into the inner recesses of their houses.

And then there were occasions when he was invited inside for a glass of iced tea or lemonade. Billy was surprised to learn that there were many lonely housewives eager to expand their knowledge of the world. In some cases, he made repeat calls—but no sales. Raymond and his friends at the firehouse warned him about the inherent dangers in those repeat calls. "Keep it up and you'll need a real cop to ride along with you," Raymond said.

For all his diligence, he never sold another encyclopedia. Encyclopedias did, however, lead him to a job that offered a decent wage on a regular basis. He became a driver for Bluff City News, delivering newspapers and magazines all over Memphis. There was one drawback: Billy was required to have his truck loaded and on the road by five o'clock in the morning, roughly three hours after the band left the stage at the Little Black Book. It was a critical detail he had overlooked in the job description.

Still, he was off by two in the afternoon and didn't have to be at the club most nights until eight. He decided he could make this work. He could grab a nap after the show, make his deliveries, sleep for another few hours, and make it back to the club.

By the time the band was off the stage, though, Billy was too wound up to even consider a nap. He was seldom home before three-thirty or four in the morning. He drank coffee. He tried to read. He showed up at Bluff City News glassy-eyed and jittery. He was so jumpy he made the other drivers nervous.

He was the first to load and pull out of the warehouse, but something about the sound of the wheels on the road made him sleepy. He tried everything to fight the fatigue: rolled down the windows, turned up the radio. Still, he nodded off, only to be awakened when he curbed the tires or a long blare of horns jarred him back to consciousness.

At first, Billy turned again to his grade school friend Charlie Freeman for help. He asked Charlie to follow him on his delivery route. If he thought, for any reason, Billy was asleep at the wheel, Charlie was to honk the horn on his car. Charlie was quick to oblige but said he didn't see how this solved the greater problem. What Billy needed, Charlie said, was rest, or a new job, something that didn't require him to be on the job at five o'clock in the morning.

"Yeah, but other guys do it," Billy said. "They play at night and work during the day."

"Yeah, and most of 'em have help."

"Help?"

"*Help!*"

Charlie never elaborated but Billy started asking questions around

the club, wondering quietly about the "help" that was available. His investigation didn't take long. He was soon introduced to the world of barbs, bennies, and white crosses.

"It's okay," someone said. "Truckers do these things all the time."

Billy played better, worked harder, completed his rounds on time, ate less, smoked more, found his own apartment and, when he could, crashed into an oblivious, dreamless sleep. He was 21 years old, sampling the Memphis nights. He felt invulnerable, except for those days when he couldn't keep anything in his stomach except tomato soup or when he was on the backside of a white cross. The "down" was horrible, but there was usually a cure in his pocket.

Eddie Bond and The Stompers continued to gain popularity for their particular mix of country, rock, and hillbilly-swing. John Huey was recognized as being one of the best steel guitar players in the South. Doyle Nelson could sing anything from George Jones to Carl Perkins. Hawk Hawkins, a masterful bass player, had gained the notice of Jerry Lee Lewis. Blind Jimmy Smith was a piano and alto sax player whose solos were so good—and so long—that the rest of the band often left the stage, went to the bar, or took a seat at one of the tables around the dance floor.

"Don't matter how long we sit out here," Doyle said. "Jimmy just keeps playing until we come back."

When they weren't filling the Little Black Book, they were playing at The Tropicana, The Manhattan, The Plantation Club, or Dance Land in Millington, one of the few integrated nightspots in the Memphis area. Their success at Dance Land said more about their music and style than any other accolade they received.

They owed no small part of their success to the cast of musicians who showed up night after night, constantly seeded by the enterprising Bond.

One of his established patrons bore a strong resemblance to country singer Carl Smith. Between breaks Bond would raise the house lights and say, "Ladies and gentlemen, look who is in the house. None other than the legendary Carl Smith, 'Mister Country.'"

The imposter smiled and waved to the crowd, then retook his seat, despite pleas from the crowd for a song or two. On one crowded evening at the club, Bond saw his friend seated near the stage and mentioned that once again, "None other than Carl Smith is with us again tonight."

At that point, a wild cheer went up as Carl Smith, the *genuine* Carl Smith, ascended the stage.

Bond didn't skip a beat. "Throw that other sumbitch outta here," he said. "We got the real McCoy right here. Sing a little something with us won't ya, Carl?"

The band's success was aided by Bond's radio show on KWAM and his regular mention of the celebrities who stopped by: singer/songwriters Jumpin' Gene Simmons, Ed Bruce, and Ace Cannon, who was known as "the Godfather of Sax." After a performance in Memphis, Cannon showed up at the Little Black Book. He had been drinking most of the night, but when he asked to sit in for a couple of songs, he was quickly obliged. The alcohol seemed to have no effect. Ace was blowing—pulling things from his horn like no one had heard before—but when he leaned back for a few high notes and the big finish, he fell over backwards, finishing the song flat on his back without missing a note.

"Amazing," John Huey said to Nelson. "He even *fell* in time. Right on beat."

Ernest Tubb visited, and Conway Twitty, who was trying to recruit John Huey. Singer Charlie Rich—"The Silver Fox"—came by and Reggie Young, who started his career with Eddie Bond and The Stompers, then moved on to play with the Bill Black Combo and Elvis. Loretta Lynn sang with the band and ended her set by saying, "I sure am having fun with you boys. Can we do another?"

Linda Gail Lewis came in and beat the piano just as well as her brother, Jerry Lee, maybe better, because, unlike him, she was sober. Billy Crocker was in the crowd from time to time, as well as B.B. Cunningham. Rising record promoter Eddie "Three Gun" Braddock, whom Billy had known in high school, cruised in, and when they were in town, the big time wrestlers Jerry Lawler and Jackie Fargo flexed and preened onstage, falsely threatening anyone who was not loyal to The Stompers.

Lefty Frizzell, the honky tonk singer out of Texas, agreed to play at the Little Black Book for two days. "All he wants," Bond crowed, delighted to have Frizzell on the playbill, "is $40 a night and all he can drink." But when Frizzell left Memphis, Bond was out about $400, which didn't include the cleaning bills.

One night, during a break, Billy, Doyle, John Huey, Bond, Blind Jimmy

Smith, and trumpet player Doug Kelly were sitting around a table when Whisperin' Bill Anderson sidled up, leaned down and spoke real softly. "I don't know anybody here," he said. "Do you mind if I sit with you?"

Billy, who was beginning to learn he could imitate almost anyone, leaned even closer to Whisperin' Bill and said just as softly, "As long as you don't impede our drinking."

Whisperin' Bill smiled. "Parish the thought, son," he said. "Parish the very thought. And while we are involved in this intimate conversation, may you allow me the privilege of singing with you this wonderful evening?"

Anderson sang "Tip of My Fingers" and a few of his other hits, and when he left the stage, Nelson said, "I believe he is the most polite man you could ever meet."

All the boys from The Mar-Keys stopped in: Al Jackson, Jr., the drummer who became Billy's mentor, as well as Steve Cropper, revered in Memphis for his ability as a rhythm guitar player, and bassist Donald "Duck" Dunn. Billy had known Cropper and Dunn from their days at Sherwood Elementary School. Between sets they talked about music and Messick High where their teachers always said, "Half our students go into music and the other half go to prison."

Did ya hear, one of them said, *Dago Tiller was killed in Brushy Mountain State Prison.*

Nobody was surprised. Dago had seemed to be looking for death from the day he was born.

One night after a show, Billy was in a room with four other guys he barely knew. They were telling him about the ultimate boost—heroin. He tied a handkerchief around his arm and stuck the needle into a vein. Immediately, he was swimming in a tantalizing euphoria. There was no feeling like this—none—but as the evening wore on, all he could think about was how ashamed Dot and Raymond would be if they ever learned what he had done.

When he came down, he was riddled with remorse and wrapped in a new awareness. He knew why people became addicted to heroin. He had heard the talk how the first hit is the best and how you kept trying to get back to that feeling, but you never could. You just kept pushing the "H" until you were gone. He never experimented with heroin again.

Billy was driving to the club one evening, pleased with his brand new, red Ford Falcon and—for the most part—pleased with himself. But he was also feeling jittery and off-center. He was making money, as well as a name for himself. He had friends and an apartment, but the thought kept running through his mind: *A guy could get lost out here.*

He had seen it with his own eyes. The blues guitarist Jimmy Reed had hired Billy to play drums in a Memphis bar. Reed was on the backside of his career, but Billy was still honored to perform with such a legend. If Reed wasn't Mississippi John Hurt, he was close.

Billy was setting up his drum kit when the club manager approached with a cautionary word. "Whatever you do, don't give Jimmy anything to drink." At that moment, Reed walked through the door carrying his guitar case. He stopped in the doorway, using the jams to steady himself.

"Looks to me like he's had enough already," Billy said.

"No," the manager said, "that's just residuals."

Reed made his way toward the bandstand to where Billy was standing. "You my drummer?" he asked.

"Yes, sir, Mr. Reed," Billy said, "and I know your music."

"Um-hmm. Well, let me ask you," Reed said, placing the palm of his hand on the snare drum, "can you hit dat wit your sticks?"

Billy looked at Reed's hand, which nearly covered the entire snare. "Yes, sir," he said.

"Okay, then," Reed said, "can you tap this high hat wid your sticks?" Billy assured Reed that he could.

"Now, can you kick dat bass drum wit your foot?"

"I sure can," Billy said.

"Dat's good," Reed said, smiling, "'cause if you hit any dese other drums you got, I'm gonna hit you flat upside the head wit dis guitar. We understood? Yes? Good. 'Cause Jimmy Reed is de star of dis here show."

Jimmy Reed lived up to his reputation. He growled his way through his two biggest hits, "Big Boss Man" and "Bright Lights, Big City," and, as far as anyone could tell, had nothing to drink but Coca-Cola.

The crowd loved him, but when the crowd cleared and Billy had put away his gear, no one could find Reed. His car was still in the parking lot and his guitar was on the stand. They checked the bathrooms and looked everywhere but Reed, the masterful blues guitarist, was nowhere to be found.

"Pull up the tablecloths," the manager said, "and look under the tables."

They found Reed curled up and sleeping, surrounded by empty glasses and beer bottles—drinks people had left behind.

"At it again," the manager said. "He pulls all the leftovers together, mixes 'em up. Calls 'em spiders."

Reed was huddled up like a bum in an alley.

"Let him sleep," the manager said. "Just let him sleep."

Billy had met a girl. In fact, her name was Martha Austin, she frequented the Little Black Book, and worked in pharmaceutical sales. Eddie Bond called her a "show-stopper," and Doyle Nelson said, "She got that Elizabeth Taylor thing goin' on." The boys in the band joked about Martha's job. *Billy got himself a good-looking woman and source to boot*, they said.

She was another reason Billy chose to watch his step, along with the looks he sometimes received from Dot and Raymond.

"Ya eating right, son? Getting your rest? Looking a little puny these days."

It was becoming difficult to keep the band together, too. Eddie Bond and The Stompers was becoming a victim of its success. Jerry Lee Lewis asked Hawk Hawkins to tour with him and John Huey was doing more and more sessions with Conway Twitty. The Stompers would only last as long as Huey held the band together.

Billy and Doyle Nelson toyed with the idea of starting their own band, but before anything transpired, Charlie Freeman presented Billy with an unexpected opportunity. The Mar-Keys needed a drummer for the road band, and there was the possibility—though faint—that he would be used in some recording sessions at Stax Records. This was exactly what Billy wanted, the chance to work with some of the finest musicians in the country.

What did he need to do? Audition? Who did he need to talk to? "Nothing, no one," Freeman said, "everybody knows how good you are. Just say the word."

The sessions were few and the tours were long and not always rewarding. They played large towns like Little Rock, St. Louis, Chicago, Indianapolis, Jackson and Oxford, Mississippi. But along the way, they were required to play fill dates, one-night shows in smaller towns to make more money between the larger and better paying jobs. The Mar-Keys, a traveling version of the group that made it big with the hit "Last Night," seldom consisted of the same members from tour-to-tour.

From time-to-time—but seldom always together—the road version of the band consisted of Charlie Freeman (when the mood struck him); horn players Packy Axton, Wayne Jackson, Don Nix or Doug Kelley (depending upon who was available); bass man Duck Dunn or his frequent replacement, Charlie McClure; and always Billy Purser on drums.

They roamed around in vans, reluctantly playing one-night stands in places like Farmington, Missouri; Peoria, Illinois; and Booneville, Mississippi. While the clubs were mostly the same—dingy, no place you would want to see in daylight—the crowds ranged from enthusiastic to completely uninterested.

In Corinth, Mississippi, Martha's hometown, The Mar-Keys played on a stage surrounded from floor to ceiling by chicken wire. It was not the first time the players had performed someplace where beer bottles were hurled through the air, but it was one of the first where the show was interrupted by uninvited percussion.

During one rousing tune, a large, rowdy dancer in a cowboy hat and boots managed to pilfer the security guard's revolver from his holster and fire three shots into the ceiling, a demonstration that sent the crowd into joyous celebration but affected the band's timing.

The cowboy was a hero until the moment when the security guard leveled him with a nightstick. The Mar-Keys, meanwhile, played on.

"Damn," Billy said, turning to McClure, "that was fun."

"Chicken wire wouldn't have helped much, would it?"

Corinth was one of many towns where they played and the crowd was ready to shoot at the least provocation. It occurred to Billy that of all the time he had spent in the army, he had never been threatened by gunfire until that night in Corinth.

They were on the road for days at a time, driving most of the night, sleeping most of the day. They stayed in bad hotels, ate bad food, and none of it sat well with the newlywed, Martha Austin Purser.

She and Billy had been married after a whirlwind romance, and after the ceremony, Doyle Nelson said, "Seemed like they dated about thirty minutes."

Martha had been around the Little Black Book enough to know about the groupies, the women who made themselves available to the members of the band. She knew about the drinking and the drug use, too. And she didn't

like being left at home in Memphis while Billy was off "gallivanting across the country doing God knows what."

She didn't like the fact that when he was home, he would show up at the door just before dawn and sleep until mid-afternoon. Even when he came home at a reasonable hour, he would stay up until dawn smoking and reading books.

The knocks on the door at all hours of the day and night angered her— people showing up drunk or worse, looking for another party or a place to sleep. She did not share her brother A.C.'s idea of marriage. A.C., she said, left the wedding ceremony, carried his wife across the threshold, sat her gently on the couch, and left on a five-day drunk. When he returned, worse for the wear and barreling through the front door, he said, "Well, honey, how do you like married life?"

The story made Billy laugh, which wasn't the best idea. Something, she insisted, has to change, and she was unrelenting in her demands. Though it had hardly begun, the marriage was in trouble. Billy tried to placate Martha, but he also continued to tour with the band.

Returning home in the middle of the night, he found the apartment dark except for an odd illumination that seemed to come through the bathroom door, which was slightly ajar. Martha was fast asleep and Billy didn't want to awaken her. He was too tired to fight. He gently opened the bathroom door.

Candles of all sizes had been carefully placed around the bathtub, the flames casting an eerie lambent light over the room. Inside the tub were his books: Twain, Faulkner, Steinbeck, Zane Grey—all the books David Welch had suggested he read—thrown in the tub, spines broken, pages wrinkled. He picked up one of the volumes fearing the worst. It was dry. They were all dry. Martha had stopped short of turning on the water.

The next day, he drove around town thinking. He loved playing in the band but he was tired of the road. He wasn't sure how he felt about his marriage. Maybe, it was time for a change. He had seen that look in his mother's eyes and Raymond's. And he had seen something else in his own eyes, looking into the mirror after another long night.

The Mar-Keys were booked to play a charity benefit in Somerville, Tennessee, just east of Memphis. It was a nice night and a good crowd had gathered. The Mar-Keys had gathered some of their best for the engagement, which had been broadly advertised on radio and TV.

The band took the stage and the crowd clamored for the show to start.

The promoter stalled, telling the people they were waiting on the emcee, a noted local disc jockey who had been enthusiastically promoting the show.

As the crowd grew more restless, a well-dressed man stepped out of a Cadillac and was greeted by the promoter with a handshake and two thick envelopes filled with cash. The DJ smiled. His teeth were dazzling. He put the envelopes in the breast pocket of his coat and walked to the microphone. "And now," he said, his voice deep and clear, "what you have all been waiting for. Ladies and gentlemen, boys and girls, lads and lassies: the one and only Mar-Keys of Stax Records and Memphis, Tennessee!"

The crowd cheered. Billy kicked in the drums but kept his eyes on the DJ, who quickly left the stage, jumped in his car, and drove away with all the cash—including the band's pay.

All Billy could think about was the DJ and his Cadillac, his clothes, the way the crowd reacted when he took the microphone, the way they cheered before he ever said a word. It was one of those nights when Billy was all instinct, sticks flashing, hands finding all the right places.

Lord, how he did love playing.

But it was time to have a talk with Martha.

"I'm gonna leave the band," he said.

She didn't move.

He lit a cigarette. "I'm going to go to radio school. It's what I wanted to do before I got involved in music. It's what I wanted to do when I went into the army, but I got sidetracked. If I do this, I won't be working until all hours of the night."

"When do you start?" she asked.

He laid the brochures on the table. Right away, he said. He'd already made the down payment—sixty dollars.

She loved him, she said, but she couldn't put up with the cops showing up at the front door because some trumpet player was sleeping in the back seat of their car.

Billy remembered the night Doug Kelly, drunk and high, made his way to their apartment complex and crawled into the back seat of the Falcon. A neighbor called the police, who showed up at Billy and Martha's apartment around dawn with Kelly in tow.

"This man," the officer said, "says he had your permission to sleep in your car."

Billy, in his boxers, surveyed the situation. Martha stood behind him in a robe. "Tell 'em, Billy. C'mon man."

He looked at Kelly and then the police officer.

"Never seen him in my life," he said.

"Okay," the officer said. "You're going downtown."

"Ah, man. Billy, help me out! Tell 'em."

Billy smiled as his friend was hauled away. Martha slammed the bedroom door. She didn't talk to him before he left for work. The horn player didn't speak to him for weeks.

She had not been amused, of course. She could be uncommonly cold. Sometimes he looked at her and thought her beauty would last forever, frozen by her glacial temperament.

He began classes at Keegan's Technical Institute, the same place where, as a fascinated boy, he stood for hours marveling over what he imagined was taking place inside.

In the morning and often on one or two hours of sleep—sometimes no sleep at all—Billy rushed through his newspaper route. Sometimes there was time for a quick nap. Sometimes there wasn't. There were days when he needed to reach into his pocket for help.

He played one-night shows with The Mar-Keys, drew an occasional recording session around town, and worked as assistant manager of Dance Land. His duties at Dance Land were simple: watch the till, watch the door, make sure no one was served after closing time, and stop the fights. The first three were easy.

The fights seemed to come in two varieties: large men flexing their beer muscles, or black girls swinging at one another over what man was staying with whom. The latter, he found, were less dangerous and more entertaining.

When he left in the mornings, Martha was asleep. When he got home, Martha was asleep. But when he did see her, she didn't complain.

Billy became an exemplary student at Keegan's. He seemed to have an innate understanding of everything about radio. He learned to operate a control room board, how to cut and edit tape. He was quick with the switches and adept with a razor blade, but he flourished behind the microphone. The instructors, Bill Trotter and Tyce Turway, talked to him about projection, speaking from the diaphragm, and testing his range.

Trotter and Turway amazed Billy, for in normal conversation they sounded like anyone who might be encountered on the streets of Memphis. But when they keyed the microphone, there was a miraculous change. Trotter's voice sounded like it came from the bottom of a well, and reminded Billy of Edward R. Murrow or Walter Cronkite. There was no hint of a southern accent. Every word was perfectly articulated, perfectly shaped. His delivery was measured, as if he controlled every tick of the clock that governed radio.

Tyce Turway's style was completely different: fast, clipped, nasal, a staccato delivery reminiscent of Walter Winchell: *Good evening, Mr. and Mrs. North America and all the ships at sea. Let's go to press!*"

Billy found that he could replicate either style—to the point the other students had difficulty telling Billy's tapes from those recorded by Trotter or Turway.

The instructors told Billy that, in their shared estimation, he would succeed in the business and quickly. All he had to do, they said, was pick a style that suited him, a space where he was comfortable hour-after-hour, day-after-day.

He told them he had always admired Dewey Phillips. They nodded. They knew Daddy-O-Dewey, who had introduced Elvis Presley to the country and had played an instrumental role in the careers of Jerry Lee Lewis and Johnny Cash, Booker 'T' and The MG's and so many others who sprang from the rowdy Memphis scene.

Billy said he liked Dewey's wild and loose style.

Manic, they said.

Phillips didn't seem to play by the rules, Billy said.

Irreverent, Trotter said.

Highly informal, Turway added.

Billy quoted Dewey's patter verbatim and in perfect voice: *Dis is Daddy-O-Dewey and Red, Hot and Blue brought to you by Falstaff beer. If you can't drink it, freeze it and eat it. If you can't do that, open up a rib and pour it in. Get yourself a wheelbarrow and a crazed bunch of monkeys, fill it up with Falstaff and tell 'em Phillips sent you.*

Phillips is a true talent, they agreed. "But," Trotter said, "you can't start out being Dewey Phillips."

Trotter and Turway knew all about Phillips. Of course, anyone in Memphis who knew music knew Dewey Phillips. Initially, he was a floor man at W.T. Grant's dime store at Gayoso and Main, playing records in the

store and employing a carnival barker's pitch to sell the latest hits.

"I got a hot one," Phillips would say as potential buyers walked by. "Ya got to hear it."

He began to use loudspeakers, blaring music and his pitch into the streets, stopping traffic. He had a following before he began his radio career. People—both black *and* white—thought he was crazy.

WHBQ was in competition with WDIA, "The Mother Station of the Negroes," and was losing money. So WHBQ hired Dewey to balance B.B. King and the greats at WDIA, and he was an instant success, even though he couldn't cue a record without scratching it. He was a wondrous anomaly and successful, in no small part, because of his friendship with record producer Sam Phillips, who literally delivered new artists to the door of his studio. There was never anyone who was in the right place at the right time more than Dewey Phillips.

For most people in this business it's nothing like that, Trotter and Turway said. It takes time and luck to build a name and a style. And most of all, it takes patience.

Billy wasn't sure what they were trying to tell him.

"Look," they said, "the market doesn't want another Dewey. The market wants someone who will compete with him, be better than him—new and different. And that's down the road. The first step is getting a job."

"So what do I do?" Billy asked.

Learn every aspect of the business from sign-on to sign-off, they said. Be clear. Stick to the middle of the road. Get that first job and then start developing a personality. What good is it to have a great character if there's never an opportunity for the character to be heard? Success is determined by the tastes and whims of program directors.

There was one thing Trotter and Turway wanted Billy to do right away. They wanted him to choose an on-air name. Billy Purser wouldn't do. It was too next-door, too corner soda shop. He needed a name that would help him get where he wanted to go.

Meanwhile, Billy prepared air-checks that Keegan's routinely sent to stations throughout the region, most of them the smaller stations throughout Mississippi, Tennessee, Arkansas, Louisiana, some in Texas and Missouri, but few in Memphis—something Billy didn't tell Martha.

Billy came in early and stayed late, checking the mail every day for an offer. Trotter and Turway assured Billy he would get a call.

Still, he needed a name. Billy thought about it running his route, the sun just coming up. *Billy Sunday?* No, that was some evangelist. He thought about it at home, knocked it around with Martha. "Why do you need another name?" she asked.

He studied the crowd at Dance Land, searching the atmosphere for a name that would play to the crowd that enjoyed the same music he did. *Nothing.* He was too busy following another rule of being an assistant manager, which was to avoid the next missile hurled his way. Various antagonists certainly had some names for him.

As his time at Keegan's shortened and he was placing the last of his air-checks in the mail, Turway and Trotter called him into the office.

"We got it," one of them said. "It's perfect. Fits for what you want to do. Comes from a movie back in 1940, starred Tyrone Power."

"What is it?" Billy asked.

"Ready? Johnny Apollo."

Billy smiled. He liked it. He rolled it off his tongue. He dropped down to his deepest, clearest, most resonant bass: *Johnn-nny AAAAAAAPOLLO!* He rolled back to a black/blues, high, southern register: *Hi, chil'ren. Dis is your slippin', slidin' soul searchin', rollin', rumblin' Johnny Apollo.*

"Still working on that one," he said.

"Good," they said. "It needs work."

In the next few days, air-checks—samples of his work and what he had done at Keegan's—were cut, re-cut, and sent to various stations. They clung to a conservative approach, Billy working in his deepest octave, pronouncing every syllable of every word.

Still, there were no calls or letters, and he was worried about getting a job. Maybe he wasn't as good as he thought. Maybe he should have been more creative. Could Trotter and Turway have overestimated his ability? Worse, were they exaggerating his skills because he was paying them? Mostly, he worried about Martha. What if no job came? What then?

With little over a week left in his course at Keegan's he was called to the office once again. He assumed it was regarding his delinquent tuition payments. He had made the first two installments of $60, but was behind on the third. As he walked down the hall, he thought about how he would explain.

Bill Trotter was seated behind a desk. Tyce Turway sat on a couch.

"So, Billy, how are you?" Turway began.

"You know you're about to finish the course," Trotter said.

"I know," Billy said. "About the tuition . . ."

They didn't give him a chance to finish the sentence.

"We've got a job offer for you."

He felt unsteady. He glanced down at the return address on the envelope they handed him—Lake Providence, Louisiana. His stomach dropped. He looked at the call letters: KLPL.

He wasn't sure what he expected, but this wasn't it. Once more, his dreams of grandeur interfered with the reality of his situation. He tried to hide his disappointment from Trotter and Turway , both of whom seemed genuinely pleased with the offer.

"It's a small station, doesn't pay much," one of them said, "But it's a start, the beginning of a career. We're proud of you. And about the tuition— pay us when you can. We're not worried about it. You've been a great student. You'll graduate at the top of the class."

He shook hands, offered many thanks, all the while thinking: *And graduating at the top of the class has landed me some place I have never heard of in my life?*

There was a voice in the room, buoyant, confident. "Do well there and you'll move up. Succeed and move to a bigger market. Do it fast. Don't get bogged down. That's what the business is about."

What will I tell Martha? he thought. *How will she react?*

That night, after the supper dishes were cleared, he made a fresh pot of coffee and told her he had good news. He told her about the offer.

She looked at him sternly through the steam rising from her coffee. "Billy," she said, "where the hell is Lake Providence, Louisiana?"

Chapter nine

Praise be, Bill Williams

He was in a new place, with a new name. He was dismayed when he found out how *small* the listening audience was. Then he was elated. If no one was listening, he could do anything. He could <u>be</u> anyone. So he became Lipton Dink.

It was not a hard drive, just 150 miles due south, straight

downriver, a shotgun run on Highway 61 from Memphis to the very northeast corner of Louisiana. It was a distance just long enough for some time to think, and there was plenty to think about—some of it good, some of it not so good.

The windows were down. The air smelled sweet and wet. There was a thunderhead rolling in from the west, and the radio crackled with static. Billy searched for a clear channel. He looked for KLPL, his future home, but found nothing without interference.

vOices in mY heaD

Chapter nine

Praise be, Bill Williams

He was in a new place, with a new name. He was dismayed when he found out how *small* the listening audience was. Then he was elated. If no one was listening, he could do anything. He could <u>be</u> anyone. So he became Lipton Dink.

It was not a hard drive, just 150 miles due south, straight

downriver, a shotgun run on Highway 61 from Memphis to the very northeast corner of Louisiana. It was a distance just long enough for some time to think, and there was plenty to think about—some of it good, some of it not so good.

The windows were down. The air smelled sweet and wet. There was a thunderhead rolling in from the west, and the radio crackled with static. Billy searched for a clear channel. He looked for KLPL, his future home, but found nothing without interference.

vOices in mY heaD

93

He switched off the radio and leaned back against the driver's seat, trying to relax. Had he made the right decision? He wasn't really sure, but he was determined.

Were things going to work out with Martha? Did he want things to work out? He really wasn't sure. He thought about how she reacted when he told her about the job. She wasn't angry, really. She was exasperated. He told her Lake Providence wasn't far away. The money was steady and he would come home on his off days—whenever he could.

It was a starting point and if he was lucky and good enough, he would move up, go to a bigger station, maybe back to Memphis.

She said it again. She didn't want to leave Memphis. She wanted a regular life. It was her mantra. He knew it by heart.

In the end, sitting at the kitchen table, she relented. She was resigned to his decision and moved, he thought, by his clean break with the band. He was done. He sold his drums. He told the guys he wasn't coming back. In the days before he left for Lake Providence, there were no late night knocks at the door, no drunks clattering around in the hall yelling, "Bil-ly. Hey, man. Open up."

"Go," she said, "I know this is what you want to do and it beats hell out of playing music and living on the road and in clubs: the booze, the drugs, the girls throwing themselves at you all every chance they get."

He thought she loved him, or perhaps she believed that she loved him. His thoughts on the relationship were equally confused.

She helped him with his bags, gave him a kiss. "Call me," she said. "Let me know how it is. I'll come down after you get settled."

She was a good woman. Lord knows he had given her reasons to move out. But she stuck it out and here she was, steadfastly supporting him as he began a new career.

He lit a cigarette and watched the countryside roll by. It reminded him of Water Valley, the trips to see Uncle Winford and Aunt Irene, fried chicken dinners and sweet tea, and afterwards, watermelon on the gallery, everybody sitting and talking, spitting seeds in the grass.

It seemed so long ago. And now what? He knew next to nothing about KLPL. He didn't know what kind of music they played, what his duties would be, or how much latitude he would be given on the air. All he knew is what Bill Trotter and Tyce Turway had told him: "It's a typical small station in a typical, small Louisiana town. 'Bout everybody knows

everybody and newcomers are best advised to watch their step."

Yep, Billy thought, Water Valley, Mississippi, like going back home. He felt his insides slow down. The thunderhead had turned north and the sun was starting to slip away to the west. Still, you could smell rain. He took a long breath and leaned farther back in the driver's seat. He felt at ease, calm—peaceful. He had not felt like this in a long time.

It was dark when he crossed the Mississippi and passed sprawling Lake Providence, the town nestled quietly at its side. It was Sunday night and there was hardly anyone on the streets. He stopped the car and looked around. The town looked like any one of hundreds where he had played with Eddie Bond and The Stompers or The Mar-Keys, but there was no hint of a honky-tonk on the air, just a car here and there, dogs barking, stirred by something only they could hear.

He pulled the letter from the glove box, studied the address, and drove around until he found the little block building with KLPL on a big sign out front. He stood looking at the station and the small tower there in back. He was to report the next morning at 5:30.

He was hungry and needed to find a place to stay. He drove around looking for a restaurant or a diner. Nothing was open. He finally found a gas station on the outskirts of town. When he pulled past the gas pumps, a bell rung, and an attendant stirred inside, under a stark light bulb hanging from a single, bare cord.

Billy stopped the car and offered an apology. He didn't need gas, didn't mean to be a bother, just got into town and was looking for a place to eat and a motel.

"Not gonna find no place open this time'a Sunday night," the attendant said. "As for a place to stay, might wanna try the Palomino Hotel. Probably still be open. If not, knock right hard, and you'll 'rouse 'em. Got some Cokes there in the cooler. Some candy bars and crackers. Not much of a dinner, but it'll get ya through. Ya been here earlier could'a had some Sunday dinner leftovers—meatloaf and biscuits."

Billy wrote down the directions to the Palomino Hotel, bought two bottles of pop, a couple of candy bars, and a package of crackers. He thanked the man and headed downtown.

The Palomino wasn't far. In Lake Providence, nothing was far. He checked in and paid for the room a week in advance, fifty bucks. Though the Palomino was less than opulent, it wasn't bad: private bath, a desk with a straight-back chair and a lamp, a phone, a rickety ceiling fan, a black and white television with rabbit ears, and a double bed with a worn chenille spread and a reading lamp on the headboard. He had stayed in worse places.

He opened a Coke and stretched out on the bed to a supper of Hershey Bars and peanut butter crackers. He tried the television and found one Pentecostal preacher in full fervor, but nothing else, just that odd whining sound and test pattern that looked like targets on a shooting range. Except for the preacher, full to bursting with the Lord, everyone had signed off for the night. He looked at his watch. It was after midnight. He needed to sleep. He needed to be sharp in the morning. He wanted to impress his new bosses.

He couldn't sleep. He tossed. He turned. Too much sugar, he thought, two Cokes, two candy bars, and peanut butter crackers. He sat at the side of the bed. He read Zane Grey. He stood at the open window listening to the night: crickets and dogs. Someone, far away, had a hot rod or a pickup in dire need of a muffler.

It was two o'clock, then three o'clock. The ease he had experienced earlier in the day was gone. He tossed and turned. He wished he had some pot. Pot was better than drinking. He had never liked the grogginess that came with booze. Pot didn't leave you shaky and thirsty. Smoke some pot and you awakened sharp, hungry, and ready to go.

Finally, he drifted into a fitful sleep. It was nearly 4 a.m. The alarm went off about forty-five minutes later. He was not sharp. He was hungry. He was not ready to go. He shaved, showered, threw on a coat and tie, ate the last of the peanut butter crackers, drank what was left in one of the Coke bottles, and struggled out the door.

When he arrived at KLPL, he met the boss, Gene someone. He didn't quite catch his last name. He called him Mr. Gene and Mr. Gene smiled. He was a proper Louisiana gentleman given to impeccably pressed seersucker suits and the occasional cigar.

He showed Billy around the station. Not much to show, really, he said. The control room was small, the studio smaller still. The disc jockey on the air was Lanny James, who, Mr. Gene explained, was a pillar of the community, married with kids, born and raised in Lake Providence, and decided to stay, unlike most. Lanny, he added, pretty much kept things together there at KLPL.

"You can learn a lot from him," Mr. Gene said. "In fact, I think he's counting on you doing a newscast later this morning."

Billy was suddenly nervous and Mr. Gene picked up on it right away. "You'll do fine, son, just fine. By the way, I really liked your tapes. Very talented. Hope we can keep you around for a spell. By the way, did you drive in last night? Do you need to get some breakfast? Coffee? Anything?"

Billy assured Mr. Gene that he was just fine, just a little nervous. Mr. Gene chuckled. "Understandable," he said, "first job and all."

They went into Mr. Gene's office, where he explained Billy's duties. He would sign on at 5:30 a.m., and do the morning show until noon. After lunch, there were spots to cut, and once in a while, after he had been on the air awhile and people got to know him, he would be asked to go out and pay a visit to folks, advertisers, that kind of thing. "And, of course," he said, "Lanny will have some things for you to do from time to time.

"Sunday," he said, "will be your busy day. You'll have to produce for all the ministers who come in and preach. Goes on most all day. But, I do believe, you'll find it entertaining, especially our guitar-playing minister, who is extremely gifted. Most of the ministers are black. Good people, all of 'em, just trying to out-preach whoever came before 'em. Big money-maker for us. Yessir, you'll be just fine. All you got to do is run the board. Run 'em in, run 'em out."

Mr. Gene had an assuring smile, and he made everything sound simple. Billy figured him to be the best salesman in all of Northeast Louisiana, and certainly, in all of East Carroll Parish.

"So," he said, "ready to go meet Lanny and do that first newscast? I believe he has already written it for you."

Billy cleared his throat and said he was ready to go. His hands were cold and clammy.

"Oh," Mr. Gene said, as he stood from behind his desk and ushered Billy toward the door, "the name on your tape—Johnny Apollo, was it? Well, we don't think that will work here in Lake Providence. Here at KLPL, you'll be Bill Williams. That okay with you?"

Billy said that would be fine. "Mr. Gene," he said, "anything you want. I'm just happy to have the job."

Lanny James was in a commercial break when Mr. Gene opened the studio door and introduced Billy Purser. Lanny took off his headset, laid it on the console, and shook Billy's hand.

"Mighty nice to meet you," he said. "Glad to have you with us. Gonna free me up to sell."

Lanny was a handsome man with a nice voice. Billy liked him immediately.

"We got about a minute and then you can do the news," Lanny said. He handed Billy a script. "Give it a look. When we come back from commercial, I'll introduce you and you can have at it."

Mr. Gene excused himself. "I'll leave you all to it," he said. "Good luck, Bill Williams. I know you will make us proud."

Billy's heart was racing. He glanced at the script and then up at the clock. Lanny James had the headset on one ear, kind of tilted back on his head.

"You got about thirty seconds," he said.

Billy's eyes trained in on the words but he wasn't really seeing. He looked for words he didn't know and words difficult to pronounce. He didn't see any problems.

"Ten seconds," Lanny said.

Billy felt a catch at the back of his throat. He swallowed and thought about Bill Trotter and Tyce Turway.

Which way to go? Trotter with the deep voice, or Turway with the Winchell style?

"Five seconds," James said.

Billy swallowed again and took a deep breath. He chose Trotter—the Edward R. Murrow voice.

"Welcome back, folks. This is Lanny James and you are listening to KLPL in Lake Providence, and now with the morning news, our newest addition: Bill Williams."

Billy spoke from someplace deep down. He was surprised how his voice sounded in the headset. He struggled at points but made it through. When he was done, there was sweat on his forehead. It had taken all of a minute, maybe less, and he was exhausted.

"Thank you, Bill. That's your morning news. Bill will be back in a half hour with the latest. Please welcome this young man from Memphis, Tennessee, to Lake Providence and the KLPL family. This is Lanny James and now, a little something from Tony Bennett."

When the record was cued, Lanny removed his headset, and smiled at Billy. "Well," he said, "you just made it through your first newscast. And, frankly, I'm surprised."

"Why's that?" he asked.

"'Cause your hands were shaking so bad I'm surprised you could see the words. You'll get over all that. By the way, nice voice. How you get down so low? That's serious baritone. Hey, you'll get over the nerves and in short order. We got about a dozen more of these to do today. By that time, you'll be fine."

They laughed. Lanny told him to get them some coffee and check the Teletypes, and that he probably needed to rewrite the next half-hour's news. Billy walked out of the studio, looking for the Teletype machines and a coffee pot. His shirt was damp with sweat. He needed a cigarette and ducked outside the door to have a smoke. He was thrilled and he was anxious. He knew he could be better. He stubbed out the Marlboro, found the coffee pot, ripped off the sheets from the ticker, and went back to the studio.

He read the news all day long and each time he was more professional. "Pretty smooth," Lanny James said. "You're getting there."

They signed off at sunset.

Lanny James stood and stretched and said he was glad to have him on the job.

"Tomorrow morning," he said, "it's all yours. I'm way behind on my sales calls. You got it all day."

That evening, Billy found a beer joint with a menu that broke his heart. It had fat juicy burgers, fried chicken and mashed potatoes with cream gravy, and lemon icebox pie.

There was a basket of boiled peanuts on every table, and the beer was so cold it made his teeth hurt and the roof of his mouth go numb. He was starved. He ate fast but not so fast the flavor was lost. He cleaned several plates and bowls and sopped up the juices with fresh bread, deciding that— while it was damned hard to beat Memphis barbecue—Louisiana cooking was some of the best he had ever tasted.

The joint had pool tables and a jukebox with records by everyone from Ferlin Husky to The Platters. He wondered if Hank Williams's classic was on the juke, and before the night was over someone punched up the Louisiana anthem.

Jambalaya and a crawfish pie and file' gumbo
'Cause tonight I'm gonna see my ma cher amio

Pick guitar, fill fruit jar and be gay-o
Son of a gun, we'll have big fun on the bayou . . .

Billy took a swig of his beer and looked at the man closest to him. The man was bent forward, broken somehow, with a loose grip on a short glass.

"You de new man on de radio?" the man asked.

The question surprised Billy. He had talked with no one outside the station except the gas station attendant and the clerk at the Palomino.

"How did you know?" Billy asked.

"Saw ya talking to Lanny James dere in de parking lot. News gets 'round real good here in Lake Prov'dence. Good man, Lanny James. Well," he said, tipping his glass, "good luck to ya."

Billy stayed later than he planned, shooting a little pool, drinking more than he intended, making acquaintances, and finding out about Lake Providence. When he got back to the hotel, it was after midnight.

He kicked off his shoes, climbed under the worn bedspread, and tried to sleep. Hours later, he was still lying there, looking at the slow turn of the ceiling fan. He was too anxious to sleep, too excited. What was it Lanny James had said? *Tomorrow morning, it's all yours . . . you got it all day.*

He got up and flipped on the television. Nothing. Test patterns. The same minister, wiping sweat and castigating sinners.

You MUST renounce the devil . . . and receive the Lord. Say it with me.
Billy gave up. He turned off the television and took a shower. He wondered if he would ever sleep again.

He pulled into the parking lot at the station at four o'clock in the morning. He made a pot of coffee and began to page through the reams of overnight news from the Teletype machines. He wrote a news report, checked the weather, looked over the morning play list, and double-checked his breaks and commercial spots. He was confident that he was ready to change KLPL and Lake Providence, Louisiana, certain that by the end of the day, adoring fans would be lining up outside the station waiting to meet him.

He sipped black coffee and smoked, wondering when Mr. Gene and Lanny James would arrive. Fifteen minutes before sign-on, he looked around—there was not another soul in the building. No one was coming to oversee his first shift. He was on his own. The station was his, his alone.

It was a good feeling but frightening, too. Sitting by himself, he yawned and yawned again. Two days with no sleep was catching up.

He drank more coffee and at 5:30—on the dot—he hit the proper switches and put the station on the air. He did commercials without a hitch and made his way smoothly through the news and weather. No bumps. Then, he introduced his first record of the day, Andy Williams. He cued the record and rested his chin in his hand on the console. As Williams crooned, Billy's eyes grew heavy.

I'm gonna close my eyes for thirty seconds, no more.

He felt as if he was floating, then falling. When he snapped to, the record was tracking.

Whick!

Whick!

Whick!

Whick!

He jerked up and looked at the clock on the wall. It was 6:15. He had been asleep for forty-five minutes. He rubbed his eyes and tried to clear his mind. He lifted the needle on the record, grabbed the microphone, and said, "And that, folks, was Andy Williams. It's 6:15 in the morning. Gonna be a beautiful day here in Lake Providence and Ark-La-Miss."

He cued the next record and looked out the window. It was clouding over and looked like rain. He paced around the studio.

First day and you screw it up. Mr. Gene and Lanny are gonna come in here and fire you on the spot. What the hell are you gonna do? What are you gonna say?

He spun records, hit his spots, did the farm reports, all the time waiting for a door to slam or the phone to ring.

Nothing.

The phones didn't ring. Mr. Gene didn't come storming through the door. Lanny didn't call. He worked the entire day, fearful. The office girls came and went, offering shy smiles. Mr. Gene stopped by and offered his compliments, said he'd been listening since about 6:30. Sounds good. Lanny waved on his way out the door to a sales call. There was not a word regarding the forty-five-minute lapse.

When the day was over, Billy sat in his car in the parking lot, thinking. Not one mention. He couldn't get over it. It could mean only one thing. No one was listening. He thought it over for a minute or two, and while he was disappointed, he was also pleased.

If no one was listening, he had the perfect testing ground. He could do what he liked, maybe not just yet—but soon. This was good, perfect. He picked up a sandwich on the way home and called Martha.

"You sound tired," she said.

His eyes felt as if they were filled with gravel. That night he slept in his clothes, never moving.

Weeks later, he was settled into the routine of KLPL, the pace of Northeast Louisiana, and a small, shabby, furnished apartment on the edge of town. When his shift was over, he ate, then sat at the kitchen table making notes and thinking about voices—voices from Memphis and Water Valley, Raymond's slow, syrupy Mississippi drawl, the Jersey Boys from boot camp, Michael Vozelli from Philly, Frau Bressler, Jimmy Reed, Whisperin' Bill Anderson, Elvis and, of course, all the ministers he had met in his life from Brother Vernon Cannon at Beverly Hills Baptist to the unending string of evangelicals who paraded through the station every Sunday.

He practiced each voice, sometimes blending them together, mixing southern words with eastern attitudes and accents. He liked the idea of pairing the likely and unlikely, wedding Frau Bressler's thick German accent, for instance, to a bit on crayfish pie and collard greens.

He made up names, scribbling them down the side of the page: Delbert Coggins, Lipton Dink, Cletus Thrumple, Herman Weems. When he came across one he liked, he imagined how each looked and sounded. He stood in front of the bathroom mirror and slipped into character, practicing the voice and expressions. Often, he laughed out loud.

There was the obvious question, of course: would anyone else think any of this was as funny as he did? Was this the right place to try it out? He loved being on the air and had already started putting together air-checks to send to larger stations. He didn't want to do anything that would jeopardize his position. Then again, there was little evidence anyone was listening to his show.

He wasn't recognized on the street. There were no phone calls, no fan mail. His measures of performance were limited to Mr. Gene's ever-present smile and Lanny James's encouragement. Otherwise, his daily show on KLPL offered small favor. On the rare occasion when Billy was recognized, it was hardly a feast for his ego.

Billy's greatest popularity rested with the preachers of Ark-La-Miss, who started showing up at the station around five o'clock on Sunday morning, all grateful for Billy's patience and expertise. Without him, they could not spread their message to the souls of the region—and in the mid-'60s their message went beyond The Word, though in Northeast Louisiana it was carefully cloaked.

Bless you, Mister Williams, and all you do. May God smile on you each and every day of your life. Praise be! You are a true friend of the church. A true friend. Hallelujah.

They came in all shapes and sizes, the best-dressed men in the area, always looking good, smelling good, no sign of sins of the flesh. Their shoes shone, and their smiles sparkled until the gravity of the sermon overcame them.

Billy studied the preachers from the tiny control room, fighting with the sound as their voices rose and fell. He watched them work themselves into a frenzy, the sermon rolling upward to a summit, then descending into the lower registers of relief and forgiveness. He admired their fervor more than their message.

One of the ministers brought the best of his choir to the broadcast, nine large—very large—women, whose gowns could not disguise the ample benefits that God and fried food had given them.

As they were about to go on the air, something broke down in the studio, leaving Billy with the problem of getting the show back on. He grabbed a live microphone and called the preacher and the choir to the control room.

The minister, not a small man, and nine ladies—none of whom weighed less than 200 pounds—pressed into the small booth, which was perhaps eight-by-fifteen. All of them surrounded Billy, who found himself engulfed in a virtual tsunami of corpulence.

"So I'm standing in the middle of this room, the microphone in my hand," he said to Martha on the telephone, "and they're all around me. Up real close. Everybody jammed together. The preacher lets go, gets everyone all stirred up and happy, and then the choir cuts loose and they are good. I mean *real* good.

"But as they begin to sing and they get filled with the joy and the spirit, they start crowdin' in on me. I'm getting knocked around by big breasts, big bottoms and big voices, knocked around like a leaf in a storm, and I start slidin' down to the floor, doin' my best to keep my feet and that microphone

in the middle of the mix. Ends up, I'm on the floor, flat on my back and all these gals are right in my face singin' their hearts out.

"The minister is dancing. The choir is belting it out and I am utterly helpless. When it's all over, I stagger up off the floor, a little breathless, and say, 'That's the damndest preaching and singing I've seen in my life.' They all laugh and say, 'Praise be, Bill Williams.' That day, I saw a whole new side of race relations, and I liked it."

Martha laughed, imagining her diminutive husband being jostled about a tiny room.

"I'll see you soon," she said. "I think we have some things to talk about."

He had never heard that tone in her voice.

"What is it?" he asked.

At first, she said nothing. The line seemed dead.

"Are you there, Martha?"

"I'll be down soon, Billy," she said. "We'll talk. I'm happy for you."

He hung up the phone and went back to the kitchen table. He turned on the radio, spun through the dial, and found John R., out of Nashville, WLAC, spinning records and pushing Royal Crown Hair Pomade and baby chicks, delivered straight to your door.

He turned through the pages of his notebook, scribbled some names on the page and went to the bathroom to practice, thinking all the time that if anyone saw what he did—how he roamed about the apartment, talking out loud, laughing to himself—he would surely be committed.

One name kept coming back to him: Lipton Dink. Billy had given Lipton Dink a New Jersey accent. In his mind, he saw those tired-looking cab drivers around Fort Dix, a cigarette dangling from their lips.

Wher' to?

Bridge or de tunnel?

He had the voice down, borrowing from the boys from basic training and Vozelli.

So Lipton Dink it would be. He had been at KLPL about six months. It was time for a coming out party.

The next day, he put the show in motion. What had originally been so taxing was, by then, a matter of rote. He opened with the news and farm reports, did the weather, and played the first few records. When the first

batch of commercials came up, he did the first two in his own voice. The third was for a local seed and feed store.

"And now," he said, "the new spokesman for Burley's Seed and Feed—Lipton Dink."

Lipton lashed into the copy. He was straight Newark, fresh from the docks. The lip was curled, his attitude was curt.

"See, dis here, is what's gonna make you money, gonna make dem cows of yours PRODUCE—know what I'm saying . . . So's when ya lookin' for what dose pigs need to get fattened up, go to Burley's . . . And tell 'em, yea, Lipton Dink sent you. Bill, back to youse."

"Thank you, Lipton. Glad to have you with us. Lipton Dink will be back later in the show."

Billy listened for the phones. None rang. One of the office girls walked by the studio laughing, giving him a thumbs-up. For weeks to come, Lipton Dink made cameo appearances with Bill Williams, pushing everything from car dealerships to grocery stores, and no one said a word.

Finally, one afternoon during a shift change, Lanny James complimented Billy, mentioning how much he had improved in just a few months. "Oh," he said, finally, "just wanted to tell you. Lipton Dink—funny."

Not long after the introduction of Lipton Dink, Billy received two phone calls. The first came from Howard Griffith and Bob Tucker, who operated KUZN in West Monroe, Louisiana. They had heard Billy on KLPL and wanted him to send them an air-check, what he viewed as "his very best stuff."

The second call came from Martha, but before she could begin, Billy started talking about the new job possibility. It was more money—$66 a week—and not that far away, about eighty miles down the road. It was a bigger station, and it sounded as though he was going to have more freedom to do the kind of show he wanted.

"See," he said, "things are working out."

"Billy," Martha said, "that's great. Good for you. I have some news, too."

"Yeah, what's that?"

"You're going to be a father."

Chapter Ten

Sean & points beyond

> He wanted something else. He didn't want to be just a broadcaster. He wanted to be funny, but not in any normal way. He wanted to put on a show. He wanted to sit in the middle of an *eccentric* cast of characters, all of whom were, well, expressions of himself.

Billy didn't know what to say. It didn't matter anyway.

His vocal cords seemed frozen, along with every other muscle in his body. The phone felt heavy. He stared at the wall and his silence alarmed Martha.

"Billy, are you there? Did you hear me? You're going to be a father. I just found out. The baby will come in late August or early September."

"My God," he said. "How did this happen?"

They laughed.

They talked for a long while, both of them nervous, uncertain. He heard a tone in

Martha's voice that was new. There was no edge, nothing accusatorial.

"I know things haven't been great," she said, "but I believe they will be better." She said she would drive down to visit in the next couple of days.

"Wait," Billy said. "How do you feel?"

"Fine, Billy, I feel just fine. There's a lot we need to talk about. We need to make plans. I'll see you in a few days."

He hung up the phone and sat there for a moment, still shaken by Martha's news. He was 24 years old. His career was just beginning and he was going to be a father. Was he ready for this? He paced around the apartment, thinking about money, his job, new responsibilities. He added to every over-crowded ashtray in the apartment, filling the place with a blue haze. He was excited and scared. What to do first?

He called Dot and Raymond.

When Dot answered, he said, "Mom, guess what?" He sounded as if he was 15 years old and had just made varsity.

They congratulated him, asked him about the due date. "We're so happy for you both," Dot said. "Son, this will change your life in ways you can't imagine."

They talked about the treasures and trials of being a parent. "So far," Dot said, "you have lived for you and only you. That's gone, or it should be."

Raymond got on the phone. "Now," he said, "two people are dependent on you. And you know what makes me sick—we've talked about this before—those folks who don't stand up to their pledge. And, boy, it ain't always easy."

Billy smiled. Raymond had a way of breaking the larger abstractions down to a few spare words.

He told Dot and Raymond about the interest from KUZN in West Monroe.

"It's a bigger station," he said, "more money—more opportunity to move up."

Dot and Raymond handed the phone back and forth, repeating questions and answers across the room.

He heard Raymond's voice, coming from somewhere in the kitchen: "More money. That's good. Gonna need it now."

"Tell Dad I think it will be a good place for me," Billy said. "I can try some new things I've been thinking about. I've been working on some voices."

"Voices?"

"Yeah, you know how Jack Purnell there in Memphis does Thurlow Beaver? Like that, but different."

"Think that's a good idea?"

"I think it will be fun. I think I can make it work."

They were quiet for a moment. It was a comfortable silence. "You might want to call Martha and congratulate her," Billy said, finally.

"We'll do that," Dot said. "But when I've called in the past, seems like she doesn't want to be bothered, doesn't visit either. Spends a lot of time with her people in Mississippi, down in Corinth."

That had always been a point of friction in the marriage. Martha seemed to resent how close Billy was to Dot and Raymond. From the time they were married, Martha didn't want to go to Sunday dinner at their house and didn't like it when Billy went to see his folks without her. It was something he had never understood and Martha had never given him a reasonable explanation. She was as tough and stubborn as she was beautiful. Once set, she rarely bent.

"Maybe the baby will change that," Dot said. "Of course, son, that's the last thing you need to worry about right now."

Billy had forgotten how much he missed his parents. Whatever they said always helped. It didn't matter how old he was or how long he had been away from home. He could admit his fears to his parents—even in his 20s—and they understood.

"It's natural, Billy," Dot said. "Being a parent is wonderful, but it's scary too."

It was good talking to them, and he told them so.

"We love you, son," Dot said. "Let us know what we can do to help. We'll tell your grandparents the good news."

Off in the background, Raymond yelled, "I'll spread the news at the firehouse!"

Billy hung up the phone and sat on the edge of the bed. He thought about Dot and Raymond and Grandpa and Grandma Wells, Uncle Winford and Aunt Irene. He thought about Martha and the baby.

He got up, washed the dishes in the sink, and emptied the ashtrays. He swept the floors and wiped off the furniture, his mind running through all he knew about being a father and a parent.

He was making the bed, sorting through what he wanted to do with the rest of his life, when the thought came to him. He desperately wanted to be a good father, a good parent, like Dot and Raymond. He wanted to be dependable and trustworthy.

Suddenly aware of how he had spent the last hour or so, he smiled.

Jesus, he thought, looking around him, I'm nesting.

Billy thought about Raymond and the hours Raymond spent adding the extra room to the house so he and Glenna could have separate rooms. He thought about how his mother always struck a perfect balance between steering and riding in the back seat with him and Glenna. They preferred her in the back, of course.

And now Billy, himself, was driving. He looked around the apartment. Everything was clean and straight, even the books on the shelves. He found his car keys, drove to the station, and began cutting tapes for KUZN. He wanted to make sure they were in the morning mail.

Back in Memphis, Dot made coffee and asked Raymond what he thought about the news from Billy.

"Well," he said, "maybe *this* will settle him down."

Somewhere in the middle of the night, Billy finished the tapes. He worked fast but meticulously, dubbing in new opens, introducing himself as Johnny Apollo. He selected the material carefully, picking his best shows, making sure to include Lipton Dink.

He needed a strong closer, and he turned to the Sunday morning show when everything went wrong and the rejoicing choir buffeted him about the control room like a twig in a high wind. He listened closely. Below the lyrics, somewhere in the rests, his plight was discernable.

First, there was his simple introduction. The minister set the choir to song and the fervor began to build. There was slight laughter; then, a muffled groan and a rumble, the sound of someone falling and, finally, when the choir was finished with the hymn, the sound of rustling robes, titters from the choir, and then a halting, beleaguered baritone: "Wasn't that—uplifting! This is Bill Williams. Whew, we'll be back right after this word. Hallelujah. I got the spirit!"

Perfect, he thought, *it's unexpected. It spurs curiosity. There's no need for an answer. The question is enough, provided the hook. Pique the interest of the listeners. Don't supply an explanation; provide, instead, something that tugged at natural curiosity.*

Do that, he believed, and the audience would sit tight, wondering what might come next.

His thoughts turned on what he wanted to do in radio. He wanted to be entertaining. He wanted to be funny, but he wanted to do so in an unconventional manner.

Humor, he decided, didn't have to be the standard joke: set up and punch line. There was room, he believed, for conceptual humor even though the medium of radio offered no visual support. He often thought about the times he had sat with his mother watching Ernie Kovacs on television—Kovacs and guests such as The Nairobi Trio, three characters in gorilla suits doing musical shtick, not speaking a word and yet, somehow, rendering them—and thousands of others—helpless with laughter.

What was it about The Nairobi Trio that grabbed them so? He could arrive at only one answer. There was nothing else like it anywhere on any stage. It was—unexpected, beyond the norm. You would never see it on The Ed Sullivan Show.

He remembered watching Steve Allen, whom he always thought was imitating Kovacs, although he couldn't come close were it not for the characters who surrounded him, such as Don Knotts, Bill Dana, Tom Poston, and Louis Nye.

All of it spun through his mind: Brother Dave Gardner; Kovacs's Percy Dovetonsils, poet laureate; Jonathan Winters's salty Maude Frickert; and Bill Dana doing José Jiménez on *The Steve Allen Show*. He was searching for something in that heady mix, and he was convinced that what had taken place in that control room—the rollicking choir and the dancing minister, the music, and the chaos—held the key to what he wanted to bring to radio every day.

Billy didn't want to do a broadcast. He wanted to do a *show*, to be in the center of a collection of characters—his creations—and sharing the stage with the people who were beginning to take shape in his mind. That's what he wanted to do, but could he make it work, and could he make it work at a small market station?

The next morning he told everyone at KLPL about the good news from Martha. Mr. Gene and Lanny James congratulated him. The girls in the office wondered when his wife would be moving to Lake Providence.

"Not just yet," he said. "She's going to stay in Memphis for the time being."

Days later, he had more news. He had been offered and accepted a new job, the morning shift at KUZN in West Monroe, Louisiana. No one was surprised. They were more surprised that Billy had stuck around for six months. In the estimation of most, he was too talented—and far too fidgety—for Lake Providence.

New things were happening for Billy just as old things resisted change. Driving from Lake Providence to West Monroe, crossing the Ouachita River, he was struck by a large billboard by the side of the road. It pictured Martin Luther King, Jr., in a classroom. His face was particularly attentive, and he was portrayed as a star pupil, one with an acute interest in the subject matter.

The caption below the picture, in letters big and bold enough to ensure the notice of even the fastest drivers, read: *Martin Luther King, Jr., in Communism School.*

Billy slowed down, studied the sign briefly. The picture could have been taken in any classroom anywhere, but the divisive message was decidedly clear, and it saturated the South.

At every turn there was another troublesome event, and none shook Billy more than James Chaney, Michael Schwerner, and Andrew Goodman, civil rights workers—"freedom fighters," they were called—killed near Philadelphia, Mississippi, dragged out in the woods, and shot by Klansmen.

Billy didn't quite know what to make of the Civil Rights Movement and the violence that came with it. He didn't know where it would lead, or how it would end, or if he had a place in the conflict.

He did know that the entire matter left him with an anxious, uncomfortable feeling. He couldn't ignore what was happening in the South. No one could.

But wouldn't it be nice, he thought, if that were possible.

Suddenly, he was embarrassed by that idea. It made him think of Frau Bressler, sitting in her parlor in Germany and the pain that sometimes crossed her face when she talked about her homeland during the war, tragedies committed and ignored in the interest of personal well-being.

He saw faces and heard their voices: Robert, the janitor at Beverly Hills Baptist and Buddy Pearson, one of the most sophisticated people he had ever known. He remembered how Grandpa Wells would rise from his chair and turn off the television when a black man appeared on the screen. He remembered Norman White, who sometimes sang with The Mar-Keys, and a night in Arkansas—maybe Jonesboro—when the clerk at the Holiday Inn turned him away and how, late that night, they had secreted Norman into one of the rooms so he wouldn't have to sleep in the van and how he had cussed and bitched about "white folks," and all the while, it was "white folks" hurrying him through the night to the comfort of the hotel room.

"You're not really white folks," Norman said, cussing all the while. "You're musicians. There's a difference."

Lines were drawn and re-drawn, strained and broken, and the terrain seemed to change every day.

Billy remembered his mother, angry over something she had seen on television, getting that stern and determined look on her face, and saying: "If I were black, I would want to be the blackest person on the planet."

The constellation of race, racism, segregation, bigotry, and violence threw a disorienting fog over the world he knew. It was early spring of 1965 and Billy was confused about many things.

He had a child coming. He needed to find a good place to live, somewhere comfortable that Martha would enjoy. He needed to work and be successful. He was determined to try new things at KUZN, and he hoped management would be supportive.

He turned up the radio and spun the dial until he landed on KLIF out of Dallas. Russ Knight, "the Weird Beard," was on. Billy listened closely, studying Knight's style and delivery. He leaned on the gas, leaving the billboard and the Ouachita River in the rearview mirror, another part of the Louisiana landscape sliding by.

The people at KUZN—Howard Griffith, the owner; his son Arthur, the chief engineer; Bob Tucker, the programming director; and Chuck Morgan, the general manager, were kind people. They helped him find a place to live, a small carriage house not far from the station, and they made sure he had time to get settled before putting him on the air.

Tucker encouraged him to take risks but to be smart about what he said on the air. It was exactly what Billy wanted to hear. It was a great time to be in radio, an odd, bewildering time in the world—and somehow radio, whether it was in West Monroe or Detroit—provided a welcome adhesive.

Good mornin', West Monroe! This is Johnny Apollo, putting some slide in your glide and dip in your hip . . .

Martha moved to West Monroe and everyone remarked on her beauty. "We are happily, blissfully pregnant," Billy would say. She busied herself around the carriage house and Billy worked. When he wasn't working, he was working on work: making notes, listening to the competition and the clear channel stations he could dial in from around the country.

At night, he read: newspapers, novels, history, biographies, and something new—psychology. His old classmate David Welch was studying to be a psychologist. That was the word from home, prompting Billy to prowl the stacks at the West Monroe library for the thick translations of Freud and Immanuel Kant. Billy wasn't learned but he wanted to be, and he thought that if he read enough, he could sound as if he were—close anyway.

He had another, simpler motive. He wanted to be able to hold a conversation with David when their paths crossed again. So he tackled Freud, eventually felled by the doctor's inscrutability. Maybe, he mused, he and David could talk about Huck Finn when next they met on common ground. Twain, Billy had decided, was more philosopher than satirist, and he planned to run that assertion past David when he saw him.

Surely that will impress him.

Billy's books didn't seem to bother Martha any longer. Maybe it was because she was focused on the baby's arrival. Maybe it was because there were no more parties and late nights. When Billy walked away from the music and its lifestyle, he made a clean break and she gave him credit for that. He drank hardly at all, there were no drugs, and his wandering eye seemed focused on her and his work—if you could call radio "work," and she didn't know that you could. To her, radio seemed mostly tomfoolery, though she didn't deny the paychecks.

Billy, for instance, was forever practicing voices, giving her a fright and the idea, from time to time, that someone else was in the house.

There was a crusty cowpoke, a cross between Gabby Hayes and Walter Brennan, the creak of worn saddles and old bones evident in every word. *Hello buckaroos, boys and girls—all you kids, too. Gather round the fire here and let me tell you a story . . . First, how 'bout a little harmoniky music? Yes, siree . . .*

There was a woman who spoke with a knowledge born of reckless nights in the clubs and bars. *Look at you! Yum, yum. Here I come. I'm a hog for you, baby. Now, here's that recipe for lemon meringue pie I been bragging about . . .*

Occasionally, but at the wrong times, it sounded as if the evening news was on, as if some twisted version of Chet Huntley or Walter Cronkite had just strolled in and sat down on the couch. *Good evening ladies and gentlemen, this news just out—er—in! Let's go live to Washington, D.C., and the White House. But, first—Erie, Penn-syl-va-nia . . .*

He began to drop the voices into his show. Sometimes it was a phone call. Often they clattered through the studio door, and with each appearance Bob Tucker offered an encouraging smile. Johnny Apollo came with a company that seemed to grow in number with each show—including a raving minister who preached from The Book of Hominomonees. Not your Old Testament. Not your New Testament, but your Present Testament, where God's messenger sayeth: *What is stronger, rubber or skin? And go on to sayeth, to providith the word, the truth: Moses tied his ass to a tree and walked forty miles. Amen, brothers and sisters . . .*

Billy quickly gained an audience at KUZN, and while he was still rough around the edges, he was tireless in preparation and without immediate peer when it came to throwing himself into his performance. More often than not, his bits worked, and when one or another didn't, Tucker continued his reassurance.

On September 15, 1965, at Ouachita Memorial Hospital, William Sean Purser, kicking and screaming, entered his new world at seven pounds, six ounces. Martha was exhausted and Billy was giddy with joy.

While Martha rested, Billy stood outside the nursery, tapping on the glass and smiling. A nurse gently lifted Sean from his bed, holding him up so Billy could see him. He was pink and pruned and thrashing about.

"Is that your little brother?" someone asked. Billy turned to see a woman standing to his side, smiling. She wore a well-pressed print dress, hat, and white gloves. He guessed her to be 55 or 60 years old. It was hard to tell.

"That's my son," he said.

"Dear me," the woman said. "You can't be more than 18."

Even in his 20's, Billy was sensitive about his youthful looks. He believed people didn't take him seriously because he looked so young, but for some reason he didn't see this as an occasion for serious behavior.

"I'm 14," he said. "I'm from Mis'sippi and in Mis'sippi, we get an early start. Fact is, I'm running behind."

The lady flushed, raised a gloved hand to her mouth, and started to move away.

"Ma'am," he said, "my boy's Caesarean. From here on, you reckon he'll be trying to leave by the window?"

The woman pushed through the large doors at the end of the hall, looking back over her shoulder as if she had encountered someone curiously foreign to her. Someone, perhaps, from another galaxy.

Billy hosted the Sunday morning ministers and then visited their churches at night, sitting with the congregation, singing along with the choir and bringing the experience back to the studio in one form or another.

When he wasn't on the radio, he was listening to radio—but never idly. For Billy, it wasn't entertainment or simply background. He was studying, analyzing, scribbling down notes, and sticking them in his pockets. He wanted to take all his observations and translate them into something . . . phosphorescent. Yes, that was it. He wanted—*incandescence*.

He wanted the voices in his head to burn with originality, become a flaming nova that blew out the ceiling tiles of the studio, and exploded through the roof, and then the entire world could laugh along with him. That's what he wanted.

Like most program directors, Jim McCullough spent a part of each day driving around, spinning the radio dial and searching for new ideas and talent. He was the program director at WWUN in Jackson, Mississippi, one of the more prominent Top 40 stations in the entire Ark-La-Miss region. The station catered to a broad, young audience mixing rock 'n' roll with rhythm and blues, making it a fixture on car radios and transistors in and around the Jackson area.

He was on a business trip driving through northern Louisiana when he rolled up on KUZN. The voice he heard was a bit forced, but the material and delivery was good. Then, there was another voice—an old cowboy who talked back and forth with the jock and then started playing a harmonica.

Two people?

Had to be.

If not, it was on tape, and whoever did it was a wizard at production.

McCullough stayed with KUZN as long as the signal held. He liked this Johnny Apollo. He had to find out who he was.

A few days later, Billy received a phone call.

"Johnny, this is Jim McCullough. I'm the program director at WWUN in Jackson. Heard your show the other day and I was wondering if you could send us an air check? You might be just right for our station."

"Uh, WWUN in Jackson? Listen to you guys all the time. Uh, yeah, sure, Mr. McCullough."

"Good! Glad to hear. Get that tape out as soon as you can. Okay?"

Days later, McCullough was back on the phone with a job offer: $100 a week to do the four-to-eight shift, drive-time Monday through Friday. As McCullough spelled out the details of the offer, Billy's mind raced.

Great offer at a great station and a big raise. The only station bigger was WNOE in New Orleans. Martha will be thrilled. It's closer to home. I can't believe this is happening.

Billy was bursting with excitement. He wanted to run down the hall yelling his good fortune to everyone in the building.

Then McCullough said something that seized Billy's attention and all the excitement, all the energy, was gone—instantly.

At first, the conversation was light and enthusiastic. Then McCullough said, "I'm assuming you have a first class radio license."

When Billy said he did not, McCullough was silent. "That's a problem," he said. He went on to explain that WWUN was a directional station and his disc jockeys were required to hold the first class license so they could redirect the transmitter at the proper times.

Billy's heart plummeted.

"Tell ya what," McCullough said. "I like your work enough that I'll hold the job for you until you get the license. I've got some friends down at Elkin's in New Orleans. We'll get you in a class straightaway."

Billy assumed that meant McCullough would foot the bill. His assumption was incorrect.

Tuition for the course was $500—paid in advance. In what seemed to be the briefest amount of time, he was driving from KUZN to New Orleans where he found a tiny room for $25 a week—paid in advance. He was not completely tapped out, but he was precariously close. It was not life in New Orleans as he had ever imagined it. And if it had not been for saltines, Vienna sausages, and stolen bananas, he would have been a dead man.

Chapter eleven

Going to Jackson

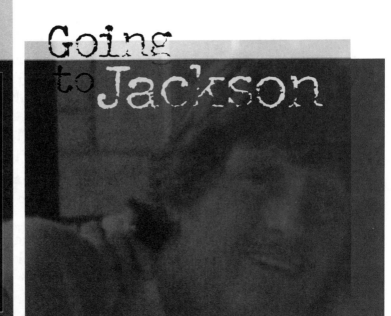

There was a brief sojourn in New Orleans, then he was in Jackson, Mississippi, where he met the *Fun Boys*. For a time, it was all fun, but the Civil Rights Movement was underway in the recalcitrant South, and it was serious business.

He had a job waiting on him in Jackson, Mississippi, but he

was stuck in a small, dingy, rundown, second-story room just off St. Charles Street in New Orleans. It was hot, he had no money, and the fact that he was living on Vienna sausage and crackers was made even more grievous by the heavenly aromas that filtered through the air from the city's Creole and Cajun kitchens.

Often, late in the afternoon on his way back to his room, he got off the streetcar and stood outside Pascal's Manale on Napoleon Avenue just to smell the barbecued shrimp. After a few torturous minutes, he generally found a market or fruit stand where he could swipe a banana, then he slipped away to the boarding house on Liberty for another dinner of wieners in a can. He wondered if they were sausages at all, taking pause over their colorless skin and jellied jackets but never quite brave enough to ponder the actual ingredients.

He envied the proper patrons of Antoine's, and even those fortunate enough to be sitting down at home to a bowl of gumbo. Being broke and hungry in New Orleans was like being the tease pony on a stud farm.

On rare occasions, he ventured over to Jackson Square and treated himself to a beignet, savoring the deep fried dough covered with confectioner's sugar. More often than not, he was in his room counting crackers, always careful to save some for the next day, and washing down his misery with another glass of tap water.

One evening, shortly after he had arrived in New Orleans, he was walking to his room when he smelled something delicious cooking in the landlord's kitchen: red beans and rice. Nothing had ever smelled so tempting: garlic, onions, peppers, ham, scallions and parsley, all simmering together.

"Say der, Bill," the landlord said. "Care ta eat wid us dis evenin'? It's a Monday. Red beans and rice. Tra-di-she-on dese parts. C'mon an' eat. Got de big ol' ham bone in der."

The landlord and his wife watched as their guest hurriedly went through one plate full, then a second, and a third. He longed for a fourth but the missus started clearing the table—a clear signal that their hospitality had come to an end.

"My, my," the landlord said. "You go tru dat red beans and rice like a wood chipper. And ya such a small fella. Gracious!" Billy was a little embarrassed. The landlord and his wife were polite, smiled when he walked by, and asked how things were going. But they never invited him to dinner again.

Probably figure I'd eat the legs off the table, Billy thought.

Billy had been in New Orleans for nearly four weeks, attending Elkins' Radio Institute, going to school five hours a day and wandering the city at night, wishing he had the wherewithal to enjoy this place that seemed like a foreign country. Not since Stuttgart and Böblingen had he seen a city like this—filled with architecture he had never seen and a culture he didn't understand.

He found himself having conversations with people and comprehending about every other word.

Cho! Co! Dat your beb back der?

Translation: *Wow, that your sweetheart back there?*

Uh, hey! How you doin'?

Translation: *I'm trying to be polite but I have no idea what you are saying.*

Generally, these exchanges resulted in curious glances and more indecipherable language.

You coo-yon or sumpin?

Translation: *You stupid or something?*

Good talkin' to you. See ya.

Translation: *This is awkward and I'm going to move on.*

The bedeviling words and phrases were as intriguing as the accent, which held no hint of the South he knew. Instead, it was touched by something of the East, a tone he had heard in the army: the boys from Brooklyn and Jersey, from Michael Vozelli—clipped and short.

What was "gris-gris?" And a lan' yap? What was *that*?

And who was Marie Laveau and why was she regarded with reverence and trepidation from St. Louis Cathedral to Congo Square?

In time, he learned that Madame Laveau was the Queen of Voodoo, that "gris-gris" was a charm used by her and her followers and that a "lagniappe" was a small gift.

He watched Dixieland bands and strolled by Preservation Hall in the French Quarter, listening to jazz. He became acquainted with zydeco, all the while wondering: *Who can get that kinda sound from an accordion, and who decided to turn a washboard into a musical instrument?*

New Orleans was a wide-open mystery, and were it not for the business at hand, Billy was ready to get lost in its dark, inviting caverns. Only problem was—he was too busy, too hungry, and too poor to make the plunge.

How had it come to this: Vienna sausages, saltines, and tap water?

No income. Car payments he couldn't make (Raymond had warned him). Martha and Sean back in Memphis, living with her relatives.

Once more his aptitude for radio carried him. The work came easy and when he wasn't in class or studying, he walked around New Orleans ruminating on his future.

One afternoon, as he walked alone along St. Charles, streetcars clattering by, folks moving here and there, laughing, he made a promise.

Someday, I will be somebody in this town. I'm going to have one of the biggest, nicest offices in the city: ferns and a big oak desk and a leather couch, and I will eat anything I want.

He returned to his room, ate some crackers, and went to bed. Soon enough, he would be in Jackson, and working. And, the Lord willing, eating. No gumbo in Jackson, he guessed, but surely he could find a good plate of biscuits and red-eye gravy.

Dave Warnock, who worked WWUN's evening shift, happened to be in the lobby of the Jackson station when he noticed a new maroon Chevy Nova pull onto the circle driveway and stop. The car, Warnock thought, was among the nicest in the parking lot, which was filled mostly with a collection of clunkers, a dented, dilapidated testament to WWUN's payroll practices.

A young man stepped out of the Nova and flipped a cigarette to the pavement. He adjusted his sports coat, ran his hands through his hair, and started for the door.

He was a good-looking sort, Warnock thought, somewhat on the short side, and dressed well but not too well. He looked friendly, and he walked confidently. *That must be him, Bill Purser—Johnny Apollo*, he thought. Warnock couldn't get over the car. *Damn, they must pay well in West Monroe.*

Warnock and Billy hit it off immediately. They were close to the same age and shared interests beyond their unspoken but common belief that they would someday be stars in radio. Warnock noticed how easily Billy smiled and laughed and why the program director, Jim McCullough, had emphasized Purser's energetic nature. Even seated motionless in a chair, Purser seemed to percolate. (Warnock knew McCullough was excited by the way he worked his fingers round and round one another, as if he were winding yarn. It was a nervous habit that, frankly, was hard to watch.)

Billy seemed to have his own nervous habits. "Can't wait to get started," he said over and over. "Man, can't wait to get to work. Can't wait until tomorrow."

Warnock soon learned there was an additional motivation to Billy's refrain, one that exceeded Billy's excitement for the job. Billy's first day on the air, two men walked in the front door of the station and asked for

William Purser. They said they had come from West Monroe and needed to talk to him. They were polite but stern.

"It's important," one said. "Is he here?"

One wore a suit. The other was dressed in work clothes, his name stitched in red script on a white oval sewn to the breast of his jacket: *Ed*. Ed chewed gum. His boss was all business. The receptionist knew trouble when she saw it.

Billy entered the lobby smiling and shook hands with the two men, then ushered them out to the parking lot where they stood and talked. Billy nodded while the man in the suit addressed him. Ed stood back with his hands in his pockets.

The man handed Billy a piece of paper and Billy handed the man something in exchange. They shook hands again and Billy walked back toward the station. The two men from West Monroe talked for a moment. The well-dressed man

Dave Warnock worked the evening shift. At first, he thought Billy was odd. In truth, the WWUN jocks made up an entire covey of oddness. The station called them "the Fun Boys." And Jackson had never seen— heard—anything like them.

Jesse James

walked to an Oldsmobile and drove away. Ed took something from the man in the suit, walked to Billy's Nova, climbed in, started the car, and drove off. Billy turned and watched, then shrugged.

Warnock was standing in the office when Billy walked through the door on his way to the production room. He looked at Dave and smiled. "Repo man," he said. "Gonna have to find a new car."

A few hours later, Johnny Apollo hit the air on WWUN for the first time. He was unfazed, as if life were perfect. He was, Warnock thought, everything McCullough had said—and a bit unusual.

The next day Billy showed up driving a beat-up Ford station wagon with a glove box that wouldn't stay closed.

"Won't have to worry about anybody stealing it," he said.

Odd bird, Warnock thought. *I like him.*

Soon, Warnock, Billy, and Joe Fisher, whom McCullough found in Orlando, were inseparable—self-proclaimed "radio freaks." When they weren't working at WWUN, they talked radio, studied radio, practicing their craft for one or the other, all the while determined to be better and more entertaining than their crosstown competition, WRBC, and together Johnny Apollo, Jesse James, and Jimmy Rabbit succeeded in that endeavor.

To Jim McCullough's delight, there was never a conflict of ego. "The Fun Boys," as they were known, worked as a team, pushing one another. When they could, they got together and dialed in KAAY from Little Rock, "The Mighty 10-90." Around midnight, they listened to Clyde Clifford's Beaker Street Show, when KAAY abandoned Top 40 and turned to new music and R&B.

WLAC out of Nashville was a staple: Gene Nobles, John R. (John Richbourg), Herman Grizzard, and Bill "Hoss" Allen. They listened to WLS and Art Roberts in Chicago and KILT in Houston, especially Russ Knight, "The Weird Beard."

They worked the dial, trying to find Wolfman Jack, Robert Weston Smith, broadcasting on XERB from Rosarito Beach in Mexico: *Who's this on the Wolfman telephone?*

They took notes. They drank a few beers and smoked funny things and every time they located Wolfman, Billy took umbrage: *He's great, but he's doing Howlin' Wolf, the blues man, that's what he's doing.*

They learned to borrow and steal, to adapt, that it was all part of the craft—Alan Freed had stolen schtick from Moondog, a New York City street musician, Wolfman had borrowed from Freed and added an extraction of Howlin' Wolf.

They were consumed by the industry, each searching for a recipe that would play on a national stage. They sent air-checks to WLAC, WLS, and WABC in New York. They heard nothing. They kept working.

They took to the air each day with an energy matched by their naiveté, fully believing that no one could possibly be listening to anyone other than them. They suffered and succeeded from blind enthusiasm and WWUN, at the time, the best small station in the tall shadow of WNOE in New Orleans, was the benefactor.

The Fun Boys were attuned to the cultural climate surrounding them—from the Civil Rights Movement, which had made Jackson and Little Rock focal points, to the music that swelled from the black community and

enveloped young whites from coast-to-coast.

While WRBC ignored the rising popularity of soul music, McCullough allowed The Fun Boys to embrace the new sound and its popular turn from R&B, and they obliged. Jackson's population at the time was nearly 40 percent black, a fact WRBC dismissed, sticking to traditional Top 40. While Jackson was far from integration, the studio at WWUN became a haven for equality. Every Top 40 record was followed by a soul number. Dusty Springfield preceded Wilson Pickett. The Rolling Stones were followed by Aretha Franklin. Depending on their mood and what they viewed as "hot," they would double up: playing an Aretha cut, then something from The Temptations, followed by The Beatles.

They named the turntables in the studio "Crackers" and "Soul." The one on the right was for "Top 40," the one on the left for "Soul," and many times, when their shifts were done, they kept their heads down. In some Jackson circles, The Fun Boys were not the least bit popular—regardless of their ratings—and while Billy's ability with language and vernacular led to praise at the station, it raised suspicions in some sectors of Jackson.

Who was this Johnny Apollo? Was he white? Was he black? Sure sounded black.

On a crisp evening, their work done for the day, Apollo, James and Rabbit were ready for a beer and about to leave the station when they saw an older Buick pull into the parking lot, lights off, driving slowly. As the car approached in the darkness, they sensed trouble. There were four men inside the car and the windows were rolled down. Apollo, James, and Rabbit hesitated on the porch, unsure of what was taking place. The car pulled closer to the porch and as it did, the barrel of a shotgun eased out a rear window and aimed clearly in their direction. They could see faces, all of them white. They waited for the blast. But all they heard was laughter as the car sped away.

The next morning they learned that a house down the street from the station had been bombed, the porch blown away, and the house set afire. The fire made the news. The fact that the home belonged to a Jewish family, new to the community, came up later, after the family had moved away.

Truthfully, they didn't pay much attention to the unrest and violence around them—unless, of course, it came in the form of a shotgun drawn their way. They were in their early 20's, bound to get on with life in spite of the bothersome and discomforting times that surrounded them. To The Fun

Boys, all that embroiled the South and exposed its meaner side was like a lingering headache. Sooner or later, it would go away and life would go on as usual. Besides, they were having too much fun at WWUN.

After nearly a year in Jackson, Billy came to work one morning with news that was both expected and stunning. He had been offered a job in Memphis and was leaving WWUN. Of course, his friends hated to see him go, but they had all expected him to land a job at a larger station. The assumption, naturally, was that Bill had a job at WMPS or WHBQ.

"Nope," he said, looking around the room, a faint smile in his eyes. "I'm going to WDIA," he said. "I'm going to be the first white guy they've ever had on the air. Can you believe it?"

Clearly, no one could. They looked from one to the other. "Jesus Christ, Bill," James said, "the first white guy on DIA. How the hell did this happen? You gotta be nervous."

Bill said he wasn't. McCullough thought otherwise and so did James, but they took Bill at his word.

WDIA was the first station in the country to feature all black programming. It was home to legends in the business, such as Nat D. Williams, its pioneer and the host of Tan Town Jamboree. Bluesman B.B. King began his career at WDIA, the beacon of the black community and a bridge to young, white Memphians who over the years listened to Reverend Dwight "Gatemouth" Moore, Maurice "Hot Rod" Hulbert, Honeyboy Thomas, and Theo "Bless My Bones" Wade.

At WDIA, Bill Purser was "Johnny Apollo, your blue-eyed soul brother," working weekend shifts, cutting spots and bits, filling in where necessary and making frequent "in-character" appearances with Rufus Thomas, who introduced him as "Johnny Apollo, my illegitimate son."

Moohah Williams—the host of *Saturday Night Fish Fry*—offered Bill a protective wing and along with Thomas they attended black clubs in Orange Mound and shows at W.C. Handy Theater. He saw a side of Memphis he had never known and delved into a type of music he had always cherished. They called it "New R&B," and traced it to Louis Jordan's "Let the Good Times Roll."

From time to time, James and Rabbit drove to Memphis for a visit. They got the sense that while he was glad to be back in Memphis and reunited with Martha and Sean, he was mostly locked down in production and didn't

have his own show. He talked about how much he had learned from Thomas and how Moohah had introduced him to people and places he never would have known otherwise, but he wondered if Jim McCullough would have him back.

He had enjoyed the status of being the first white man on the station, but he wasn't sure the position was leading to anything significant. At WDIA, Johnny Apollo was a curiosity, an aside in the shadows of black legends, and for the prestige that came with his small status there, he wanted more. Truth be told, he didn't see himself as anyone's sidekick, no matter how famous they might be.

Weeks later, Bill was heading back to Jackson. Martha told him he was nuts. She said she wasn't moving again. She was tired of it all, packing and unpacking. She said he had better make a decision. She was staying in Memphis. Sean, almost 2 years old, waved goodbye.

Billy was frustrated and angry, but he needed to press on. He was accustomed to Martha's rage, but he wondered where he would eventually stand with his son.

Hardin Browning—Cris Lundy on the air—was just settling in at WWUN, trying to make his way, and the competition—though friendly— began with Johnny Apollo.

It was Browning's task to follow Apollo, so he decided to watch everything Johnny did—from preparation, which seemed to go on twenty-four hours a day—to performance.

Bill Purser was a thing to behold. He surrounded himself with books, magazines, newspapers, and clippings. He made notes all the time and little bits of paper were always coming out of his pockets. Sometimes he would sit down and cull through napkins and envelopes—unpaid bills, more often than not—studying what he had scrawled down in some frenzied moment of creation.

Sometimes he smiled and tucked the paper back in his pocket. Other times he swore in disgust, crumbled the scribbled thought in his hands, and tossed it in a wastebasket.

He seemed incredibly disorganized—until he went on the air. Then all the little notes and clippings from magazines seemed to rise from the smoke-filled studio and become something far beyond the WWUN norm.

For all the clutter Bill brought to his show, for all the cigarettes burning

on the consoles, and the Cokes overturned during one wild turn or another, for all the papers that flew in the air and fell to the floor, no one left the studio in more fastidious condition than Bill Purser. He arrived with a profusion of papers and left nothing behind but a resonance that, Browning believed, begged anyone who followed to be as good as one could be.

"I remember walking by the studio one afternoon," Browning said, much later. "I hadn't been at WWUN long. Bill was doing his show and it sounded like there were three or four different people with him in the studio — all arguing about something. Politics, maybe, I don't remember.

"I turn back and look in and he is in there by himself holding a conversation — going from one voice to another and making it work, and there's nothing on tape. Maybe it's Granny. Maybe it's Ranger Bob. It's one voice after another and it's all just coming out of his head. He's doing it live and it's funny as hell. He made it hard to do your show prep because all you wanted to do was sit and listen to what he was doing. You'd end up laughing at what he was doing and not thinking about what you needed to do, and he came up with something different every damned day."

Bill Purser was a welcome distraction in more ways than one. He had a way of attracting characters and frequently found himself in the midst of unusual circumstances.

One afternoon, a chauffeur-driven Cadillac pulled up in front of WWUN. A tall man wearing blue jeans, a dark sports coat, and cowboy boots stepped from the rear seat of the car, adjusted his sunglasses and walked to the receptionist's desk. He identified himself as Eddie Braddock of Stax Records in Memphis.

"I'm here," he said, "to see Bill Purser/Johnny Apollo."

The receptionist politely asked Braddock to have a seat and that she would buzz the programming director, Jim McCullough.

Braddock, not bothering to remove his sunglasses, declined the seat and said thank you.

Momentarily, McCullough walked into the lobby with an air of authority, introduced himself, and said, unfortunately, it was station policy not to allow record promoters to visit with disc jockeys. As McCullough spoke, there was a hint of a smile at the corners of Braddock's lips, as though he found both the policy and the man expressing it faintly humorous.

"Is that so," Braddock said, leaning forward slightly. There was

something about the man that was unsettling—a confident kind of . . . menace. McCullough began to twiddle and wind his fingers together. He took a step backwards. Braddock pushed his sunglasses up on his nose and leaned just a bit more in McCullough's direction.

"Bill Purser is a friend of mine," he said, speaking very slowly. "Would you tell him Eddie Braddock from Stax Records is here to see him? Or,"—he softened his voice—"would you like me to break your knees?"

McCullough buckled under Braddock's subtle assault and, without hesitation, summoned Bill. When Bill was told of the incident he laughed, and said that McCullough was wise to grant Braddock his wish.

"They don't call him Three-Gun Braddock for nothing," he said. "There's a story that Eddie invited friends over to his house one night to watch something on television. They arrived finding Eddie, always a gracious host, wearing pajamas but heavily armed. He had a high-caliber sidearm on each hip and a snappy little Beretta in an ankle holster. Never took 'em off all night.

"He has a definite familiarity with firearms and no reluctance to discharge them in circumstances he deems necessary. Great guy, known him since high school. The man *knows* music."

The next time Eddie Braddock pulled up on the circle driveway at WWUN, he was in a chauffeur-driven Ford Fairlane, and before his shiny black boots with the pointed toes hit the pavement, Billy was quickly summoned. Jim McCullough was nowhere to be found.

"Bill," the receptionist said, "your friend from Memphis is back—Mr. Braddock."

"Hmm," Bill said, "business must have taken a bad turn."

"Not really," Braddock said, "I just enjoy sharing the wealth. By the way, where is everybody?"

Bill looked around. There was no one in sight.

"I don't rightly know," he said.

Even a casual night on the town—a simple trip for a bite to eat—often turned into an event—if Bill happened to be along. B.J. Thomas stopped by the station one night to see Jimmy Rabbit. James was there and Cris Lundy, and Billy was milling about rustling through papers, cutting out one thing and another, laying them perfectly straight on a table.

Thomas suggested they get something to eat, and they piled into

Thomas's car, headed for Five Points and a sleepy all-night diner that served burgers and hash browns, eggs and grits, and the best coffee in Jackson.

There weren't many people in the place, just some truckers, big boys with cut-off sleeves to accommodate arms like oak limbs, and some scrawny older ones smoking and coughing. Outside, big rigs rumbled, keeping the batteries charged. The waitresses chewed gum and wore white and pink, their hair up high. They were all somewhere between pretty and spent, and when one arrived at their table, she stopped, called by the man behind the counter, who was wiping his hands on his apron.

"We ain't serving that one," he said, pointing at Thomas. "Ain't serving no long-hair in my place."

After he spoke, there was not one rattle of spoon or fork, just eyes turning to the table where James, Rabbit, Lundy, Apollo, and Thomas sat.

"Wait a minute, y'all," Rabbit said. "This is B.J. Thomas, recording artist. You *know* him. Did that song a while back, 'I'm so Lonesome I Could Cry.' You know him."

Somebody *hrmphed*, said that was a song by Hank Williams, then chairs and stools screeched across the linoleum floor as people stood, arguing. There was swearing and fuming and talk of a haircut for Thomas.

The Fun Boys and Thomas were backing out of the restaurant, heading for the car, but Bill kept ducking back in—arguing and swearing in one voice after another, using that Granny voice: *Ya sons of bitches. Ya ugly dogs. I'll kick all your asses.*

They made it to the car safely, Bill hanging out the window, still shaking his fist, taunting their antagonists as the car headed down the highway, him screaming: *Come back here you cowards. That's right! Go ahead. Run!*

"All I wanted to do was get something to eat," B.J. Thomas said, incredulous.

They were scared, laughing, Thomas driving fast through the night, all of them glancing back now and then to see if headlights were drawing down on the car. None were. They were safe. Someone lit a joint. Someone said, "Hey, Bill, one of these days you are gonna get us killed." He laughed, but he also remembered what his mother had often said, *There's a time to stand up and there's a time to sit down, and you don't know the difference.*

One afternoon, Bill left the station to take a walk and get a sandwich at Woolworth's soda fountain.

Generally, the soda fountain was quiet; that day people were talking

loudly, jostling about, anger in the air. Bill took a seat at a four-top back in the corner, alone, wondering what was going on. At the counter were five young men. Three were black, two were white, and all of them appeared to be college boys.

They were civil rights workers, northerners, staging an impromptu sit-in. They had asked for service and when denied, refused to leave. Bill watched as they sat determined and expressionless while white customers gathered around and shouted, spouting one racial epithet after another.

Bill studied the men at the counter. He had seen them all of his life. His mother and Raymond had often referred to them as "white trash," those who felt some entitlement from the color of their skin, a birthright that permitted violence and degradation. It was the sad dirge of the South, and Bill saw something coming.

A large man approached the men sitting at the counter. He had a nasty, mean smile. He leaned down and faced all five. "So," he said, "trying to make some sorta statement, are we? Is that what y'all call it?"

They said nothing, just looked ahead. The crowd hooted and called, looking for a bloody resolution.

Still, there was no response. Unable to get a rise out of the young men, he reached for a ketchup dispenser.

"Ya want service, *here's* some service," he said, squirting ketchup on the head of one of the black men. People laughed and crowed as the young man stood and walked away to clean the mess from his hair.

Bill had seen enough. He left his table and walked to the stool left vacant by the civil rights worker. The man turned his attention to Bill. "And what are you," he said, "some sort of nigger-lover?" Spittle flew from the man's mouth as he spoke.

Bill's hand found a sugar shaker on the counter. He gripped it tightly and then smashed the man across the bridge of the nose. He went down in a tumble, blood, sugar, and glass mixing with the shock on his face.

Bill passed several people, all dazed by the fury of the blow, as he made his way to the door. He took two steps into the street and then broke into a run. To his surprise, no one followed.

Time to get out of Jackson, he thought.

Chapter Twelve

The Battle of Louisville

The best times in Memphis were the simplest times. The worst times were, well, the worst. When *Louisville* came calling, Bill was ecstatic. He was used to living in WMPS's bathroom, but surely there was a station somewhere that had a place for him.

Radio WMPS in Memphis was one of those stops in which

the bags are left in the car. Bill knew that on his first day. When Hal Smith, the program director at WMPS, offered him a job doing the morning shift, all Bill heard was "$130 a week." It was a chance to go back home, to be with Sean and Martha, and to be in a larger market.

Instead, it appeared that he was shipwrecked on a godforsaken little archipelago of sagging ceilings and stained tile, swept by sounds and smells that even he, with all his considerable netherworld experience, could identify.

Offices weren't provided, the lobby was off-limits, and when the jocks weren't on the air or in a production room, they had two choices: the men's room or a storage room where they sat on crates and boxes surrounded by a museum of vinyl tombstones honoring everyone from Billie Holiday to Buddy Holly. The big orange and black "No Smoking" sign on the door made it far less popular than the men's room.

And that was where he found himself—the bathroom—chain-smoking, trying to read the *Memphis Commercial-Appeal*, and caught in a paroxysm of laughter that was sending his male co-workers out to pee in the bushes flanking the parking lot. He might as well laugh.

Hal Smith had not mentioned the stringent personnel policies of WMPS as he lured Bill away from Jackson. He talked about Bill's voice, working in a larger market, and making more money. He weaved a persuasive argument, and Bill liked and believed him. But then, he believed *everybody*. He thought that certainly he, Bill Purser, was descended from the first guy who bought an underwater lot in Florida.

Within a week of arriving at WMPS, Bill was miserable. WMPS reminded him of the army, and once more, he was looking for a hole in the fence. Still, he followed his personal counsel: never quit a job—no matter how distasteful it might be—until you have a new one, and his search for a new job began approximately forty-eight hours after he arrived at WMPS.

The best times in Memphis were the simplest. When Bill was off work, he often stood at the kitchen window watching Sean explore the backyard. Not quite 3 years old, Sean already showed an uncanny interest in dirt and grass. He examined tree trunks as if he were studying a secret map. Sticks and stones were his toys of preference, and above all else, he loved to dig holes. The Pursers' backyard was a toddler's excavation site. Bill watched Sean with as much wonder as his son held for the world.

Martha was finally content, and largely oblivious to Bill's disquiet. Her family was together and settled in Memphis, and she was proud of his position at WMPS. Without pursuing the matter, she was certain he would spend the rest of his life there. Why not? It was one of the largest radio stations in the city. He made a comfortable living. What cause was there to go hurrying off to another city?

When he could, Bill went to see his parents. They drank coffee, talking and laughing, Dot and Raymond quizzing him about the new job, Martha and Sean.

It sure was nice to have him back and close, they said, and it was fun being able to hear him on the radio every day.

"Yes," he said, "but WMPS isn't all it seems to be."

When he described the station, Raymond went into a diatribe about the ills of the business world.

"You know what makes me sick," he began, "makes me so mad I could eat a sack of nails . . ."

By the time Raymond finished ranting about the injustice of business, both Bill and Dot were laughing.

In Bill's mind, a character began to take shape in his mind. He was a hard-bitten, blue-collared, tough-talking guy with gravel in his voice and a gritty view of the world around him. He was a confrontational social commentator who took on all wrongs and said what many thought but most were reluctant to say. He could have been a fireman, like Raymond, and he might have sounded like Raymond. Bill made himself a note, stuck it in his pocket, and said he had to be on his way.

"He won't be staying around here long," Dot said.

"Nope," Raymond said, "and that could mean trouble."

And then there occurred one of those subterranean shifts in which, unseen, the tectonic plates of one's life shifts seismically, and the geography changes overnight. This is how it happened to Bill.

In the winter of 1969, Bob "Todd" Thurgaland arrived in Louisville and set up shop in a guest room at the Brown Hotel at Broadway and Fourth. He was armed with notebooks and tapes and charged with the task of restoring the status and ratings of WAKY radio, which in the 1950s and 1960s had been Louisville's top-rated station. Since then, it had fallen upon hard times, and Todd Thurgaland's job was to rekindle WAKY's creative operation.

For one week, Todd confined himself to his room at the Brown, listening to radio night and day. He paced. He made intricate notes and evaluations, placing his assertions in orderly stacks on the desk. He ate meals in his room, piling trays of dishes outside the door. When he ventured out into the streets, with the thickening rain turning to snow, he was investigating. He listened to a transistor radio. At street corners, waiting for lights, he tried to determine what station people were listening to in their cars. He strolled Fourth Street, the aorta of the region known as Kentuckiana, and

noticed that on Friday and Saturday nights, kids in cars were all listening to the radio. Fourth Street was a rock 'n' roll caravan. Unfortunately, though, WAKY had lost its place in the parade to WKLO, Louisville's top-rated station by a wide margin.

Todd focused on WAKY's weaknesses and WKLO's strengths, which were found primarily in the mouth of the morning man, Bill Bailey, "The Duke of Louisville." Bailey's voice was made of barbed wire, sharpened by an abiding attraction to Kentucky Bourbon, ice-cold beer chasers, and a two-pack-a-day smoking habit. Bailey was unguarded, reckless, and defiant. He growled his way through every show, saying whatever came to his mind. He charged the microphone and his audience like a street fighter with razor blades in the toes of his boots:

"Tonight it's Halloween and all the little cuties will be coming around looking for candy. Ah, the little urchins, the little darlin's. I love 'em. But with the kids come the punks—looking for trouble, causing trouble. Do what I do to these punks. Shoot 'em, so you won't have to worry about 'em next year . . .

"My good dear friends," Bailey bemoaned into the microphone, "my life has come to this: a bottle of Alka-Seltzer and a stack of teenybopper records. Good Gawd."

Todd made a note and underlined it: "Hire Bailey or get him out of town." He made other notes about WAKY: Get the right people. Find the right people. Give 'em format. Give 'em air. Let 'em go. Give WAKY personality and identity.

On the following Monday morning, Todd met with Al Smith and Johnny Randolph, the music director, and outlined his plan. Afterward, Todd and Randolph, whom Todd named assistant program director, began to court Bailey, doing their best to sell him on coming to WAKY. One night, thoroughly sloshed and just hours before he was to go on the air for WKLO, Bailey signed a WAKY contract. After he sobered up, he reneged on the deal, claiming he had signed the agreement in "a state of alcoholic distress."

Todd, Randolph, and Smith were undeterred. If Bailey wasn't at WAKY, they said, they wanted him far away. So through the extensive airwave grapevine, they planted word of Bailey in Chicago, which was where he soon landed, the full extent of his peregrinations unbeknownst to his own self.

Johnny "Dude" Walker was now the mid-morning voice—"When Dude Walker came to Louisville from Memphis they brought his larynx in on a flatbed truck," Randolph said—and it was Walker who told the others about Johnny Apollo.

First, however, they had to find him, which wasn't easy. They could hear him, but no one seemed to know where he was when he was off the air.

"Why the hell can't they find the guy?" Todd said. "It's crazy."

Walker laughed. "He's in the bathroom," Walker said. "That's where all the jocks at WMPS go when they aren't on the air. It's one of the only places they are *allowed* to go."

Finally, by enlisting old friends in Memphis, Walker came up with a home number for Bill Purser, got him on the phone, re-introduced himself, and told him of WAKY's interest.

Randolph told Bill that he had two rules at WAKY. "I try to hire people that are better than me," he said, "and I try to put them in position to thrive. We don't like to restrain our jocks."

They were on the phone for more than an hour and, from time to time, Martha walked by with an irritated look. Bill waved her away and returned to the conversation. The dismissive gesture added to Martha's aggravation.

"You'll like it here," Walker said in closing. "We have a lounge for the jocks and a couch. It's a great place to work. And you can move out of the bathroom."

When Bill told Martha who was calling and why, she was incensed. "No, Bill. No!" she said. "I'm not moving again. Louisville? What's in Louisville?"

Bill lit a cigarette and thought about what Martha had said. What's in Louisville? Maybe the opportunity of a lifetime—maybe that's what's in Louisville. He was tired of arguing with Martha.

He looked at the smoke spiraling from his cigarette. No one had ever talked to him like Todd, Randolph, and Walker had. Even if this discussion didn't lead to Louisville, Bill knew it would lead to something new—even if it meant leaving Martha and taking him away from Sean. That was the ultimate conflict. Could he tolerate being away from Sean? He knew what he wanted, but he feared what it might cost.

A few days later, Todd and Walker boarded a flight for Memphis, determined to hire Johnny Apollo. They took a suite at the Peabody Hotel and stocked the bar. Ever since hearing Bill's air checks, Todd had

been puzzled. "He sounds like someone. Who is it? What am I missing?" Randolph and Walker both agreed, but they couldn't identify the similarity.

When Bill arrived at the Peabody, Todd put his offer on the table. "We want to hire you," he said. "We're offering a handsome salary. We think we can give you the room within our format to truly go somewhere in this business, but we get the sense you're hesitant to come with us."

Bill began to explain. He said that his marriage wasn't going that well and his wife didn't want to leave Memphis. He had a little boy, Sean, and he was fearful that if he moved again the marriage would be over. More than anything, he was concerned about the boy. He was pleased that Todd and Walker had so much interest, but he wasn't sure if he could make the move.

As Bill talked, leaning back in his chair and then forward, nervous about what he was saying, trying to find the right words, Todd jumped to his feet.

"That's it," he said. "*Gary Owens!*"

"Exactly," Walker said. "Gary Owens."

"You sound like Gary Owens," Todd said.

Owens was the legendary Los Angeles disc jockey who had joined the cast of *Rowan and Martin's Laugh-In*, the top-ranked television show in the country. Owens's signature line in every show was the full-throated: "This is Gary Owens speaking to you from beautiful downtown Burbank."

"Bill," Todd said, "Do this for me. Put your hand behind your right ear and say, 'This is Gary Burbank speaking to you from beautiful downtown Louisville.'"

Bill did the line several times, each time playing with it a little more and deepening his register. He paced around the room, talking more quickly. Todd and Walker sat stunned as Bill Purser metamorphosed before their eyes. They had given him a character and in a matter of minutes he was the character, and that character introduced other characters. Bill Purser was doing impromptu comedy.

"It's like he doesn't know we're here," Walker said to Todd, between paroxysms of laughter.

"It's insane," Todd said. "He's perfect."

Todd wanted Bill Purser in Louisville. He offered him $25,000 a year, which sounded like a fortune.

"And let's do this," Todd concluded. "Why don't you bring Martha and Sean to Louisville and we'll try to convince her it's the right thing for you and the family."

That evening, Bill roared into the house. He was talking so fast Martha couldn't keep up. She had seen this excitement before and, from her standpoint, it was never good.

She caught bits and pieces of the tide of information cascading her way.

"WAKY in Louisville . . .

"I spent the afternoon with Bob Todd, the PD, and Dude Walker. You remember him. Used to be Johnny Dark . . .

"Lots of money . . .

"They have this idea where I become Gary Burbank . . . *Laugh-In* . . . You know . . .

"So I just got into it. I was all over it . . .

"Martha, I really don't know that I've ever been this excited . . .

"They want us to come to Louisville . . . "

"Stop! Just stop!" Martha screamed.

"I told you before, I am not moving again. I'm happy here. I'm not going to chase around the country anymore."

She walked from the room, her heels pounding solidly against the carpet. The exhilarating wash that carried him home had vanished. He felt hollow, empty.

In Louisville, the station figured out who Bill Purser really was. Turns out he wasn't Bill Purser, after all. He was Gary Burbank—an inside joke based on America's most famous TV show. He was great in his new identity, too. But there was a cost.

He went into Sean's room and studied his face as he slept, listening to the rhythm of his breathing. He stroked Sean's hair. Sean rustled, seemingly lost in his dreams. Bill slept on the couch that night, in his clothes. He was dreaming, too, about himself and Sean, together on *Laugh-In*.

Over the next few days, Martha and Bill fought. Most of all, though, she was silent. It was her preferred form of punishment. Todd, Walker, and Randolph, meanwhile, made daily calls to Bill, reiterating their offer. Each day, Bill finished his shift at WMPS, took up residency in the men's room, and considered his options. Ultimately, there was only one.

When Martha came home from work, he met her at the door. "They are offering us an all-expenses-paid trip to Louisville," he said, "just to see if we like it there. We're going, all three of us. Pack your bags."

Todd booked a room for the Pursers at the Seelbach, the celebrated hotel on Fourth that had so impressed F. Scott Fitzgerald during a trip to the Kentucky Derby that he used it as a model for the Plaza in *The Great Gatsby*. "Make no mistake," Todd said, "this visit is about Bill's wife. She's the only thing stopping this deal. Her name is Martha . . . ."

For two days, Bill and Martha were courted by Todd, Walker, and Randolph, who functioned like painters, applying coat after coat of the most convincing arguments they could conjure. They took Bill to the station and were sure he was sold. They took Martha to lunch and were sure they were lost. Bill was exhilarated, Martha was uninterested, and when the weekend came to an end, no one had any idea what Bill's decision would be.

The drive back to Memphis was quiet. Sean slept in the back seat. Bill focused on the road, headlights rushing by, heading east. He thought about the studio at WAKY. He thought about how happy everyone who worked there seemed to be. He thought about his own happiness, then cursed himself for placing his own desires above everything else. He glanced over his shoulder at Sean, lulled to sleep by the hum of the highway.

Bill sighed. "Martha," he said, "I've made up my mind. I'm taking the job. That's all there is to it."

Bill could feel her lean away hard against the passenger's door. It was as if she were trying to get out of the car.

"You can come with me," he said, "or not."

Martha didn't say a word.

Bill worked to keep the car steady. Brightly lit semi-trailers barreled by, leaving their turbulence behind.

"Did you hear me?" he asked.

There was only silence.

Some weeks later, Bill, Martha, and Sean moved into a small place in Utica, Indiana, just a few miles upriver from Louisville. Each day, Bill hurried out of the house as eager to reach the excitement of working at WAKY as he was to escape Martha's anger. She wore her resentment like a decoration, and for Bill WAKY was a party, while home resembled a wake.

Perhaps it was that schism which fueled his performance. At home, he was Bill Purser, locked into old failures. In Louisville, he was Gary Burbank, beginning a run worthy of Seabiscuit.

He wore suits and large eyeglasses with dark frames. He studied Owens's gestures, imitating his every move, and he turned WAKY's Fourth Street showcase studios into his own personal stage, scurrying about like a gerbil in a maze, never missing an opening for a one-liner.

Teenagers, mostly girls, parked their cars and gathered outside on Fourth Street to watch and flirt with Burbank and the other jocks. Randolph loved the attention.

"The Harem is gathering," he said. The Harem translated into successful numbers for WAKY and wondrous sights for the jocks.

"I'll bet," Walker said, "we have seen every ass in all of Jefferson County."

"And beyond," Burbank said.

Nothing seemed to escape Burbank, including the fact that the NBC affiliate in Louisville—because of a commitment to University of Louisville basketball games—ran *Laugh-In* on a tape-delayed basis. While *Laugh-In* ran on Monday night across the country, WAVE-TV held the program until Saturday night.

Bill called his mother in Memphis and asked her to record the program on audiotape and overnight the tapes to Louisville. When he explained what he wanted to do, Dot was thrilled. Like Raymond, she loved a good scam.

By Wednesday morning, Bill had the tapes and notes from Dot on what she thought worked best. He listened to what Owens did, the jokes and bits Dan Rowan and Dick Martin were doing. He recognized it as a form of burlesque, a cut from Ernie Kovacs, an adaptation of Jonathan Winters's chaotic genius. He studied the material like a first-year medical student studied *Gray's Anatomy*, searching for the essential elements in his own dissection of comedy.

In twenty-four hours, he had turned the best of *Laugh-In* into *The Gary Burbank Show*. He gave it a Louisville slant, but retained *Laugh-In's* national focus—a subtlety that set him apart from most DJs in Louisville.

Todd and Randolph reveled in both the results and Burbank's ingenuity. Over coffee, they congratulated one another on their decision to hire Burbank.

"He's incredible to watch," Randolph said.

"And difficult to follow," Todd added.

"He had the audience in stitches," Randolph said, years later. "By the time *Laugh-In* aired in Louisville on Saturday night, people actually thought this nationally syndicated show was stealing Gary's material . . . ."

For all the acclaim he received at WAKY, Bill continued to test and stretch ideas. *What worked? What didn't work?* The format allowed the jocks roughly twelve seconds between songs, and Gary Burbank filled every tick with characters, voices, bits, and jokes. Every show was a laboratory filled with trial balloons. Some floated, others didn't.

This is Gary Burbank telling you and only you that this is Gary Burbank speaking to you through my mouth . . . And another thing, it is 4:23 and this is The Fifth Dimension and Stoned Cold Picnic.

Sex education classes had to be canceled today at school when two visual aides eloped. First graders were shocked because the two men hardly knew one another.

This is Gary Burbank asking you to support the rehabilitation of the criminally insane, or—I'll kill you.

Believe it or don't!
Many years ago, King Henry the VIII cut off his maid's head. You knew that. Yes. He thereby created the first topless waitress.

And now time for today's Unquestioned Answers.
Today's answer: Manila Folder.
The question: What do you call a bad Filipino poker player?

This just in . . . Count Dracula is looking for the world's greatest juggler!

Gary: What have you got there?
Wonder Mother (Formerly Thelma Hooch): This just in . . . Sister Mary Louise has announced she is going to quit and marry Rabbi Raymond Klinger, who is also giving up his religion. They plan to be married in the Baptist Church and bring up their children to be atheists . . . God willing!

Gary: I think you offended just about everyone you could.
Wonder Mother: Oh, good!

Gary (as Maw Harishi Diaper Rashi): The world's greatest mystery. It is written: What does a nudist do with his keys after locking his car?

In 1969, his audience consisted mostly of teenagers and young adults, short on sophistication and weary of baritone voices delivering hits, time, and temperature. They wanted excitement. They were cruising from The Kingfish Restaurant on River Road up Fourth Street, radio blaring, taking a right on Chestnut, headed for Consolidated Liquors on 15th where if you could see over the counter you could buy a six-pack of Falls City beer and a fifth of Heaven Hill whiskey.

They were drinking and driving, experimenting with pot, and they weren't wearing seatbelts. Their life was letter jackets and draft numbers, slow days and unfulfilled nights. Gary Burbank gave them what they wanted: antics and improvisation, and each day—from three to six—he was there with the music they wanted to hear and a new batch of material that perfectly fit their world, no matter its sense—or lack thereof.

And now just back from the Tijuana Kaopectate Festival after a six-day run, it's me, Gary Burbank!

After each show, he straightened the studio and graded his performance. He wasn't always pleased, but he was constantly reassured by Randolph, Walker, and Todd—especially Walker, who seemed to have a certain sense for Bill Purser's insecurities. "You have the personality and the ability to drive a radio station," Walker said. "No one is doing what you do. Build on that. Believe in your talent."

Each day Bill Purser went back to work as Gary Burbank with renewed energy. *I've never been in this position before,* he thought. *I've never thought of myself as an integral part of anything—just a spoke in the wheel. Here, I'm at the hub.*

It was a good feeling.

In a matter of weeks after Bill's arrival in Louisville, WAKY began to move up in the ratings. The crowds outside the studio became larger.

Requests for personal appearances began to stack up on Randolph's desk, coming in from small towns and villages that surrounded Louisville and comprised Kentuckiana. Everyone wanted to see the WAKY jocks, and they especially wanted to see Gary Burbank. Todd and Randolph sent their jocks out in waves, saturating the region with WAKY's presence.

People on the street knew Gary's name. There were billboards everywhere, and surveys with his picture were displayed in Louisville record shops. Sponsors wanted him to do commercials. Other stations wanted to talk with him about jobs—Chicago, Philadelphia, and Kansas City. He was overwhelmed. He had never worked harder and never been happier, but for all his professional success, and in part because of it, there was trouble at home.

Martha hated their life. Gary—Bill—was never home. She wanted to go back to Memphis.

"This is too much like the music business," she said. "I want to go home," she said. "I want to be with my family."

Bill spent as much time as he could with Sean. They played in the backyard, rolling balls back and forth, playing with sticks and stones, Bill trying to teach Sean about baseball—telling him about Luis Aparicio, the Memphis Chicks, and those days when he sat with the shortstop at the drugstore marveling over the wonder of air conditioning.

Bill was never sure that his son was hearing what he had to say or understood, but it didn't matter. He enjoyed every moment.

On Sundays, he drove Sean through downtown Louisville. He told Sean stories, often rolling into one character or another—some from the past and his youth, and others he had created along the way. He told Sean about Memphis and Mississippi, and who his people were. He told him about how the magnolia trees smelled and how their scent mixed with that of the honeysuckle. He told Sean all these things because he knew he was about to lose him.

At a stoplight, Sean began to laugh. He raised a small hand to the window and pointed at a Louisville Metro bus.

"Daddy," he said, laughing. "Daddy!"

Bill turned to look. On the side of the bus, there was a large portrait of Gary Burbank wrapped in a banana skin, eyes wild.

"Daddy," he said, laughing. "Banana."

Bill laughed, too. The bus pulled away and he turned the car toward home. Sean fell asleep. Dot was right. He had never loved anything more than he loved the little boy sleeping at his side.

One Sunday night, Bill, Martha, and Sean were riding in the car, Sean in the backseat. Martha and Bill were arguing over something. He had no idea why. Martha was fed up. She was taking Sean and going back to Memphis.

"Go to hell," Bill said. The next thing he knew, Martha was holding a .22 pistol to his head, the barrel squarely planted just above his right ear.

"I'm gonna kill you," she said, cocking the revolver.

Bill drove, staring intently at the highway. He thought he was going to die in front of his son.

"Martha," he said, "is this the way you want your son to remember his father?"

She pressed the barrel of the gun harder against his head, then slowly pulled it away. She dropped the gun to her side and tears ran down her face.

"Tomorrow," she said, shuddering, "I'm taking Sean and I'm going home. Screw you, Bill Purser. You will never see your son again."

The next morning, Bill went to work. When he came home, they were gone. The drawers and closets were mostly empty, some left ajar. Clothes were on the floor. Toys were scattered about. Bill saw a toy soldier, and a baseball, and a rock.

He picked up the rock and sat down on the floor. The funniest man in all of Louisville, Kentucky, began to weep.

Part III

The War years

Phyllis Chapman, ingénue

For a time, Phyllis was the girl in Gary's life. Well, she was the girl in Len's life, too. After all, the two of them slept in the *basement*. She also had a thing for Turley. So she was everyone's girl. That alone was enough to suggest things wouldn't end well.

They were in the basement, as they were most nights:

Gary, Len King, Marty Bass, and Phyllis Chapman. They were—with the exception of Phyllis—sprawled across the furniture, drinking Dad's Root Beer and sampling from the bags of cookies and chips strewn about the room on counters and tabletops. Clouds of sweet smoke rolled about the basement, engulfing Len, Gary, and Marty, who was on the couch humming a tune no one seemed to recognize.

The television was on but there was no sound, just images blinking back and

adding shadows to the smoke hovering in the room. Phyllis, meanwhile, chattered and squealed, jumping with great agility from one piece of furniture to the next.

Marty paid little attention to Phyllis—even when she came close and gently touched his cheek or nose. Marty wasn't particularly fond of Phyllis. Len and Gary were more tolerant, knowing that sooner or later she would breathe enough of the smoke in the room and eventually settle down. Of course, they lived with Phyllis and were accustomed to her.

Marty worked with Gary and Len at WAKY, and while he was a frequent visitor to their house on the east side of Louisville, he never quite understood why they had taken Phyllis in. She was unpredictable. She broke things. And she didn't always smell good.

Marty roused himself from the couch.

"How long has she been here?" he said.

Len looked at Gary.

"Not quite sure," he said.

"A while," Gary added.

"Hmm," Marty said. "What ever possessed you to get a monkey?"

"Phyllis Chapman is a rare species." Gary said. "She's a stump-tailed Macaque."

Phyllis raced across a coffee table, knocking over bottles and glasses as an ashtray spun to the floor.

"Len," Gary said, "would you kindly give Phyllis a shotgun hit so she'll quiet down."

"Your turn," Len said.

"We were out on our motorcycles one day," Len continued, "and we decided to go look for some fish for the aquarium, that one over there with the Red Tail Sharks and Neon Tetra."

"Neon what?" Marty asked.

"Fish," Len said. "So we go to the pet store and there's Phyllis and she's smiling at us."

"We thought," Gary said, "she looked a little like an old lady with that crinkly little face."

"Yeah," Len said. "So we look at one another and say, 'Why not?' We buy her and bring her home. Two hundred dollars, wasn't it?"

"Something like that," Gary said.

"You brought her home on a *motorcycle*?"

Marty was sitting up listening to the story. He was just out of high school and fascinated with his older friends.

"Sure," Len said.

"Just put a leash on her," Gary added. "She sat on my shoulder all the way home. I worried that she needed goggles. You know, little monkey goggles. They didn't have any."

"Almost caused a couple of wrecks," Len said. "Dumbasses yelling at us: 'Hey, ya got a monkey on your shoulder.' Like we don't know. 'No, man. You must be hallucinatin'.'"

"Uh," Marty said, laughing, "I think I need another hit."

"Let us partake," Gary said.

"What about the fish?" Marty asked.

"What fish?" Len replied.

"The fish you went to get in the first place."

Len was handsome with dark hair and a heavy, dark beard. "Man," he said, turning to Gary, "what is he talking about? Marty, you are stoned."

Gary heard a rapid clatter. "What's Phyllis doing now? Is she typing again?"

"Yeah," Marty said. "She's at your Selectric."

"Good," Gary said, "material for tomorrow. Anybody want to go out?"

"No," Len said, "put that Monty Python record on again."

"John Cleese," Gary said. "Ya know, if somehow I had known what they were doing, I would have given up everything I had, left everything, done anything I could to be a part of that."

"I want to know about the fish," Marty said. "What about the fish?

"What fish?" Len asked.

Phyllis often accompanied Gary and Len on their late-night runs, riding along in Gary's 1968 yellow Cadillac convertible, a ship of a car with faulty electric windows. Sometimes the windows went down and wouldn't come up. Sometimes they went up and down on their own. Gary figured it was some "electronic thing" exacerbated by his failure to put the top up on nights when it rained.

Len agreed that the idiosyncrasies of the Caddy had something to do with wiring, but rather than take it to a mechanic, they were pleased by the sheer intrigue of it all. *What would work today and what wouldn't?*

Often, they rolled up in front of the local convenience store, stoned,

made their way into the store, and stood, smiling, Phyllis in tow.

"Oh, my God," the clerks muttered, "they're back."

Gary and Len would look at one another, puzzling over what had brought them to the store in the first place, while Phyllis chattered and screeched.

"Shush, Phyllis," Gary said. "Len, what did we come here for?"

"Not sure. Let's just look around."

Then Gary and Len proceeded to fill the counter with pop, chips, crackers, cookies, batteries, toothpaste, ChapStick, aspirin, brake fluid, popsicles, and light bulbs. When it seemed as if they were finished, the clerks would patiently ask, "Is there anything else?"

Gary and Len would study over the question, then make another round through the store, Phyllis riding along, chattering away, snatching whatever might catch her eye.

Gary and Len, meanwhile, stocked up on other things: hot dogs from the rotating spit, lighter fluid, flints, cigarettes—lots of them—peanut butter and tanning lotion. They moved through the aisles of the store as if they were on a scavenger hunt, and when they were finally done, Gary would appear at the counter and hand his wallet to the attendant.

"Take what it costs," he said, "'cause, right now, I can't afford to frivolously waste any more brain cells on mathematics."

He leaned forward and smiled. "Honestly," he said secretively, almost whispering, "I've always been challenged when it comes to money."

As far as Len and Gary could determine, the attendants never took more than the two of them spent, and they always smiled as the WAKY boys drove away in the yellow Cadillac with the monkey leaping around and the windows going up and down independently.

No matter how they pretended otherwise, the clerks were secretly pleased about whatever mayhem might have ensued, for Gary and Len were local celebrities who turned tedious nights at the convenience store into a festive event.

Gary and Len gained a reputation for being two of the largest consumers of marijuana in the Louisville area, though they never used it on the job. Johnny Randolph knew about their recreational habit, and he even joked about it. "While it never affects their work, it may very well enhance it," he said.

Before Martha took Sean and left for Memphis, Gary felt as if he was in

a continual fight to preserve his talent, as though he had to hide his success and disguise what and who he was. To Martha, Gary's success in radio was nothing more than a paycheck—and a source of continual displacement. He was always feeling a need to apologize for what he did and that he was good at it.

Sometimes Gary talked with Johnny Randolph about the conflict at home. Randolph served many roles at WAKY, including Father Confessor. "Radio," Randolph said, "is Martha's demon and that's unfortunate. But you know that, don't you?"

Gary nodded.

Although he missed Sean horribly, the separation from Martha freed Gary to submerge himself in his work. And his play. Since Len King had arrived in Louisville, he had gotten better at both.

It was nearly six o'clock. Gary was wrapping-up his shift at WAKY and he was tired. The show was good, but not one of his best. It had rained all day, and all day he felt as if he were reaching, not completely owning the show. He glanced out on Fourth Street. Headlights formed odd reflections off standing pools of water and the wet, grey pavement. He was one of the most sought-after radio personalities in the country and one of the most noted personalities in Louisville, but there were times when he felt oddly alone. He had always needed to be surrounded by people and friends. As much as he delighted his listeners, he was subject to periods of self-doubt and insecurity.

At a commercial break, he noticed a disheveled figure outside the studio window. The man was dressed in a shirt and tie but drenched and dirty. He tapped on the window and smiled weakly.

Gary had never seen such a forlorn look. He went to the door and invited the man in. He looked to be about 30 years old.

"Thanks, man. My name is Len King."

"Hey. Gary Burbank."

"Gary Burbank! Man, I admire your work."

"You in trouble?"

"Uh, no. I was supposed to have an interview with Bob Watson, the news director, at four. But I had to finish my shift in Niles, Ohio, and then I got stuck in traffic in Cincinnati and I get a damned flat on the bridge. So I'm trying to change the tire just off the bridge and these idiots are about to run me over, and now I'm here and I'm two hours late. People in Cincinnati don't seem too nice. Is Mr. Watson still here?"

Gary smiled. "No, man," he said, "Bob is gone for the day. You want a cup of coffee? Need to go back to the restroom and dry off? Do that, why don't you? This break is about over. I need to get back to the board."

King had grown up in Mayfield, Kentucky, a small city in the western part of the state, and attended Murray State University where he majored in radio/communications. In college, he became aware of WAKY and the more he listened to air checks from stations around the country, the more he believed WAKY was on par with any station in the country. In some ways, he thought, WAKY was better. The jocks had more edge, more intellect. The format was tighter. The music was more avant garde. WAKY was not bound to the confines of Top 40. If The Rolling Stones had a hit, WAKY jocks explored the depths of their music, especially Burbank, John W. "Dude" Walker, and Cris Lundy, all of whom, King learned, had roots in the Memphis music scene.

They played "Satisfaction," but then reached back for "Walking the Dog," written and originally performed by Rufus Thomas, or "Honest I Do," the work of Jimmy Reed and Ewart Abner, both covered by The Stones. From King's perspective, WAKY's jocks, especially Burbank, seemed to have a deeper connection to the heritage of popular music than most, and it came across in their presentation.

King wanted the job badly. He wanted to work around first-class talent. On the seven-hour drive to Louisville he wondered if he was getting in over his head, if WAKY might be too sophisticated for a small town guy with little experience. His palms were damp and his heart thumped. He thought about what he wanted to say and the kind of impression he wanted to make. And then, in the middle of the Brent Spence Bridge, over the Ohio River in Cincinnati, four lanes full and pushing south . . .

Thump . . .

Thump . . .

Thump . . .

The flat. He would never make it on time. Who would hire someone who couldn't be punctual for a first interview—no matter the circumstances?

King was sitting in the lounge, downcast and depressed, when Burbank entered the room with a Coke in one hand, a cigarette in the other.

"Well," he said, "you're almost dry. So tell me what happened again."

King went through the story once more. He was sure he had blown his chance at the job. Burbank smiled. He felt sorry for King.

"Look," he said, "Bob is a good guy. He'll understand. If you need a place to stay, you can stay at my house, and I'll make sure Bob sees you tomorrow morning."

King was shocked. He said nothing for a moment. This was Gary Burbank, known throughout radio as one of the top DJs in the country. They had just met and Gary Burbank was offering him a place to spend the night.

"You would do that," he said, "talk to Mr. Watson?"

"Sure," Burbank said. "Why not?"

King expected WAKY to be populated by people filled with ego, but, thus far, he was badly mistaken.

"So, what do you say?" Burbank said.

"Uh, thanks," King said, "I really appreciate it. But I have to drive back to Niles tonight and do the news first thing in the morning, six o'clock."

"Damn," Burbank said. "How long is the drive?"

King said it was close to seven hours, depending on the traffic around Cincinnati.

"Don't know Cincinnati," Burbank said.

"From what I saw today, you don't want to," King said. "They tried to kill me. Hell, nobody even slowed down. Seems like everybody there has vehicular homicide on the brain."

Burbank laughed. "That's good," he said. "Tell you what. I'll call Bob in the morning and tell him you were here and what happened. I'm sure he will be in touch to set up another interview. When you come back to town you can stay at the house, it's a pretty big place, and I'll show you around Louisville. You'll like Louisville. It's a great place to work."

Burbank talks, King thought, *as if I already had the job*. He was taken with Burbank, his unaffected nature. He was funny, down to earth, someone you immediately liked.

By the time King was driving back to Niles, Ohio, he wanted the job more than ever. King didn't sleep much that night and shortly after his shift was complete, his phone rang. It was Bob Watson calling from Louisville.

"Len? Sorry to hear about your bad luck," he said. "Gary Burbank told me all about it. Glad you weren't killed in Cincinnati. Hey, when can you make it back down here when you can spend some time?"

Within weeks, King was a member of WAKY's news department and living in Burbank's basement, where he eventually shared space with Phyllis Chapman and a coterie of characters who were drawn to Burbank. They became inseparable friends and it surprised no one, particularly Johnny Randolph. Burbank and King were equally eccentric, fiendishly clever, and hell-bent on enjoying what life had to offer. At one of Gary's parties, Marty Bass looked around the room admiring the women in attendance.

"You know," he said, his voice strained to compete with the music blaring from the stereo, "if the Hunchback of Notre Dame worked at WAKY, he could get phone numbers."

The phone seldom stopped ringing at Burbank's house. Usually, it was someone calling from Los Angeles, New York, Chicago, or Philadelphia, urging Gary to leave Louisville and come to work in a "Big Market." The pitch was always the same: "Why do you want to stay in a podunk town like Louisville?"

Gary's reply was as consistent as the pitch. "Because I like it here," he said. "I like the people. I like the station. I'm happy here."

When friends learned he had received offers in New York but had chosen to stay in Louisville, they were pleased but didn't understand. Why didn't he take a stab at the big time? Gary smiled patiently.

"One of the few times I was in New York my clothes were stolen at the train station," he said. "I figured if you lived in New York, your clothes would be stolen everyday, and I don't have that many clothes.

"Besides," he continued, "remember what Bill Bailey said when he quit WLS in Chicago and came to WAKY: 'I got tired of those suits who knew nothing at all about radio telling me, Bill Bailey, The Duke of Louisville, what to do.'

"There's something to what Bill said. I don't think there are too many places in the country where you have the kind of freedom we have here."

The phone rang on. If it wasn't another job offer, it was a friend, often Turley Richards, a successful singer and guitar player with a particularly warped and self-deprecating sense of humor. Turley would call and announce his imminent arrival. "Thought I'd come over and have a beer, maybe watch a little TV with y'all," he'd say. "How's Phyllis? Can't wait to see her."

Turley would come in the house, find his way to the basement, fetch

a beer from the fridge, and after a word or two with Phyllis—who had a particular affinity for Turley—would take a standing position directly in front of the television, slightly swaying back and forth.

"Dammit, Turley, sit down," Gary said. "I can't see the television."

"Neither can I," Turley replied.

Then the chorus from Gary, Len and Marty: "Well, no shit, Turley, because you're *blind!*"

"Yep, blinder than a bat," Turley said, smiling. "Just love to screw with you boys."

They laughed, and Phyllis screeched, finding her way to Turley's shoulder.

There were also calls that sent Gary into fits of anger and frustration. Martha was on the line with another complaint—or threat. The divorce was in the lawyers' hands, and Martha wanted money, but she would not allow Gary to see Sean. Gary refused to make any payments unless she permitted him to see his son. Their conversations degenerated into rancorous shouting matches.

Len turned up the stereo, attempting to steel himself from the conflict. The conversations always ended the same way—Gary slamming the headset into the receiver and unleashing a string of obscenities.

"She's not getting a penny until she lets me see Sean."

"You have to be done with this," Len said. "It's not good for anyone, not you and not Sean."

"It's like she enjoys making me miserable. I'll give her anything she wants. I just want to see my son."

"Yeah," Len said. "You got to push it, see the lawyers—come to some resolution. So you wanna get high?"

The smoke rolled and the pain went away.

"Hey, Len."

"Yup."

"Thanks, man. You are a good friend."

"Yup."

They listened to ACE Trucking Company, Cheech and Chong, and pretty soon, the world came right again. Phyllis sat in Gary's lap, nibbling on a cracker.

Johnny Randolph knew about the phone calls. The ones that troubled him most were the repeated offers from other stations. While Martha's calls unsettled Gary, he never allowed his personal angst to erode his work, and the parties never spilled over into his workday.

Never in its history had WAKY offered contracts to its disc jockeys. But Randolph convinced management to make an exception with Burbank. "He's getting calls every day," Randolph said, "and we can't lose him. Ultimately, someone is going to lure him away."

Randolph not only admired Burbank's work but felt he owed him a debt of gratitude. After Bob Todd's departure as program director, there was talk that WAKY was considering an outsider as a replacement. When management's intentions were met with a disgruntled response, a meeting was called to discuss the situation.

"Tell ya what," Gary said, five minutes into the meeting. "I'm gonna walk down to the corner and have a beer. When I come back, if Johnny Randolph is not program director, I'm quitting."

While WAKY was not a union shop, and Gary Burbank and Bill Bailey served as the unofficial shop stewards. Burbank left the meeting followed by several other jocks. Within minutes, Randolph was named program director.

Gary was already one of the most highly paid people at WAKY, but Randolph persuaded Smith to up the ante. They were prepared to increase his salary by as much as $10,000, if they had to go that far, as well as throw in a series of perks.

"The money will help," Randolph said. "But Gary is not really motivated by money. He's motivated by performance and a sense of pride in his work. Most important, he needs to feel that his work is appreciated."

Nonetheless, Smith and Randolph had contacted a number of sponsors who were more than willing to offer all manner of things in trade in order to keep Burbank in Louisville: car dealers, clubs and hotels, furniture stores, a Harley Davidson motorcycle dealership, music stores, restaurants. One way or another, they could provide enough material motivation to keep Burbank at WAKY.

They arranged an early evening meeting. After four hours on the air, Gary arrived spent, disheveled but laughing.

"You wanted to talk to me, fellows?" he said, pushing his hair back from his eyes. "What's up?"

"Gary," Smith began, "we want to offer you a one-year contract. You're important to this station and we want to keep you around. Johnny tells me you're getting offers from all over the country."

Gary nodded. "That's true," he said, "but I love it here."

"We trust you," Randolph said, "but we would feel a lot better if we had a contract."

"So," Smith said, "we would like to offer you a one-year deal with a $5,000 raise."

"Wow," Burbank said, "that's great. Thanks. So where do I sign?"

Randolph looked at Smith. They were thinking the same thing: *could it be that easy?*

"Uh, Gary," Randolph said, "is there anything else we can do for you, I mean, beyond the raise?"

"I'm not sure I know what you mean," Gary said. "I've never been good at this kind of thing."

"Beyond the raise, we're in a position to make your life easier," Smith said. "Is there anything you need or want?"

Gary thought about that for a moment. "Well, now that you mention it, my ex-wife wants a new refrigerator."

Smith made a note. "We can do that," he said.

"Doesn't even have to be new," Gary said. "It can be used, just as long as it works well."

"Sure," Randolph said, "we'll take care of that. Anything else?"

"It would be great," Gary said, "if I had a permanent slip for my boat at Cumberland Lake. I'm always towing it back and forth."

"Permanent slip," Randolph said, trying to hide a hint of a smile. "Anything else?"

Gary smiled looking back and forth from Smith to Randolph. "Anything *else*? That's plenty enough. I can't think of another thing."

Randolph returned the smile. They had been prepared to offer him ten grand, refurnish his house, grant him a free car lease—and more—and they were getting by with five grand, a used refrigerator, and a boat slip.

Randolph remembered something: one of Gary's first personal appearances. The mayor of Lebanon, Kentucky, Hylean George, an affable cigar-loving character with a paunch that prevented him from completely zipping up his pants, had invited Gary and Johnny to be his special guests for a charity event. Gary, proud of his 1968 Caddy convertible, insisted

on driving. From the outside, the car looked grand. When they got in, Randolph noticed a back window was open.

"It's pretty cold," he said. "Better close that back window."

"Can't," Gary said, "it's broke or something. I'll just jack up the heater."

Inside, the car was filled with an impressive library of books and papers but the interior was falling apart. The seat covers were worn and the dashboard looked as if it had been bleached.

"What's wrong with the interior?" Randolph asked.

"Oh," Gary said, "sometimes—well, lots of times—I forget to put the top up and it rains. I keep meaning to get that fixed."

The image left an impression on Randolph: records and books in the back seat—Santana mixing with Steinbeck against cracked and worn leather.

"Tell ya what," Randolph said, "I know how much you love the Caddy. Why don't you let us have it completely detailed for you and the interior repaired? Maybe they can fix that window."

"Windows," Gary said. "There's something contagious going on—an epidemic. Now, all the windows are acting up. That would be great."

"Our pleasure," Randolph said. "Gary, you are really important to this station and what we do."

In the coming days, a deliveryman in Memphis dropped off a shiny, used refrigerator at Martha's. Gary's boat was safely moored in a permanent slip at Lake Cumberland, his paycheck took a nice bump, and there was an important phone call for Randolph.

"Uh, Mr. Randolph, this is Alton over at Ned Couch's, The Seat Cover King. Well, sir, we were working on Mr. Burbank's car getting it all cleaned up just like you asked and we found something."

"Found something? What?"

For a moment, Randolph's heart dropped.

"Well, sir, looks like a bunch of payroll checks. None of 'em cashed or signed. All made out to Gary Burbank. They was stuck back under the seat. Found a couple in the trunk, too. We'll hang on to 'em. Just thought you might want to know 'cause it's a considerable amount of money."

Johnny hung up the phone, smiling. He had never known anyone quite like Gary Burbank. He walked down the hall and told Gary about the checks.

"Yeah," Gary said, "I didn't need them yet. See, Johnny, this is how I know when I need money: when I walk in the house and flip on the lights and they don't come on, or when I pick up the phone and it doesn't work, or I open the refrigerator and there is no food in it. Then I take one of the checks and I cash it."

He smiled and laughed. Randolph didn't know if Gary was joking or not. He seldom did.

Not long after Bill Bailey returned to Louisville to work for WAKY, he walked into Randolph's office and took a seat on the couch.

"What's up, Bill?

"Ya know," Bailey began, his voice sounding like a gravel road, "I've been back awhile and I don't quite get this Burbank kid. Don't get me wrong. He's great, but he's out there, way out there."

"Yeah, that's true."

"But, seems like every time I see him in the lounge he is either sleeping or meditating, got his fingers together in that Dalai Lama pose. Or, he's got out that old Broadman hymnal and he's wailing out the Lord's hit parade: *There's a Fountain* or *The Old Rugged Cross*, something like that. Is he whacked?"

Randolph laughed. "I know," he said. "He has a great singing voice."

"I like him," Bailey continued, "don't get me wrong. I just like to steer away from crazy."

"Yeah," Randolph said, "I guess you could say he is a little whacked. But, it's a good whacked. You know, he's got a monkey. Lives in the basement of his house."

"A *monkey?*"

"Yep, her name is Phyllis Chapman."

"A monkey? Jesus," Bailey growled, "they sure as hell gave this place the right name. Everybody is whacked."

Gary and Len were distraught. They had searched the house and scoured the neighborhood. Here and there, they stopped people, asking for their help.

"Have you seen a monkey running around loose, about yay-high, reddish brown hair? Wait—come back—her name is Phyllis."

Phyllis was nowhere to be found and no one had seen her.

"I'm worried," Gary said. "She's been gone for hours. How the hell do you think she got out?"

"No idea," Len said. "Maybe we should make some posters, offer a reward. Do we have any pictures of her? Should we call the cops?"

"I don't think they have a missing monkeys division, Len. You think they are going to send a sketch artist over? Maybe she'll get hungry and come home. Cats come home. Dogs come home."

"Sometimes," Len said.

"If she's not back in the morning, we'll do something about it. Call the SPCA, somebody."

"I think a lot of that monkey," Len said, "even though she is starting to stink this place up pretty bad. I think her smell is beginning to seep into my clothes. Do I stink? Just the other day I passed Dude Walker and Bill Bailey in the hall and they stopped and looked at me kinda strange. I can't afford to stink."

"You don't stink. If you stunk, believe me, Bailey would be the first to tell you."

"Seriously, Gary, I think I stink. Still, I'm gonna miss her. Hey, remember how she used to get up by the wheel of the boat when we would take her down to the lake, screeching into the wind?"

"She's not gone yet," Gary said. "We'll talk about it in the morning."

"I always wanted to take her to the zoo, but I was afraid they would keep her."

"Or us," Gary said.

The next morning, Len was drinking coffee and cruising through the local television news channels when a live report caught his eye. It was WHAS and the news team was just a few blocks down the street.

The well-coiffed reporter was saying that people in the Cherokee Park area had reported seeing a wild monkey running loose through the neighborhood.

"Gary! Quick. You gotta see this. I think it's Phyllis. She's on television!"

Gary hurried into the room. "What the hell are you talking about?"

The reporter was talking to an older looking woman, ringed by friends and neighbors.

"Ma'am, you say you have seen this monkey?"

"Yes, several times. It's been running around here for a day or so."

"Is it a large monkey, a chimpanzee? Did you feel threatened?"

"Why, no. It's just a small thing. Doesn't have a tail. Seems pretty tame."

"I see."

"Of course, I have seen it before."

"You've seen it before?"

"Yes, I've seen it riding with that disc jockey and his friend in that big, yellow Cadillac. They live just down the road there. They take it out on their motorcycles sometimes."

"Disc jockey? Motorcycles?"

"Yes, I'm quite sure the monkey belongs to Gary Burbank, the young man on WAKY. I listen to him everyday. Nice young man. It's his monkey. There's no doubt in my mind. He's probably very worried."

The reporter had his headline: *Gary Burbank's Monkey Loose in Louisville.*

Len turned to Gary. "It's always about you," he said. "I'm the one who lives with the monkey in the basement. I'm the one who stinks and you get all the publicity."

That day, Phyllis, a nervous wreck, was retrieved and returned to the safety of the basement. WAKY turned the story into a promotional event. Gary spent much of his day doing interviews with news outlets while Len walked around the station polling his co-workers.

"Do you think I stink, you know, smell bad, like monkey urine?"

Phyllis returned from her two-day excursion neurotic and incontinent. Nothing seemed to calm her nerves or her bladder. Gary and Len decided they needed to find Phyllis a new home. They fretted over it for a few days and finally paid a visit to the pet store where they found her. They talked with the manager, told him about what had happened and how Phyllis's behavior had changed. They asked about donating her to the zoo. The manager said she would never adjust. Phyllis seemed to sense that something was about to change. She chattered incessantly and soiled the counter of the store. The manager said he knew some people who lived in the country with all sorts of pets. He would talk to them.

"You're sure they will give her a good home?" Gary said.

The manager said he was sure.

Len was depressed. "Make sure they know her name is Phyllis Chapman. We named her after a girl in my high school marching band. We were very good, good enough that we were chosen to represent the state of Kentucky in a regional competition in Mason City, Iowa. We worked real hard but during our performance one person turned the wrong way, just one person. That person was Phyllis Chapman."

"I see," the manager said. "Have you been feeding her anything special that we should know about?"

Gary and Len looked at one another. "Dad's," Gary said.

"She loves Dad's Root Beer," Len said.

"I see," the manager said, when it was apparent he did not. Phyllis was agitated. Gary and Len said goodbye and didn't look back.

On the way home, Len and Gary decided the manager felt they were unfit parents. They knew better, of course, but the manager wouldn't understand.

They were in the basement, sprawled across the furniture, peacefully high.

"I really am gonna miss her," Len said.

"I know," Gary said, sighing. "Me, too. But first thing we have to do is get this place cleaned up. Shampoo the rugs and the furniture. Get all your clothes washed and drycleaned."

"I knew it! I *stink*," Len said. "Dammit."

"Her going to the farm, it's probably for the best," Gary said. "Besides, I've met someone."

"*Met* someone? A *woman*? Hell, you meet a woman everyday, more than one. We all do!"

"Yeah, but not like this one," Gary said.

Leaving the clubhouse

Gary met a woman he couldn't seem to impress. She impressed him, though. She even showed up at the house, *navigated* the wreckage of his lifestyle, and showed him how to balance his checkbook. If that wasn't love, whatever could love be?

One fall night, Gary and Len were sitting around the house.

The air was clear and the windows were open, and they could smell the pies Mrs. Sharp was making next door. Mrs. Sharp was a widow in her 70's, as broad as a sedan, the product of her fabulous pies and cakes. (Lard was her medium, cherry pie her masterpiece. Len and Gary guessed she ate as many as she sold.) Tonight, the pie smelled like pumpkin.

Outside, children were laughing and playing. Then the doorbell rang. When Gary opened the door, a ghost, a doctor, a cat, a ballerina, and two soldiers huddled on the steps.

"Len," Gary yelled.

"Ah, crap," Len said, appearing at the door. "It's Halloween. I completely forgot."

"Hang on kids," Gary said.

Len ran to the kitchen and rifled through the refrigerator and the cabinets. He searched the recesses of the freezer. He returned with a loaf of Wonder Bread and dropped a slice into each bag and pillowcase. The children watched closely. For a moment, no one said anything. Then the ballerina reached into her trove of treats and retrieved the slice of bread.

"Bread? You're giving us *bread*?"

Len looked at Gary. Gary looked at the ballerina, the ghost, the doctor and the cat. The soldiers, brandishing cap guns, seemed most displeased. Gary cleared his throat.

"Uh, would you like some butter with that—or some jelly?"

The kids turned and walked away.

"Thank God," Len said. "We don't have any butter."

They turned off the lights, jumped in the Caddy, and drove to the convenience store.

"Oh, my God," the clerk said. "There they are. Hey, I been meaning to ask you guys: where's Phyllis?"

"Can't talk now," Gary said. "We need some treats."

"She went to the farm," Len said, dumping an armload of Reese's Cups on the counter.

At a WAKY function in downtown Louisville, Gary met a tall, elegant, impeccably dressed woman. She was well spoken but aloof. While they talked, her eyes drifted around the room. Her name was Deana, and she looked like a model. He asked her if she was alone. She smiled.

"For now," she said.

When she moved away, Gary followed her. He was drawn by how she moved, the way she tossed her hair when she spoke. She smiled a lot and had a way of turning on the barstool, her legs wrapped around one another just so.

Gary asked her if she would like to go somewhere else and have a drink.

"Not tonight," she said, sliding him a cocktail napkin with a telephone number written on it. "But call me. I need to go."

When she left the bar, climbing the steps that led to the lobby and Fourth Street, her exit was prolonged and wonderfully rhythmic. When she was gone, it was as though she had taken something with her. Only one barstool was empty but the place seemed suddenly vacant.

Over the next few days, Gary called her, never getting an answer. He thought she had given him a phony number, but he kept dialing. Finally, one day, she answered. She said she had been out of town on business. Gary asked if she would like to go out. She hesitated, then said yes.

They met several times at discreet locations. Gary wondered why she would not let him pick her up at her home. He asked if she was married. She laughed.

"No," she said. "Hardly."

First, she said she was in public relations. Later, she told Gary the truth. She was a call girl and her "boss" refused to let her date men on her own.

She asked Gary if he still wanted to see her. He said he did but he was tired of sneaking around.

"The next time," he said, "I'm picking you up at your apartment."

Deana told Gary that her boss could be dangerous.

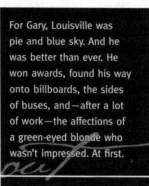

For Gary, Louisville was pie and blue sky. And he was better than ever. He won awards, found his way onto billboards, the sides of buses, and—after a lot of work—the affections of a green-eyed blonde who wasn't impressed. At first.

"I have friends," Gary said. "In fact, your boss will not want anything to do with these guys."

When Gary showed up at Deana's apartment in the yellow Caddy, he had a police escort—two members of the Jefferson County Sheriff's Department. Deana was impressed. The sheriffs, meanwhile, kept an eye out for the belligerent ex-husband Gary had told them about. Their hats were tipped forward as they gazed up and down the street.

"Gary, you need us later tonight you just call," one of them said.

The romance didn't last long, however. Deana would disappear for days, generally when conventions were in town. Nothing of consequence would come from such a relationship, Gary decided, and told Deana. To his surprise, she was angry, revealing a hard edge that belied her beauty. She shouted and threw things around the room. Gary was glad it was over.

A few days later, after work, Gary and Len pulled up in front of their house. They saw a car sitting near their front door. The trunk lid was open and so were the car doors. Deana and two other girls, equally beautiful, were loading things into the car: a television, a stereo, speakers, a toaster, and a vacuum cleaner.

At first, all they noticed were the girls' tight jeans and high heels.

"Damn," Len said, "take a look at that. Wait! That's our stuff."

Gary wasn't sure.

"We don't own a vacuum cleaner, do we?"

"Come on," Len said.

"Dammit," Gary said. "We need to change the locks."

The next day, Mrs. Sharp was at the door with two pies straight from the oven, one cherry and one apple.

"Here," she said, "these are for you."

Gary took the pies and thanked her.

"Those girls," Mrs. Sharp said, "they told me they were helping you boys move. I told them I hated to see you go."

Len and Gary glanced at one another.

"You would hate to see us go," Gary said.

Mrs. Sharp smiled and walked away.

Another day, Len was driving home—Marty in the car, smoking a joint—when Len suddenly hit the brakes and made a sharp turn. He wheeled the Caddy to the curb directly in front of a bus stop where an aged woman clutched her purse with both hands. Len put the car in park and jumped out, smoke drifting behind him.

"Hey, baby," he yelled.

Marty was sure Len had lost his mind.

"Need a ride?"

She looked at the Caddy and then at Len.

"Len," Marty said, "what in the hell are you doing? Who's the old woman?"

The lady smiled and made her way toward the car.

"Why, thank you," she said. "That's very kind of you."

Len opened the back door for the woman.

Marty was aghast and tried to slide down in the seat.

"I don't believe you all have had the pleasure of meeting," Len said. "Mrs. Sharp, this is Marty Bass."

"Pleased to meet you young man," she said.

Marty stumbled through a greeting.

"This is much better than the bus," she said, "though your car does have a peculiar smell."

"Incense," Len said.

"Oh, yes," Mrs. Sharp said. "The same stuff you burn at your house."

"Yes," Len said. "Exactly."

Marty started to laugh.

"Mrs. Sharp is our neighbor; she makes pies for us," Len said.

"I charge them five dollars," she said. "I can't just give them away. I charge most people ten dollars."

Marty tried to restrain his laughter.

When they pulled up in front of the house, Gary was standing outside.

"Hey, guys," he said. "Mrs. Sharp, how are you?"

"Len was kind enough to give me a ride home from the bus stop," Mrs. Sharp said. "I met your other friend. He's certainly a happy young man. He laughs an awful lot. Well, I best be getting inside."

"Mrs. Sharp," Len said, smiling. "How much is bus fare these days?"

"Why, forty cents," she said.

"Well, that will cost you twenty cents—the ride home," Len said. "You know, I can't do this for nothing."

"Gracious me," she said. "You boys do go on. We'll just take it off the next two pies. Thanks, again. It's blueberry pie tonight."

Len laughed. "She's sweet," he said.

"Yes, she is," Gary said.

Mrs. Sharp reminded Gary of home—Memphis and Mississippi, Mamaw Wells, calmer times.

"You seem quiet," Len said.

"Just thinking," Gary said.

More and more, he wondered: *Do I need to slow things down a little?*

And yet, all was going well in Gary's professional life. He was named Medium Market Radio Personality of the Year, a prestigious national award that brought acclaim to WAKY and impressed everyone but the recipient. His picture was on billboards and buses. He made appearances on local television and at concerts introducing national acts. When he made an infrequent stop at clubs around the city, he was generally the center of attention. Calls from large market stations continued to come in, like the uninvited guests at his door.

But there was one person he could not seem to impress. Her name was Carol Anderson. She was just out of school, a 1970 graduate of Jeffersontown High School and working at Triangle Talent and Allen Martin Studios where Gary and many of the WAKY jocks recorded commercials and jingles.

She had long, blonde hair and penetrating green eyes, and while she was cordial, she was plainly unimpressed with Gary Burbank. His first attempts at conversation were politely brushed aside. On every occasion, she smiled and said she needed to get back to work. Finally, there was a small relenting: "It's been nice getting to know you," she said.

Carol was pretty and unpretentious, qualities that were often mutually exclusive. She was also unimpressed with Gary, impressive in itself. Almost as impressive as Carol imposing a semblance of order on his disorderly lifestyle. So he married her.

Little by little, Gary gained her confidence. With each visit, she seemed more comfortable with Gary's attention.

Of course, she listened to WAKY, she said, but she listened for the music and to find out where the bands were playing.

Gary couldn't keep from laughing. She had a disarming nature that prevented anyone from assuming a lofty perch. She was sensible, down to earth. She had been a cheerleader in high school and loved sports, especially college basketball, and liked watching the University of Louisville's games. Her family had been in Louisville for years.

Gary told her a little about growing up in Memphis and Mississippi, but mostly he listened. There was something about this girl that made him want to be quiet. Finally, he summoned the courage to ask her out on a date.

She wasn't sure. There was a significant age difference, she said.

"Ten years," Gary said.

"Let me think about it," Carol said.

She told her friends about Gary's invitation. They were excited for her and asked questions about him. He was, after all, a celebrity, but he wasn't quite as crazy and off-the-wall in person as he was on the radio. She had made up her mind about Gary, but she wasn't going to be quick about it.

Gary told Len and Marty about Carol. Their reaction was mutual.

"She's how old, 19?"

"You've got to be kidding."

Johnny Randolph, Gary's boss, had a different reaction. *This is good*, he thought, *on two fronts. She is a Louisville girl and she might just keep him around here longer than we can.* Randolph knew that Gary's big market suitors were intensifying their efforts. WLS and WCFL in Chicago were in the mix, as well as WABC in New York and KLIF in Dallas.

In meetings with Don Meyers, Randolph expressed his concerns about Burbank. "Honestly," he said, "I lay awake at night worrying about losing him to a bigger station. They can pay him more than we could ever hope to, and I think he is beginning to feel confined by our format."

Randolph knew Carol from his meetings at Triangle Talent. She seemed to be a good girl from a solid family. If she and Gary were seriously involved, it would be in the station's favor.

His other concern went unspoken. As much as he admired Gary's work, Randolph feared that Gary's lifestyle might hamper a promising career. While Gary wasn't self-destructive, neither was he the embodiment of normalcy.

Burbank's shows were a model of precision and orchestration. Everything had a place and everything fit. His life at home was a glaring contradiction. When it was time to do laundry, Gary bought new clothes. When it was time to buy groceries, he tried a new TV dinner.

His closets were cluttered. The lights were always on and his refrigerator, gas tank, and checking account had one thing in common: they were generally empty, a product of nothing more than a lack of interest. Gary had little room or time for anything that didn't nurture his purpose, which was his show.

Maybe, Randolph thought, *this girl can put some order in Gary's life.* He thought about that for a moment, ultimately aware there was a flaw in his theory. He was applying commonplace values to an individual who was anything but ordinary.

Ah, hell, he decided, *it'll all work out for the best.*

At first, Gary and Carol went out for burgers and to the movies. They caught most of the important musical acts that came to Louisville and Lexington. Slowly, Gary cut ties with other women he knew and dated. As time passed, Gary and Carol spent more and more time together.

Soon, she was a frequent visitor at the house and as she became more familiar with Len and Marty, she began to offer her opinions on anything and everything.

"Ever notice," Gary said, "how she's the first to tell you when you have said or done something stupid."

"No shit," Len said. "She is sure as hell not afraid to speak her mind."

She picked up and she cleaned. Once in a while, she did laundry.

Marty told Len he thought this was a serious thing between Gary and Carol. Len didn't buy it.

"Nah," he said, "it'll pass just like all the rest. Gary's too crazy to get married again."

Marty told Len he was in denial and Len began to doubt his own assessment of the situation when Gary took Carol to Memphis to meet his parents and Sean. When they got back to Louisville, Gary was beaming.

"My parents loved her," he said, "absolutely loved her, especially Mom. And the coolest thing was," he said, "how great she was with Sean."

"See," Marty said. "I told you, Len. Look at 'em. They're happy."

Len watched Carol sit at the kitchen table and help Gary pay his bills, write checks, place them in envelopes with stamps, and address them to the proper parties.

"What are you guys doing?" he asked.

"She's helping me pay the bills," Gary said. "We went to the bank and deposited a bunch of checks."

Len looked around. There wasn't a single dirty dish or glass in the sink. Towels were folded on the kitchen counters.

"Jeez," Len said, "what is happening?"

"See, I *told* you," Marty said.

"Damn," Len said, "is the leader leaving the clubhouse?"

Gary, Carol, Len, and Marty had spent a weekend at Cumberland Lake. They skied and partied, sunbathed, and when it was time to start home, they secured Gary's boat in the slip and climbed in the Caddy. No one was looking forward to the three-hour drive. The sun and the two-day party had taken its toll. Gary and Carol were in the front seat, Marty and Len in the back.

As they passed Woodson Bend, an upscale group of condominiums overlooking the splendor of the lake, Gary turned to Carol.

"You know," he said, "we could buy one of those places. It could be our getaway. I could put down a few thousand."

"And," Carol said, "I could add a few thousand."

"Of course," Gary said, hesitantly, "we would have to get married first."

"Yes," Carol said, "we *would* have to get married first."

Marty smiled.

Len, shirtless and sunburned, grabbed the back of the seat.

"Will someone," he said, loudly, "tell me just what the hell is going on?"

On July 1, 1972, after a nine-month courtship, Carol and Gary were married. It was a civil ceremony held just across the river from Louisville in Jeffersonville, Indiana. Turley Richards served as best man and his wife, Adrienne, witnessed the service. Carol's brother, Larry, was there but her parents were away on business.

"I guess," Gary said, "they think it won't last long."

"I wonder," Carol said, "if we're legally married since Turley, our chief witness, is blind?"

After the ceremony and amidst the celebration, Gary realized he had made crucial mistakes in scheduling.

"Uh, Carol," he said. "I just remembered that I am supposed to make an appearance tonight at Club 68 in Lebanon. I'm supposed to introduce Tom Dooley and The Love Lights."

"Yes," she said, looking at him, her eyes passive and cool.

"And," he said, "I'm also supposed to introduce The Exiles at The Golden Horseshoe. So I'm going to call one of the other guys at the station and see if they can cover for me. Or, I'm just gonna call and cancel."

Carol asked Gary how much he received for the introductions. He said that each appearance paid $75. Carol considered the situation for a moment.

"The clubs are close together aren't they?"

"Less than a mile," Gary said.

"We're doing them both," she said. "Let's go. That's $150. It'll pay for the wedding. We can celebrate another night."

Turley heard a ruckus.

"What the hell is going on?"

"I'm not sure," the justice of peace said. "They appear to be in a hurry." Turley, Adrienne, and Larry were left at the altar. Gary and Carol were gone. *It's a good thing mother and dad weren't here*, Larry thought. *It's been an unusual afternoon.*

Carol and Gary raced back to the apartment, changed clothes and jumped in the Caddy. Lebanon was, at a push, an hour's drive southeast, state roads most of the way, Kentucky State Troopers around every turn.

Gary drove while Carol came up with a plan. The clubs were competitors and Gary had mistakenly double-booked himself. Both acts were to be introduced at eight o'clock. "This has got to be quick," she said. "We'll go into one club a few minutes early and say we just got married, see if they can hurry things along. As soon as you're done, we'll scoot out the door and go to the other club. If we're a few minutes late, we'll say 'Sorry, we just got married.'"

The plan went off without a hitch. Everyone congratulated Gary and Carol and thanked them for showing up on their big day. On the way home, Carol counted the cash, folded it neatly—all bills facing the right way—and tucked it in her handbag.

"See," she said, "there is *always* a way."

Chapter fifteen

Shootout in Falls City

The voices crowded into Gary's head. The station guys thought he had a multiple personality *disorder*. In a way, he did. Where was there a place for all of them? First, though, there was Carol. And the new voice in their own immediate family.

By the spring of 1973, Gary was looking at WAKY and his life

in a different way. He was in his early 30's. He had been in radio for ten years and Carol was pregnant. He knew he didn't want to be a teeny-bopper disc jockey all his life. He was, in fact, coming around to Bill Bailey's way of thinking.

"My God," Bailey often growled, "who among us aspires to such an inauspicious fate? Oh, please let me play 'Crocodile Rock' one more time. Christ!"

Gary wasn't bored at WAKY, but he was living with a growing sense of frustration. WAKY was the top-rated station in the

market, recognized nationally. Because of WAKY and the people there, he had gained national acclaim and formed friendships he was certain would last forever. He made more money than he ever expected to and enjoyed life more than he ever had before.

Offers continued to come his way, some more intriguing than others, some completely unexpected. Hanna-Barbera, the creators of Scooby-Doo, offered him a job in Los Angeles doing cartoon voices. Gary respectfully declined, rejecting a sizeable salary.

He wanted to find a place where he could expand the repertoire of his comedy. He wanted another challenge. Carol had her own challenges; she was in her third trimester. Len and Marty, on the other hand, were confused.

"Wait," Len said, "you've turned down offers from East Coast to West Coast, and now you're thinking about leaving. Where?"

"I don't know," Gary said. "I just know that I need to do more than I'm doing now. I'm not sure what, but something. I want my show to be comedy, not records. I want to play a record when I want to or when I need a break. Maybe I should be a program director."

Marty and Len laughed.

"C'mon," Marty said, "*you* dealing with suits and advertisers?"

"I could do it," Gary said. "I'd have to do it my own way, but I could do it. Yeah, with a big office and bookshelves, ferns everywhere, and a big leather couch, and a bar."

"Yeah," Len said, "we know. But guess what? I was talking to Lee Masters the other day. He says he wants to go into management. I told him we would have him over to celebrate."

"More like a wake," Marty said.

"Lee said he's making us banana nut bread cake to mark the occasion— with secret ingredients," Len said.

"Bet it will top anything that ever came out of Mrs. Sharp's oven," Marty said.

For a moment, Gary forgot about his frustrations.

"Lee's banana nut bread may not be a match for Mrs. Sharp's culinary delights," he said, "but I'm sure it will serve to enhance our appetites."

Len looked at Gary. "You've been watching PBS again, haven't you?"

Lee Masters was another Johnny Randolph find. He was tall and handsome with curly brown hair, and everyone thought he resembled Eric

Clapton, the lead guitarist in Cream. He was polished and superb on the air, and he viewed radio and music as a platform that would allow him to enter the larger, more profitable world of television and entertainment.

On a sunny Saturday afternoon, Masters showed up at Burbank's house for the celebration of his new career path. Gary had laid in the necessary provisions. There was Dad's Root Beer, of course; Cokes, beer, and whiskey, even a freshly brewed pot of coffee, another example of Carol's impact on the household, which was pristine except for the basement where Len lived and Marty was a frequent overnight guest.

The *piéce de resistance*, of course, was Lee's perfectly browned loaf of banana nut bread replete with five-inch sparklers spraying phosphorescent flames in every direction.

"It looks fabulous," Gary said, proposing a toast.

"To you, Lee," Gary said. "We should all be so smart as to follow your lead."

Marty nudged Len with an elbow. "What's got into Gary? He's talking crazy."

"I'm not sure," Len said.

They raised glasses and bottles toasting Lee. It was as if he were sailing off to Madagascar.

Sometime later, Gary was picking the last remnants of the cake from the pan. "I do believe that is the best banana nut bread I have ever had in my life," he said.

Lee was looking around the room, counting empty pop bottles. "Gary, he said, "I've always wanted to ask you: why do you always have root beer in the house?"

"It's Dad's Root Beer," Gary said. "Isn't it great? I get it free. I sing their jingles."

"There are so many benefits to this business," Lee said.

"Here's what I loved about that banana nut bread," Len said. "It had just the right amount of cinnamon."

"No," Marty said, "nutmeg. Right, Lee?"

"I'm not sure," Lee said.

"You know," Gary said, breaking into a large smile, "if I hold my head just right, I can see my own nose."

"Really? I'm gonna try," Lee said. "My God! You're right!"

Around two o'clock the next day, Lee called Gary's house. "Thank

you," he said. "It was a great party."

Gary hung up the phone, wondering if he should follow Lee's lead. *What the hell*, he thought, *the monkey is gone*.

More and more, Gary's frustrations came to the surface. One day at the studio, Gary decided to consult "The Big Cherokee."

John "Dude" Walker was relaxing in the lounge. He was tall and slender with long, dark hair, deeply proud of his Native American heritage.

"Dude," he said, "I think I want to be a program director." Gary was pacing. He had a book in one hand and a cigarette in the other. Dude said nothing. Gary didn't give him an opening.

"There are things I know can be done in radio: things that will work, things I want to try and that I know I will be good at, you know, theater of the mind, comedy, an extension of the things I'm doing right now."

Dude studied Gary. *This is real*, he thought.

"I want to take the characters I've developed, like Wonder Mother and Ranger Bob and put them together in sketches.

Then came a conversation: Wonder Mother talking with Ranger Bob about campfires, recipes, and available cowpokes.

"Firesign Theater, Monty Python, The Ace Trucking Company—that kind of thing," Gary concluded.

Dude smiled. "Wait," he said, "do you want to do a different type of show, or do you want to be a program director?"

Gary said he wasn't sure about anything other than his wish to try new things.

"I understand," Dude said, and asked if Gary had spoken with Johnny Randolph. Gary said that he had not.

"That's just it," he said. "I like it here and I love Louisville. Carol is from here. Her family is here. We are about to have a child. But I can't do what I want to do here at WAKY. The format doesn't have room for sketch comedy."

Dude listened.

Unfortunately, he thought, *this sounds all too familiar. This guy is about to bounce.*

Later that day, Dude sat down with Johnny Randolph. "I had a conversation with Burbank today," he said.

"Oh, yeah," Randolph said, "how many voices?"

"Two. Maybe three," Dude said.

"Slow day," Randolph said.

"Yeah," Dude said, smiling, "I think anyone who has ever held a conversation with Gary has been confronted by multiple personalities."

"Kind of like talking with Sybil," Randolph said. "You want to say, 'Hey, can you all clear out for a minute so I can talk with Gary.'"

"Know the feeling," Dude said, smiling. "But this was a pretty serious conversation."

"Serious? *Burbank?*"

"Yeah," Dude said.

Suddenly Dude had Randolph's full attention.

He related the gist of the conversation.

"A program director?" Randolph said. "Gary said *that?* No way can I imagine him wanting to deal with all the ancillary crap that comes with the job."

"I don't think that's what he really wants," Dude said. "Sounds to me like he wants to find a format where he can do comedic repertory theater."

Randolph was perplexed.

"You know," Dude said, "the stuff he and Len and Marty are always laughing and talking about."

"I always thought they were just screwing around," Randolph said.

"They are," Dude said, "but if you listen to them it's really funny stuff."

Randolph thought for moment. "So what do we do?"

"I'm not sure there is anything we *can* do," Dude said. "He's frustrated; wants to try new things."

"Dammit," Randolph said. "I knew this day would come."

"Well," Dude said, "it's not here yet, but it's coming."

On July 23, 1973, Tracy Lynn Purser was born at Methodist Hospital in Louisville. A nurse wrapped her in a soft, pink blanket, placed a pink striped stocking cap on her head, and gently handed her to her father. He wrapped his arms around her and held her close, softly touching her cheeks and her fingertips. "I don't think I've ever seen anything more beautiful," he said, barely above a whisper.

Through her exhaustion, Carol managed a smile. She was drifting off to sleep.

"Daddy's little girl," he said. "Daddy gonna take good care of you. Yes,

he is. You gonna be my little rock star."

He couldn't hold her close enough. He tucked her more snuggly inside her blanket. He was filled with new emotions. Throughout the pregnancy, he was confident this child would be a boy, a younger brother to romp and play with Sean, and that somehow he would bring his children together and give them everything they needed. Now, he had a daughter, and he wasn't prepared.

He thought about the hardest days of his childhood: Wolf River, Mud Island, and Junior Askins—days of wanting and uncertainty.

Gary held the child closer. Little puffs of breath caressed his cheek. She seemed to wink at him. Her lips parted in the slightest smile. His stomach trembled and warm tears pooled in his eyes. There were crazy things in his head, new things in his heart.

The nurse appeared. "I need to take her back to the nursery," she said.

He kissed Tracy on the cheek, wiped a tear from his own. "I love you," he said.

He looked at Carol, sleeping.

He stroked her hair and kissed her softly. *You don't know it*, he thought, *but someday—years from now—they will dig me up and find a deep love for you in the marrow of my bones.*

He patted her on the hand and drove home.

Len and Marty were sitting at the kitchen table drinking coffee.

"Congratulations," Len said.

Gary hugged them both.

"Thank you," he said. "You are good friends. You know what, I need to do one thing. I need to get Sean back."

Len cuffed something from his eye.

"Yeah," Len said. "You do."

"You want some coffee?" Marty said.

"Coffee would be good," Gary said.

In New Orleans, Bill Thomas had taken on the daunting task of saving WNOE, a station of proud tradition that had fallen behind the times and plummeted to seventeenth in the ratings. The station was founded by former Louisiana governor and state senator James A. Noe, an independent oilman whose career had benefited from his longtime association with "The Kingfish," Huey P. Long.

In a day when rock 'n' roll had swept the nation, Noe's massive portrait was the dominant fixture in the station's lobby. The first thing anyone saw when they walked in the door was the imposing countenance of the governor: blue suit, striped tie, just the right amount of silk showing from his breast pocket. He seemed to be smiling. Or perhaps it was a grimace at the new music coming from down the hallway. His thinning hair was combed straight back. His jowls nestled atop his collar. His right hand was in his pocket, hidden from view. His left rested on a desk, exposing short, thick fingers and manicured nails.

Jesus, Thomas thought, pondering the portrait, *is this the image you want for a rock 'n' roll station? The kids don't want to trust anyone over 30 and the guv has got to be twice that. Someone the kids wouldn't trust twice.*

The portrait of the founder was the least of Thomas's troubles. The station itself was dreadfully dull. The older jocks had settled into a stilted style, and the newcomers had succumbed to the approach of the veterans: time, temperature, anemic joke, song.

Thomas, a veteran of WDIA in Memphis where personality ruled the airwaves, was shocked when he listened to WNOE's air checks.

"It's as if they are sleepwalking," he said, "and in New Orleans, of all places. It's no wonder they're failing."

He had enlisted Eric Anderson, another product of WDIA, as his sales manager. Anderson was immaculately groomed with an affinity for tailored suits and Sea Island cotton shirts. He looked as though he had just arrived from cocktails with the Vanderbilts, and yet he could talk easily with anyone. Anderson was perfect for New Orleans.

"You know what we need, don't you?" Thomas said.

"I think our instincts tell us the same thing," Anderson said.

"We need some energy. We need someone who will come in here and shake this place up—not only *this* place—the entire market."

"We need someone," Anderson said, "who will come in here and do some crazy shit. Have anyone in mind?"

"Yeah," Thomas said. He handed Anderson a piece of paper. There were two names written on the paper.

"Two very talented people," Anderson said.

"And both crazy," Thomas said.

"Exactly," Anderson said.

Dude Walker thumbed through his messages. *Bill Thomas called,* one of them read. *He is trying to get in touch with you.* Walker was surprised. He had heard that Thomas had recently been named general manager of WNOE in New Orleans, but he hadn't spoken to him in years. He hoped it wasn't a job offer. He was happy at WAKY.

When he returned the call, Thomas came straight to the point.

"I've got a sick station here," Thomas said. "I need to shake things up. I have two people in mind who can do that and, Dude, you are the only person I know who has worked with 'em both. It's Gary Burbank or Scott Shannon. Who should I hire?"

"Let me give it some thought, Bill."

"Just so you know," Thomas said, "whoever I hire is going to be my morning guy and it's got to be the right person to drive the rest of the station—set the tone for everyone who follows him. By the way, I got lots of spots to fill. You interested?"

Dude said thanks, but he was happy in Louisville.

The next day, Walker called Thomas back.

"You need to go with Gary," he said. "Give him Morning Drive, give him space, there's no telling what he can do. Besides, he's ready to make a move. He's been talking about becoming a program director, but what he really wants is new creative space."

When Thomas called, Gary was surprised. He was more surprised by the offer: a generous pay increase, the title of program director, an office on the second floor, and a voice in every hire and direction the station took. It sounded too good to be true.

"An office? Ferns and a leather couch?"

"If that's what you want," Thomas said.

"It's a lot to digest. This is a great place, but I've always loved New Orleans. Let me think it over, Bill."

"Certainly," Thomas said, "but I need to know pretty soon. And one question: what should we call you? Johnny Apollo? Gary Burbank? Bill Purser?

"You forgot Bill Williams," Gary said. "But it's Gary Burbank."

"It surely is," Thomas said.

Len was excited. "*New Orleans?*" he said. "Are you seriously considering this?"

"You have to," Marty said. "It's a chance to do exactly what you want to do."

"What *we* want to do," Gary said. "They need a news director. They have a slot open in the afternoon and overnight. If we do this, Len, you'll be the news director and Marty, you'll do nights."

Marty looked at Len, then Gary. "You really think I'm ready to do this?"

Gary smiled. "You're ready," he said.

"Wait," Len said, "have you talked with Carol yet?"

Gary said he had not; that he realized it might be a difficult sell.

"Yeah," Len said, "with a new baby. Her family is here. She's lived here all her life."

Gary knew the terrain all too well. His first marriage had wrecked at a similar juncture.

This time, he thought, *things will be different.*

Carol listened closely, saying nothing. The money was impressive. The offer was inviting. She realized Gary was beginning to feel confined at WAKY, but New Orleans? She knew he was tired of being labeled: *big duck in a little pond.*

"It's so far away," she said. "We just had the baby. My family is here. I don't know anything about New Orleans. I really don't want to leave, not now. There will be other offers."

Among other things, Gary thought, *Len is a clairvoyant.*

The discussion made Gary uncomfortable. It brought back bad memories. He wanted no strife in their lives. Above all else, he didn't want anything to come between them—certainly not work.

Carol wasn't angry. "Could we wait awhile?" she asked. "This is all happening too fast."

He said they couldn't wait. "There may not be another offer like this one," he said.

"But there have been so many," she said.

"Not like this one," Gary said.

"Is this really what you want to do?"

"I think so," he said.

"If you think it's best for your career," she said, "then let's do it."

Gary took her hand. "It's like you say, 'There's always a way.'"

Part IV
Northern exposure

Chapter sixteen

Traveling Minstrel show

Finally, Gary and company was back in the Big Easy. He'd smelled barbecued shrimp cooking for ten years. They lit upon WNOE like *gypsies*. Soon after, The Governor showed up. He owned the place, after all, and he wanted to see what had finally spiked the ratings.

All the negotiations between Bill Thomas and the Burbank

Troop had been done by telephone, each trusting the other's word. This bothered Eric Anderson a bit, as he preferred to lay eyes on the unholy gaggle that was about to come down from Louisville and take charge of his radio station.

Ordinarily, Thomas was the realist and Anderson was the one-time philosophy student. Employers, he soon learned, were unimpressed with his erudition concerning Hegal and Kierkegaard, and after an instructive period of selling watches and

menswear, he landed a job selling radio advertising time. In time, he became a student of radio, and now, oddly, he found himself being the realist. He thought the station might want to take a firsthand look. *Don't buy a pig in a poke*, as those invading southerners themselves might have said.

"Bill," he said one afternoon, "I sure would feel better about this if we had met with these boys before we signed them. I have no doubt they're proficient at their jobs, but they sound absolutely wild—unruly—on the air. Are you sure we have made the right choice?"

"They are," Thomas said, "and we have."

Anderson wasn't afraid to take risks. When he first started to make money, he invested in the St. Louis Browns baseball team. People called him crazy until the team moved to Baltimore in 1954 and the checks started to roll in.

"Bill," he said, "I shall defer to your judgment."

There were seven in the troop: Gary, who was to take over the morning slot and direct WNOE; Len King, the news director; Marty Bass, hired to do late nights; Jason O'Brien, who would fill the midday shift; Gary Guthrie, for early evenings; and, of course, Carol and Tracy.

During the twelve-hour drive, everyone, with one exception, expressed some reservation about leaving WAKY. Even Tracy seemed more fussy than usual. Len, who always had Gary's ear, was the most vocal.

"We were having so much fun at WAKY," he said.

"We'll have more fun in New Orleans," Gary said.

He told them about the days when he played New Orleans with The Mar-Keys and his six-week stay living on Vienna sausages, soda crackers, and tap water. By the time they were cutting west across lower Alabama, they were as enthusiastic about the move as he was.

"You know what I'm gonna do first?" he asked.

"Go to the station, I guess," Len said.

"No," Gary said, "going to Pascal's Manale. It's a restaurant uptown on Napoleon Avenue. Best barbecued shrimp in the world."

"You've eaten there before?" Len asked.

"No," Gary said, "but I've smelled those shrimp cooking for ten years."

"Must be some serious shrimp," Marty said.

"Yep," he said, "now Gary Burbank goin ta eat all de barbecue shrimp he want."

Len and Marty had long recognized their friend's single-mindedness. Now it was more evident than ever. Traffic was light. Gary had his mind on New Orleans and nothing else.

Their first stop in New Orleans was a hotel. Gary made sure Carol and Tracy were comfortable. The next stop was 1838 Napoleon Avenue, Pascal's Manale. They ate plates of barbecued shrimp and oysters on the half-shell. Gary insisted they try the boudin and the Courtbouillon.

"It's coo' boo yon," he said. "And for dessert, beignets or the custard and raisins with rum sauce."

They ate until they couldn't eat any more. When the meal was done, they took a walk. Gary bought a copy of the *Times-Picayune*, glanced at the headlines, rolled it up, and stuffed it in his back pocket.

"C'mon," he said, "I want to show you where I had to stay when I was here."

Along the way he told them how he stole fruit from the markets and went back to his room on Liberty.

"Right here," he said, "that's where I stayed."

Inside, the television was on, flickering blue against the night. He looked at the house for a long time, unusually quiet.

"We should go," Len said, "they're expecting us at the station tomorrow morning."

"Yeah," Gary said, "we should. Wait. Somebody lit a joint. Who is it? Y'all leaving me out?"

Someone coughed.

Someone else said, "Uh, care for some dessert?"

Early the next morning, Bill Thomas and Eric Anderson were together at WNOE awaiting the arrival of Burbank and his team. When the receptionist buzzed in, there seemed to be a ruckus in the background: laughter and loud voices.

The receptionist giggled.

"They're here: Mr. Thomas, Mr. Anderson. You might want to come to the lobby. Please!"

Bill Thomas smiled.

"Here we go," he said.

Eric Anderson tried to smile, too.

"Indeed we do," he said.

Though Thomas and Anderson had tried to visualize the changes Gary Burbank and his troop would bring to WNOE, nothing prepared them for the gathering in the lobby.

My God, Anderson thought, *they look like a band of gypsies.*

Their hair was long. Some had scruffy beards. They wore blue jeans, T-shirts, and sandals. Two leaned across the receptionist's desk laughing and flirting. Three stood before the portrait of Governor James A. Noe.

"Who is it?" one asked.

"And why is it here?" another asked.

The third, the smallest of three, said: "It's the founder of the station. His son, Jimmy, runs the place now."

"This needs to go," the first one said.

"Greetings!" Bill Thomas roared. "Already thinking about changes, I see. Good to see you, Gary. It will take me awhile to get used to calling you that."

After a round of introductions, Thomas and Anderson freed Gary and the others to tour the station.

As the troop made their way to the second floor, where the studios were, Anderson turned to Thomas.

"Thank goodness Jimmy Noe isn't here," he said. "On appearance alone, there's no way he would let them go on the air."

Thomas smiled.

"And that," he said, "is precisely why this station is in the fix it is in.

"Besides," he added, chuckling, "I planned it that way."

Change came to WNOE like a storm rolling in off the Gulf.

Hurricane Burbank began with an immediate alteration in image. Governor Noe's portrait was carefully tucked away in storage, replaced by an equally large photograph of Len. Where visitors had once encountered the daunting visage of James Albert Noe, they were confronted with a young man in a T-shirt and jeans, his hands stuffed into his pockets and a sheepish, submissive smile on his face.

Len's picture was an object of curiosity among WNOE's secretaries and receptionists. "Len's a handsome man," one said while they studied the photograph. "But the look on his face, well, he seems *simple*."

"We call it 'The Grim,'" Gary explained. "We came up with that look one night when we were talking about the Vietnam War. We were looking

for a subservient countenance, a look that if you were trapped in a foxhole and someone was about to bayonet you, you would 'Grim' them and they would say, 'Nah, I'm gonna let this guy go. He isn't a threat to anyone.'"

"So it's a social statement?"

"I guess it is," Gary said. "Never quite thought of it that way, though."

Some things—and people—at WNOE resisted change more than others. There was, for instance, Len's favorite salesman, a holdover from the old regime. He was graying, middle-aged, and fervently Pentecostal. While Len regarded himself and his friends as nuts, he had quickly come to the conclusion that New Orleans was filled with people who were truly insane. The salesman, for instance, was positive that Armageddon was close at hand. Moreover, he indicated, Len and his friends were likely its agents.

He saw doom around every corner, and he quoted extensively from The Book of Revelations. The little scared man could do it by heart and did it all the time. "Sinners," he said, under his breath. And then he began: *And I beheld when he had opened the sixth seal, and, lo, there was a great earthquake; and the sun became black as sackcloth of hair, and the moon became as blood . . . .*

In the studio, the Allman Brothers played, and Leon Russell and Joe Cocker, and every few minutes the troubled salesman from the first floor ran up the stairs looking at the ticker, searching for more evidence that doom was impending.

It drove Len nuts.

"Tell ya what, Nostradamus," he said.

"The name is Harvey."

"Yeah, Harvey, I'm gonna make it easy for you. I'll cut a hole in the floor so we can just run the ticker paper from the second floor down to the first. That way, you won't always be up here bringing us down. Okay?"

The salesman looked at Len.

"It's your picture in the lobby, isn't it?" he asked.

"Yes," Len said.

"You're important," he said. "You need to be saved."

"What I *need*," Len said, "is a jigsaw."

The project was nearly completed when Bill Thomas interceded.

"I hired you to be news director, not a carpenter," he said. "No holes in the floor."

Len was disappointed. But no more than the salesman.

In less than a month, Real Rock WNOE's rating began a steady improvement. It jumped from 17 to 12 and then burst through the Top 10. Bill Thomas was delighted.

"New Orleans," he said, "has never seen anything like this."

Eric Anderson noticed a distinct change in those who wanted to advertise with WNOE.

"Bill," he said, "a guy tried to pay me for ads the other day with a bong."

"A bong?"

"I believe," Anderson said, "it is a large pipe used to smoke marijuana. I told him we preferred cash or check."

"What did he say?"

"He said something like: 'Cool, love your station.'"

On the air, Gary and The Troop leaped over every boundary that existed in Top 40 radio. While they were out of the box at WAKY, they were out of the crate at WNOE.

Gary played the hits and targeted New Orleans politics and politicians, including Edwin Edwards, the colorful and controversial governor of Louisiana, who, according to Burbank, undoubtedly rose to office through the time-honored tradition of voting by the dead.

From the Garden District to the Ninth Ward, there was no immunity— especially for the Saints, New Orleans' hapless professional football team. The year before Gary arrived in New Orleans, the Saints were 2-11-1. Only one team had a worse record, which spurred the rallying cry among "Aints" fans: "Thank God for the Houston Oilers."

When the Saints lost the first three games of the 1973 season to the Falcons, Cowboys, and Colts by an aggregate score of 116-to-20, Gary swooped in like a heron. What better way to poke fun and satirize the team and the sport than to challenge its machismo image? Gary invented Bruiser Larue. Bruiser was introduced by Bass Ackwards, another Burbank creation, who offered "Needless News Commentary" throughout the morning show.

Bass Ackwards: With us today, Bruiser Larue. Isn't he wonderful? He has four touchdown passes, picked up a fumble, and two sailors on leave. Bruiser, it's great to have you with us.

Larue: Thanks for having me!

Bass Ackwards: You're such a great football player. How did it happen?

Bruiser: When I was a boy (laughs), we used to play two-hand touch. Loved it! (Laughs) Piling on was my favorite part.

Bass Ackwards: You don't say.

Bruiser: Yes. Before that, we played kick the can and I wore my mother's high heels.

Bass Ackwards: Really? That explains a lot.

Bruiser: Yes. California oranges, Texas cactus, we play the Dolphins just for practice.

Bass Ackwards: Isn't he wonderful. Bruiser Larue, 6-foot-2, eyes of blue. How did that go? California oranges, Texas cactus, we play the Dolphins just for practice. I'm Bass Ackwards and this is Needless News Commentary.

It was live and largely extemporaneous. There was no format. Gary played a record when he wanted to or needed to. He interacted with Len King during his newscasts and kept him in the studio after the news to spoof whatever he chose. Often, Len didn't know what was coming or where it was coming from, which, Gary felt, offered more comic potential.

In no small way, they were doing exactly what they had done in the basement of their home in Louisville, creating skits on the fly, which had been too edgy and too time consuming for WAKY's orchestrated format.

To Eric Anderson and Bill Thomas, Burbank's style was thoroughly bizarre, funny, sometimes absurd, and often just plain silly. But no one else in the market was doing what he was doing and WNOE's rating continued to rise. Within six weeks of what some at the station called "Burbank's Siege," WNOE had jumped past WTIX to number one among Top 40 stations and number two, overall, behind WWL, a full-service station, an achievement that sparked two immediate developments.

"I have some news," Anderson said, walking into Bill Thomas's office. "Fred Berthelson was forced out as GM at WTIX. His replacement came in first day on the job and walked around with a pair of scissors cutting off everyone's tie. He says, 'We have to change the way we do things around here. Are you paying any attention to those people at WNOE?'"

"Oh, we have their attention," Thomas said, smiling, "and we have the attention of someone else. The governor he wants to make a visit to the station and meet the new boys who turned things around here."

Anderson adjusted his tie, which was already perfect.

"Does Gary know?" he asked.

"Haven't told him yet, but I will as soon as I have the details."

"Make certain that you do," Anderson said. "We want to make sure that when the governor arrives Gary doesn't have his wino friend in his office."

"Surely," Thomas said, "what's his name, Charlie? Freddie?"

"Charlie," he said, "but he also answers to Freddie, I believe."

Anderson started to laugh. "The other day," Anderson said, "a group came to see Gary about religious programming, of all things. Gary didn't want to be bothered. So he went down to the street, collected Charlie or Freddie and brought him up to his office, sat him down in the chair behind his desk, then brought the folks in. Gary introduced Charlie or Freddie as his 'consultant' and cautioned them that while Charlie or Freddie was 'somewhat eccentric,' he was an invaluable help in all his decisions."

"Good lord," Thomas said.

"The group began its presentation and, shortly, Charlie or Freddie starts babbling incoherently. Shouting one second, whispering the next, waving his arms, traipsing around the room. Well, his visitors were aghast and Gary's just standing there as if he is listening very intently to whatever it was Charlie or Freddie was saying. The group finally gives up and—with a collective look of bewilderment—departs. Gary thanks them for stopping by. A moment later he emerges into the hallway with Charlie, hands him a pack of cigarettes, and says, 'Thank you, man. I don't think they'll be bothering me anymore.' It was a sight worth beholding."

"That's our programming director," Thomas said, "winos as consultants, holes in the floor, and the best ratings this station has had in years. God bless him. Has he stopped hitting Don Anthony in the head with a newspaper?"

Gary hired Don Anthony away from WTIX to work the midday shift. He viewed Anthony as talented and was pleased to take away one of the competition's better DJs. But Anthony had an annoying tick in his delivery.

"Have you noticed it?" Gary asked.

"Drives me nuts," Len said.

"He always says, 'This is Don Anthony telling you it's 12:18.' Wonder when he gets home if he walks in the door and says, 'This is Don Anthony saying: Hiya, honey, I'm home.' I got to break him of that."

The next day Gary talked with Anthony. "Don," he said, "just say: 'It's 12:18. You don't need the prefix: 'This is Don Anthony telling you . . .' Okay?"

Anthony said he understood. Gary went back to his office and turned on the radio to monitor the broadcast. He had just settled in behind his desk when he heard Anthony say, "This is Don Anthony telling you . . ."

Gary grabbed a newspaper from his desk and ran down the hall, swearing. When Anthony hit a break, Gary said: "You're doing it, Don."

"Doing what?"

"You're saying, 'This is Don Anthony telling you . . .' You're saying it over and over. So here's what I'm going to do. I'm gonna stand behind you here in the studio, and every time you say it, I'm gonna whap you upside the head with this rolled up newspaper."

"Yeah, right," Anthony said.

For the better part of two days, listeners to Anthony's show heard a curious sound effect, accompanied by a devious laugh.

Marty and Len loved it. It sounded, they decided, like Anthony was killing flies. "Except," Marty said, "for the occasional whimper. That's the best part."

In preparation for Governor Noe's visit, Bill Thomas ordered the offices to be cleaned and straightened.

"Gary," he said, "could you and the boys turn it back just a notch? I'm not talking about on the air. I mean around the office while the governor is here. He appreciates success, but he's rather conservative. And one other thing. Could you see to it that Charlie—or Freddie—isn't around for any executive matters?"

"Not a problem," Gary said, "Charlie must be on leave of absence. I haven't seen him for days. Who's Freddie?"

"Charlie," Thomas said.

"No, Freddie. Who's Freddie?"

"Your friend," Thomas said.

"No, that's Charlie," Gary said. "Who is Freddie?"

"Your friend," Thomas barked. "The one you bring to meetings."

"That's Charlie," Gary said, "I don't know any Freddie."

"Does he answer to either name?" Thomas asked.

"I don't know," Gary said.

"He's on third," Thomas said, smiling. "And thank you for that Abbott and Costello moment. Just take care of it, will you? I'm tired."

"You know, Charlie is one of the most agreeable people I have ever met—and helpful, too."

"Just take care of it, Gary."

Few matched Eric Anderson for sartorial splendor, but James Albert Noe was his equal—resplendent, even at 84. The day he arrived at the station he wore a light grey, custom-made suit, white starched shirt with a royal blue necktie, and pocket scarf to match. His black wing-tipped shoes twinkled with a shine that matched the one in his eyes.

He stood in the lobby talking with Anderson. Together, they looked like men who shaped the affairs of state: powerful, influential men. The governor leaned close to Anderson. They shared a quiet word.

"You know what I always say," the governor said, "if you want to hide a law, put it in the attorney general's books."

The governor found great amusement in the thought.

Anderson laughed along.

"Sir," he said, "would you like to see the changes we have made?"

"That's why I'm here," he said. "You and Bill Thomas have lived up to your word—quite successful, indeed, and I would like to meet this Mr. Burbank. Is he responsible for that picture on the wall, the one that replaced my portrait?"

"Well," Anderson began.

"Good," the governor said. "Never liked that picture. Made me look too ornery."

As Anderson and Thomas toured the governor through the station, he said little, just nodded and smiled. He said he liked the fact the station was making money and was gaining acclaim.

"However," he said, "my daughter, Gay Noe McClendon, tells me you all are crazy." Before anyone could speak, he smiled and continued. "There is nothing wrong with crazy, not in these times. Craziness serves as a shield against those things that can drive you nuts."

When the tour was over, they gathered in a conference room and the governor was asked if he had any questions.

"I do," he said softly, turning to Gary. "How long do y'all get for lunch?"

"Most of us," he said, "take a half hour."

James A. Noe sat quietly for a moment, then rose from his chair. "Well," he said, "that just won't do. Who in this town can eat in a half hour? I know I can't. Henceforth, you will have an hour, or as long as you require.

Gentlemen, keep up the good work. I thank you and bid you good day."

They never saw him again.

Later that evening, Gary was at Len and Marty's apartment. It was after supper. Len and Gary were done for the day. Gary had eaten supper with Carol and tucked Tracy into bed.

"You know who he reminds me of?" Marty said.

"Who's that?" Len asked.

"The governor," Marty said.

"Who does he remind you of?" Gary asked.

"Cannon . . . on TV . . . William Conrad . . . only older and without the mustache."

"Great pipes," Gary said.

"He's from Louisville, you know," Marty said. "He played Matt Dillon in the radio version of *Gunsmoke*."

"From Louisville?" Gary said. "I didn't know that."

Len was confused. "The governor is from Louisville?"

"Cannon," Gary said, "He was the original star in *Gunsmoke*."

"I love Miss Kitty," Len said.

"Wonder what the real deal is between Marshal Dillon and Miss Kitty?" Marty asked.

There were other nights—many of them—when Gary and Len sat around the apartment talking seriously about the show. "It's coming to me, Len," Gary said. "What I eventually want to do on the air: the characters, the concepts."

"But what you're doing now is great," Len argued.

"No," Gary said, "it isn't. It's okay. Some of it's funny. Some of it is just shallow and foolish, too DJ-driven."

"You're beginning to sound like Bill Bailey," Len said.

Gary laughed. "I think Bill's right. There is no success without some anger and some pain. I don't think creativity is served by comfort or complacency."

"Sometimes you worry me," Len said.

"Why?"

"You think too much."

Chapter seventeen

Bon soir, Bienville

They weren't dressed for Detroit in the winter. But then who is? "*The Morning Mouth*," the billboards called him. There were even signs on the buses and cabs. Finally, perhaps, the pond might be as big as the duck.

Gary had finished his shift and was in his office opening a

large package that had arrived in the morning mail. Len was sitting on the couch watching Gary fight with the packing tape and cardboard box.

"What ya got?" he asked.

"Another shipment from the Tonto Brothers," Gary said.

"It's about time," Len said. "We were almost out."

"Well, we are flush now," Gary said.

"Score," Len said. "I was beginning to wonder what we were going use as give-a-ways for the listeners. We give away concert tickets, cash, and gift certificates, but this is what they want."

"Yep," Gary said, lifting a large jar from the box. "Pickled pig lips. Let's see, we got jars of lips, ears, pig's feet, and some snouts. We're set."

"Yum," Len said. "Looks like biology class. Do people really eat these things?"

"Sure," Gary said. "I think. Some believe it's a sin to waste anything from the kill."

In fact, the porcine victuals had gained cult status among Gary's listeners in New Orleans, with possession signaling that one was tuned in and truly in "The NOE."

Every station gave away concert tickets, cash, and cars, but the really hippest of WNOE's listeners—those who called and played along—received pickled pig lips. In New Orleans, the absurdity of the prize was duly appreciated.

A world away in Windsor, Ontario, Cosmic Bob Moody, a CKLW disc jockey, was passing Bill Hennes's office when he heard shouting. While that was not entirely uncommon, the tenor of it piqued Moody's curiosity. He tapped on Hennes's door and opened it.

"Is everything okay?" he asked.

Hennes smiled.

"Yeah, everything is fine," he said. "I just made up my mind about our new morning guy. It's going to be Bill Bailey or Gary Burbank. I'm determined to land one of the two."

"How are you going to do it?" Moody asked.

"I'm going to keep offering them more money until one of the two says 'Yes,'" Hennes said.

"Who do you think will bend?" Moody asked.

Hennes said nothing for a moment, then smiled a very small smile.

"Burbank," he said. "He's more adventurous. And if we get Burbank we get all the voices in his head. It's like hiring an ensemble. Have you heard him do this preacher, Deuteronomy Skaggs? Listen to this . . ."

This is the Reverend Deuteronomy Skaggs of the Little Radio Church of the White Winged Gospel Truth. Don't make me holler, don't make me shout, turn them pockets inside out. Reach in them jeans; pull out them greens. I don't like noisy money. I like quiet money. I'm talking about that

green salad of salvation. Say it with me: Amalulah.

"See," Hennes said, "this is where this guy is different. He is completely committed to the character. It doesn't matter who he is doing: Skaggs, Nixon, Kissinger, Ranger Bob, Thelma Hooch—doesn't matter—completely disappears into the character."

"Thelma what?" Moody asked.

"Hooch," Hennes said. "Another character he does. Kind of a raunchy Maude Frickert."

Gary glanced at the message on his desk. *Bill Hennes from CKLW called*, it read. *Will call back.*

Though he remembered Hennes from WKLO in Louisville, Gary gave the message little thought until Len came into the office.

"I got a call from Bill Hennes," Gary said. "I didn't know he was at CKLW."

"Yeah," Len said. "He's the programming director. What's he want? Is he offering you a job? Shit, Gary, I mean we're talking The Big Eight, probably the hottest, most successful rock station in the country."

"Hold on," Gary said.

"No," Len said. "Seriously, they don't call it North America's Number One Music Station for nothing. They got five towers and they bounce that signal from Canada to Kingdom Come as clear as a bell, and everybody who works there—even the news guys—are totally whacked. You got to call him back! What's the number?"

"He didn't leave a number. C'mon, let's go to lunch."

"Lunch?" Len said. "This is huge; could be the chance of a lifetime. How can you think about lunch?"

Gary smiled.

"I'm hungry," he said.

Hennes came straight to the point. He wanted to replace the morning man at CKLW.

"Gary," he said, "we want you to be our guy. It's a helluva place to work; there's no place like it in the country."

Gary listened, but he wasn't altogether certain Hennes was making a serious offer. Over the years, he had listened to so many offers from

PDs at big market stations that he was nearly numb to the pitch, but the conversation with Hennes was different. Hennes never belittled WNOE or the New Orleans market. He never came close to uttering the words that instantly annoyed Gary: *Aren't you tired of being a big duck in a little pond?*

All he did was offer Gary a job.

"Before you make up your mind," Hennes added, "we would like you to come up and visit. You'll fit right in. The people here are some of the most talented people in the country and they are crazy as hell. I don't hire jocks, Gary. I hire entertainers. *You* are an entertainer."

It was sunny and 60 degrees when Gary and Carol boarded their flight at New Orleans International. When they arrived in Detroit, it was 20 degrees and there was snow on the ground. They weren't dressed for the weather and didn't anticipate the ashen aspect of Detroit. Fog floated over Lake St. Clair, and steam rose from the sewer grates.

Depressing, Gary thought.

"Are we sure about this?" Carol asked.

"Let's go straight to the station," he said. "See what it's like. We can check into the hotel later."

Carol couldn't hide her immediate impression.

As Gary eased the rental car into a parking place on Ouellette Avenue, a figure appeared at CKLW's front door and then pounced out on the sidewalk. Teddy Bear Richards was a tall, strong man with flowing dark hair and a goatee. He looked like an escapee from either Big Sur or Big Time Wrestling. He was wearing swimming trunks, boots, and sunglasses. He was shirtless, carrying a surfboard. He was smiling, yelling, and running toward their car.

"And we thought New Orleans was crazy," Gary said.

"And we thought we were underdressed," Carol added.

Teddy Bear danced around the car, snow flying from the heels of his boots, his breath steaming from his mouth. Otherwise, he seemed oblivious to the Canadian chill.

As Gary stepped out of the car, Teddy Bear began to chant: "Gary Burbank! Ga-rryyy Bur-bank!"

He introduced himself to Gary and Carol: "Wild Willie said you were on your way, man. Wanted to make sure you got a warm welcome."

"Wild Willie?"

"Yeah," Teddy Bear said, "that's what we call Bill Hennes. Helluva PD, man. You'll find out why we call him Wild Willie. Works hard and parties hard. C'mon and meet everybody. How do you like my board? Needs to be waxed, man."

Snow cracked under their steps but Carol was smiling.

I think I'm going to like this place, Gary thought.

That evening, Gary and Carol were preparing for dinner with Hennes and Herb McCord, CKLW's general manager, as Gary chattered about the energy and the talent.

"I've never seen a group of people like this . . . Nobody relaxes, not even for a second . . . Everyone totally spends themselves . . . To work here you have got to be on all the time . . ."

Carol tried to get a word in.

"Gary," she said.

He didn't hear.

"It's an exciting place and . . ."

"Gary," Carol said.

"It rubs off on you. I could feel it and . . ."

"*Gary!*" she said. "We need to go downstairs for dinner! We are going to be late!"

"Yeah, what? Oh, yeah. But here I wouldn't have to do all those things I have to do in New Orleans, the things I hate like firing people and the meetings . . ."

"Gary," Carol said, firmly. "Finish getting dressed. We're going to be late."

For all the things she loved about her husband, there were times when he was completely exhausting.

"Yeah. Yeah, right," Gary said. "Damn, lost track of the time. I'll just be a second."

Looks like we are moving to Detroit, she thought.

Gary emerged from the bathroom.

"Does this look okay?" he asked, adjusting his sports coat. "Should I put on a suit?"

"You look fine," Carol said. "Let's go."

The maitre d' at the Viscount Hotel studied Gary dismissively.

"So sorry, sir," he said. "Your party is here, but I cannot seat you."

His tone irritated Gary as much as his pompous demeanor. He wanted to punch this ostentatious swank in the nose. Instead, he said, "I'm sorry, sir, I don't understand. Why can't you seat us?"

The maitre d' removed a pen from his pocket and tapped a small card attached to the stand before him.

Gentlemen are required to wear a suit and tie to be seated, the sign read.

"Oh," Gary said, his temper rising but in check. "I see. I'll be right back."

Then he smiled as broadly as he could.

In response, the maitre d' managed a patronizing smirk.

Upstairs, Gary selected a tie and then pulled his suit from a hanger in the closet. It was a nice suit. On the rare occasion when Gary wore it in New Orleans, Eric Anderson always commented on the fit and fabric.

"Carol," Gary said, "I'm going to need your help."

"What are you going to do?" she asked.

"There," he said, "button that for me. Now, pull that zipper back there. Easy. Yow. Okay, let's go."

"You look ridiculous," Carol said, smiling.

"Absolutely," Gary said. "But I'm adhering to the rule."

Herb McCord and Bill Hennes were well into a second cocktail when the maitre d' approached their table, Gary and Carol walking closely behind.

"What the hell?" Hennes said, smiling. "Your suit is on backwards."

"Completely," Gary said, turning to the maitre d', "but I *am* wearing a suit and tie, in accordance with house standards. Thank you, my good sir."

"Your waiter will be with you momentarily," the maitre d' said, retreating from this menace before him.

"I love it," Hennes said, "but what led to this contrarian attire?"

"I have sublimated qualities," Gary said, beginning the story.

Hennes and McCord were delighted.

By night's end, Hennes was convinced Burbank was the right man for the job. "He's an entertainer," he told McCord during their drive back to the station. "He's competitive, and most important, we get along. How much can we offer him?"

On the flight back to New Orleans, Gary thought about Hennes's offer. It was as exciting as Detroit was dismal, and even the dreary downside of Wayne County was inviting. Other than the occasional

Tigers game, he wouldn't be tempted to explore. He could bury himself in performance; find out just how far his talent could take him.

There was one problem. What about the people who trusted him and followed him to New Orleans: Len, Marty, O'Brien, and Guthrie? What about those he had hired: Don Anthony and Dr. Grady "Wildman" Brock, the most insecure individual he had ever encountered in radio?

How would they feel if he left? They were friends, especially Len and Marty. They were also gifted people, capable of succeeding without him. He didn't know what to do. He wasn't sure how Carol felt. FM radio was on the rise and steadily eroding WNOE's market share. Did he truly want to be involved in the managerial decisions required to stave off FM? Was that even possible? What he wanted to do was work. How had Hennes put it? *Be the entertainer you can be and want to be. You don't need the distractions.*

When the plane touched down in New Orleans, the sun was shining.

"It's pretty, isn't it?" Carol asked.

"You know who I really liked?" Gary said.

"Who's that?" Carol said.

"Cosmic Bob Moody," he said. "He's from Arkansas. We have a lot in common."

"Something bothering you?"

"In a way," Gary said. "I have to talk with Len and Marty."

"I know," Carol said.

"You've got to do this," Len said, "even if it's just for a while. Who knows where it could lead? Gary, CK' has what—the second largest cumulative audience in the country—people everywhere will hear you."

"Besides that," Marty said, "that's some serious money."

Gary reminded his friends of what they already knew; he had never been motivated by money.

"Maybe it's time," Len said. "You got a family. You have to think about things beyond what makes you happy."

"All that is true," Gary said. But he still wasn't sure. He didn't know how Carol felt about moving to Detroit.

Len and Marty laughed. "That girl is in for the haul," Len said. "If not, she would have already dropped you like a dirty shirt. Besides, Detroit is closer to Louisville than New Orleans. You can drive it in about seven hours."

"And what about you guys?" Gary asked. "You left Louisville to come down here and work for me and we haven't even been here for a year."

"And it's been a party from day one," Len said, "Hell, we'll be fine. Don't worry about us."

Marty was uncommonly quiet. "Tell you the truth," he said, "I've been thinking a lot about quitting the station and going back to school at Southern Illinois."

Gary and Len were surprised.

"I mean, I appreciate everything you guys have done for me," he said, "but I'm thinking I want to finish my degree and try television news. I think that might be my future. Don't get me wrong: everything I know I learned from you guys, but this FM thing is happening and radio is going to change."

"Wow," Gary said, "are you serious?"

"Yeah," Marty said. "I'm going back to school, back to Carbondale."

"Man," Len said, "our naive little friend is growing up on us."

Marty smiled.

"That's great," Gary said. "We're proud of you, aren't we Len?"

"Always have been," Len said.

"So," Gary said, "should we have a party?"

"What a question," Len said.

They gathered in Bill Thomas's office. Thomas sat behind his desk. Eric Anderson occupied a large armchair, absently adjusting the crease in his meticulously pressed trousers. Gary slouched back into the corner of a large leather couch.

"I hate to see you go, Gary," Thomas said

"I wish we had the money to keep you around," Anderson said, "but we can't approach the salary CKLW is offering you, and even if we did . . ."

Gary stopped Anderson in mid-thought. "It's not really about the money," he said. "It's about where I am in my career. I hope you know that."

Thomas and Anderson said they understood.

"It's also about leaving New Orleans," Gary said. "I love this city, but it's killing me."

"How so?" Thomas asked.

"There's something happening all the time, day and night. For almost

a year, I've been afraid to go to bed—afraid I'd miss something. I got to get some rest."

"I don't think you missed much," Anderson said.

"I do have a question," Gary said. "Since I'm leaving, are you going to take down Len's picture in the lobby?"

"Not a chance," Thomas said. "The Grim is there to stay. So let's go have a drink and toast your future."

"There's one thing I need to do first," Gary said, "I'll be right back."

They shook hands and Gary scurried out of the front door at 529 Bienville.

"Where do you think he's going?" Thomas asked.

"No idea," Anderson said.

Gary looked up and down the street. Nothing. He walked around the building and scanned WNOE's parking lot—no luck there, either.

He walked a few blocks checking the usual haunts but to no avail. He was looking for his friend, Charlie the wino. Gary wanted to say goodbye and to see if he needed anything.

At CKLW, Bill Hennes and Herb McCord launched a massive promotional campaign advancing the arrival of "The Morning Mouth," Gary Burbank. They bought ads in newspapers and spots on every television station in the immediate area. There were billboards and signs on buses and taxis in Detroit and Windsor. They spent tens of thousands of dollars. The "Go Bananas" campaign reached into Cleveland, Toledo, western Pennsylvania, and parts of Illinois. Every jock at CK' pushed Burbank's imminent arrival as far as the signal carried their voices: from Ontario and Quebec to the Dutch Antilles. The blitz went on for weeks, culminating in a lavish cocktail party at the Pontchartrain Hotel in downtown Detroit.

Cosmic Bob Moody got an early peek at the guest list. It included the usual array of advertisers and clients but beyond that, it was a Who's Who of Detroit.

"Impressive," Moody said.

"We've invited everyone from the media," Hennes said, "everybody from the music world, and the politicians. Everybody who is anybody and anybody who even thinks they *might* be somebody. We got 'em all."

Edsel Ford II was on the guest list, along with Detroit rock stars Bob Seger, Ted Nugent, and Mitch Ryder. Hennes and McCord had also invited

Berry Gordy, Jr., who had recently moved Motown Records to Los Angeles; legendary songwriters Eddie Holland, Lamont Dozier, and Brian Holland; and newly-elected Coleman Young, Detroit's first African-American mayor. The Four Tops was the evening's featured act.

On the night of the party, limousines rolled up end to end in front of the Pontchartrain on Washington Boulevard as turned-out folks disembarked, shaking hands.

It was one of those events when friends and enemies gathered together, an appearance often necessitated by image rather than a genuine desire to be present.

That's the way Gary saw it as McCord and Hennes ushered him through the crowd, making introductions.

Others saw it differently.

Bob Moody, Teddy Bear Richards, Super Max Kinkel, Brother Bill Gable, and several other CK' jocks congregated by the bar. Teddy was wearing one of his long, cashmere coats, which had become a signature piece of his apparel. After seeing *Superfly* and Youngblood Priest's attire, Teddy rushed out and had three coats—black, gray, and tan—made by a Detroit tailor.

Around the station, he wore the coats and went bare-footed. No one was sure what else he did or didn't wear under the coat, and no one asked. For this occasion, he had opted for shoes, socks, and pants—even a shirt.

"You know," Moody said, "I think most guys in Burbank's position would be a little intimidated by all the expectations, but he doesn't appear to be fazed. He's either a real pro or he's numb."

Hennes joined the group after handing Gary off to a clutch of particularly cloying advertisers.

"He's a real pro," Hennes said, after a sip from his glass. "A rare combination: professional, talented—salt of the earth." Hennes laughed. "You know what he just told me? We're meeting all these people and he says, 'Everybody is treating me like a movie star or something. So I guess I better act like one, a very friendly movie star.'"

Just then, Byron MacGregor, CKLW's legendary news director, joined the group. "Let's talk about me," MacGregor said, loudly, pressing his thumbs against his chest.

"Me! Me! Me! Let's talk about me!"

His friends laughed.

While CKLW listeners regarded MacGregor as a serious professional, the golden throat who had recorded Gordon Sinclair's *The Americans* and sold millions of copies, everyone at CK' knew the truth. MacGregor was a wag who regarded his own acclaim and good looks somewhat suspiciously; even *he* wasn't sure from whence it all came. This knowledge endeared MacGregor even more to his friends.

"Once we've survived this soirée," MacGregor said, "let's throw Gary a real party, the kind he'll truly enjoy."

"Now," Teddy Bear said, "you're talking."

"In the meantime," MacGregor said, falling into his deepest baritone, "I believe I will walk over there and allow those good citizens to be thoroughly taken with the proximity of my presence."

Cosmic Bob Moody was one of several great jocks at CKLW. He was, like Gary, a transplanted southerner. The shirt Bob's mother made for her boy—with its "Woo, pig, Suey" emblem—made Gary feel right at home, even in the frozen north.

Gary had never shaken so many hands, nor had he seen so many hollow smiles. Other than the fact that his arm was as dead as a pump handle, the party was a blur. What he wanted to do was spend time with the other CK' jocks, get over by the bar where they were all standing, and talk about work, maybe slip outside with them for a quick smoke.

They were in the ballroom, then gone, then back. With every exit and re-entry they were happier, louder. They were surely having a better time than he was. He was never fully at ease in circumstances such as these, whether it was Garden District parties in New Orleans or the long parade of Derby parties in Louisville.

Still, he knew the party had to be endured, no matter how uncomfortable and surreal it seemed. For all those who welcomed him and wished him good luck, Gary knew most didn't care if he fell on his face at CKLW.

But he was just a southern boy with rebellious country roots, satisfied

only when he followed his own direction, not theirs. His new job was all about producing and performing. It was what everyone called "The Big Time," and he knew he would be in direct competition with Detroit radio favorites, WXYZ's Dick Purtan and P.J. McCarthy at WJR. They were entrenched in the market, but Gary came as advertised. "A smart aleck, wise-cracking semi-hippy from out of town—New Orleans no less," McCord said. "But we believed Detroit was ready for something new."

And Gary was ready. Right now, though, he'd had enough of the spotlight. He wanted The Four Tops to sing. He just wanted to go to work. His spotlight was the microphone.

Finally, the group took the stage, and Gary went to the bar to find more comfortable company—the CK' jocks.

"I need a drink," he said.

"After you've finished your drink," someone suggested, "how 'bout we all slip away?"

The Four Tops opened with *I Can't Help Myself*. The crowd sang along:

Sugar pie honey bunch.
You know that I love you
Can't help myself.
I love you and nobody else . . .

By the time Gary and the jocks returned to the gala, most of the audience was standing, dancing and swaying to *I Got a Feelin'*. Gary felt almost at home then, like he was back in Memphis or New Orleans. He had never appreciated The Four Tops more than he did at that moment.

Na, na, na, na
Na, na, na, na
Hey, hey, hey
Goodbye!

McCord and Hennes slipped back into the crowd to meet and greet. Gary turned to Brother Bill Gable, a noted CK' jock.

"Wonder if I can just get on out of here," Gary said. "I just . . ."

"We know," Gable said, "but you better stick around awhile longer. Know what I mean?"

Gary understood.

"So," he said, "let's work the crowd."

"Let's," Gable said.

Gary spent the rest of the evening studying faces, accents, postures, and posturing. He met Detroit's most prestigious and most pretentious. By the time the party was over, his mental notebook was filled front to back with material. His pockets contained notes on cocktail napkins: names, impressions, thoughts.

"So," McCord said, at evening's end, "you ready for this?"

"Oh, yeah," Gary said. "I'm gonna like it here."

Big duck, Big pond

The studio at CKLW was not that much different from any

Gary had worked in before. The equipment was a little more advanced, and for the first time, he was not entirely on his own. CK' was a union shop and every jock was assigned a board operator.

Gary's board op was Jose Llombart, a strong, thick man of Hispanic descent. Jose reminded Gary of Glynn Bishop back in Memphis: broad sloped shoulders and thick hands, scars decorating some of the knuckles. Jose was not one to be challenged and no one in full capacity of his senses would dare to do so.

There was one difference between Jose and Glynn. Jose smiled all the time, and somehow, that made him all the more intimidating, as if there were something sinister hiding behind that smile.

Of course, Gary and Jose hit it off at once.

Jose made it clear that his job was to make Gary sound as good as he could possibly sound.

Gary was equally clear. "I'm glad you're here," he said, "'cause you never know who might come through that door wanting to beat my ass."

"Won't happen," Jose said.

Gary scanned the studio before taking his seat and awakening Detroit.

"Everything okay?" Jose said.

"Everything's fine," Gary said. "We got everything I need: a microphone and a nice big studio. Let's fill it up."

Jose flashed his wide, bright smile. It was a few minutes before six in the morning. Gary looked out the window at Detroit, sitting across the river, large and gray under a blue-black sky. There was no color except for the distant traffic lights.

Gary stubbed out a Marlboro in an already crowded ashtray.

"Let's do it, man," Jose said. "Let's blast America."

Jose's words gave Gary a bit of a jolt.

His heart fluttered, but he had the microphone and a big room—all he needed. He closed his eyes and opened a door in his mind. That's the way it had always been, as if he were not really in control—thoughts and ideas coming from God knows where. Sketches and characters on paper began true to script, then cavorted off in their own direction.

In his first days at CK', Gary introduced a large portion of America to Deuteronomy Skaggs and "The Healing Hour," during which the reverend promised to free the afflicted of any and all ailments. Listeners in Detroit—and as far away as Boston—played along.

They asked to be healed of bunions, tax problems, hangnails, hangovers, hemorrhoids, chronic infidelity, various forms of fungus, and depression stemming from the performance of Detroit's professional sports teams: the Tigers, Lions, Pistons, and Red Wings.

The Tigers had a convicted felon named Ron LeFlore. The Wings had Bart Crashley and John Lochead. The Pistons had Bob Lanier, 6-foot-11 with size 22 shoes. The Lions had cool-as-could-be Lem Barney out of Gulfport, Mississippi, as well as Bill Munson, a stick straight, flat-topped

quarterback from Utah State University.

Detroit was a city filled with contrasts and conflict, presenting Gary with a mountain of material. He lampooned Coleman Young, the city's first African-American mayor, who, until Gary's arrival at CK', enjoyed a free pass from the local media. Though Young was viewed as unassailable, Gary created Soul Man Young, who discussed the foibles and faults often associated with the mayor but never publicly aired.

Soul Man was a self-avowed charlatan and philanderer, determined, nonetheless, to do his part to save Detroit. Soul Man called Gary's show each day with a new plan to exorcise the city's demons, from potholes to cops watching him "too damned close, making it hard to do 'bidness,' if you know what I mean. Dem and de damned FBI."

Except for the mayor's office, the spoof was an immediate hit in Detroit. Young was so incensed he dispatched one of his largest aides, a former University of Michigan football player, to have lunch with Herb McCord and to instruct him that action would be taken if Burbank didn't desist.

The luncheon was cordial enough until the plates were cleared and coffee served.

"You know," Young's aide said, "we can cause you a lot of trouble."

McCord listened, not really surprised.

"Oh," he said, "how so?"

"We want this Burbank to stop the Soul Man routine. Otherwise, we'll call in the Federal Communications Commission, the FCC."

"Yes," McCord said, "I am familiar with the FCC. Do you know what our call letters are?"

The aide said he did: "CKLW."

"Do you know what the 'C' stands for?" McCord asked.

The aide was silent.

"The 'C,'" McCord said, "stands for Canada. We are licensed in Canada. We're not governed by the FCC. We are governed by the CRTC. Now, unless you have any connections in Ottawa, I'd say our conversation is over."

Back at CKLW, McCord told Hennes how the mayor had tried to muscle him into gagging Gary.

Hennes was concerned. "You are not going to tell Gary about this, are you?"

"No, no way," McCord said. "I don't want him to know. I want him to

keep on goading the giants. The audience loves it. Besides, Gary has Young dead-on. You can't tell if it's the mayor talking or if it's Gary."

Young was merely one who felt the Burbank barb. Gary took aim at virtually anyone in Detroit who had either prestige or position. He satirized veteran Detroit TV anchorman Bill Bonds, suggesting that Bonds's guttural voice and well-documented quick temper was the result of prolonged dipsomania.

Bonds would burst into the studio, chastising Gary for his lack of knowledge regarding Detroit.

"You don't know *anything*, boy. I'm Bill Bonds. I rule Detroit. I *am* the news. Ya got a stash around here? Sure you do. Bill needs a little bracer. Whatcha got in that coffee cup. Give Bill a little taste. I like mine half-and-half. Yes, indeed: half coffee and half bourbon. Yum. That gets Bill going."

Bonds frequently called the station telling McCord and Hennes how much he liked the bit.

"There's one problem, though," he said. "I can't get a straight cup of coffee anywhere in the city . . . ."

Bob Talbert was a well-known columnist for *The Detroit Free Press*. Talbert, who came to Detroit in 1968 on the heels of the riots, was regarded as one who helped bring the splintered city back together.

By the time Gary arrived, Talbert, a South Carolinian, was revered not only for his folksy column but his numerous community activities and volunteer efforts. Where Talbert and Burbank parted ways was the columnist's self-anointed status as Detroit's media watchdog.

Talbert found Gary somewhat reckless, his double entendres bordering on blue and not quite fitting for public consumption.

Burbank viewed Talbert as genteel and friendly enough, but another example of someone who had become a little large for his trousers.

"First of all," Gary said to Bob Moody, "I don't want *nobody* being my watchdog. Second, what's with those shirts and jackets Talbert wears—all the sequins? Who does he think he is, Porter Wagoner? He ain't Porter Wagoner."

It was a line that made the air many times in many forms and one that infuriated Talbert, who was far more comfortable wielding the critical brush than being tarred by it.

Staffers at The Big Eight were surprised when anyone took umbrage with anything that occurred during Gary's show. He was never vulgar, never mean-spirited, and even his most outrageous takes were steeped in either an element of truth or a quirk of human nature. Beyond that, there was nothing on CKLW's air more outrageous or more popular than *Byron MacGregor's 20/20 News*. MacGregor was hired as news director when he was 21 years old. He was handsome, with an inimitable voice and dramatic delivery. "If there is a God," McCord said, "He sounds like Byron MacGregor."

While his voice had the tone of omnipotence, his words were laced with a tabloid syntax, and he hired people who could follow his lead. While every other news outlet in Detroit delivered the news dolefully, in linear fashion, Byron MacGregor took the news to new heights.

It's 20 minutes before 8. This is Byron MacGregor, CKLW 20/20 News. A gang that went fishing this morning pulled up something they weren't planning on for dinner: 'The kids were fishing in the canal over there, and they spotted something wrapped in a blanket. And it wasn't the first time this thing was spotted. A day or so ago, one of the kids mentioned it. But this time it came up to the surface, I guess, and one of the kids got his hook caught in it.' It turned out to be a rotting body. Eyewitness Charles Evens tells the 20/20 hotlines that the stiff sank to the bottom. That's when police were called in. The worm-baited hook belonged to Victoria Findley who tells us what that floater looked like: 'He was black. He had short hair and rags tied around his neck and rope tied around his legs and his hands was tied up.'

That thrilling catch pulled from the water along Harding between Jefferson and the canal . . .

When you see it happen, the Big 8 wants to know about it on the hotlines at 254-CKLW in Windsor and 961-NEWS in Detroit.

We offer a weekly cash award and pay $1,000 each year for the year's biggest story.

It's 20 minutes before 1. This is Grant Hudson, CKLW 20/20 News, and you heard this first on the Big 8: Accommodations are getting tighter at the Wayne County Morgue as officials stare at sixteen new feet peeking out from those rubber blankets. Eight murders since midnight—three of them happening a short time ago in an attempted quadruple blowout. Two women are dead, one man is dead, another man now under the knife at Ford Hospital—all suffering multiple stab wounds.

Another deadly duo of Detroit dastardly deeds as the dice decree death. A disagreement over 7-Come-11. Now she's in heaven. The man who delivered that double-barreled death with his package of penetrating pellets has been pounced in the pen.

In another case of hot lead in the head, a heavy-handed hitchhiker tipped with a trigger and paid his bill in bullets . . . .

Thelma Hooch, Deuteronomy Skaggs, Ranger Bob, Soul Man, Bass Ackwards, and Captain Gorgeous—"Gary's People," as they came to be known at The Big Eight—paled in comparison to the alliterative, blood and guts style of CK's *20/20 News*.

Given Gary's appreciation for language and the absurd, Byron MacGregor's newscasts were a feeding ground. He seldom allowed MacGregor to walk away from the newscast cleanly.

Invariably, Gary had a follow-up question.

"Byron, wait a second."

"Yes, Gary."

"You just said this guy was strained through the grill of a Lincoln."

"Yes."

"So how was the Lincoln running after that, a little rough I'm thinking?"

"Uh . . ."

"Had to be some REAL problems. My Cougar doesn't want to start when it rains. Of course, it's a Ford product. What should I expect?"

Gary's trump card was his irreverence. Byron's ace-in-the-hole was his connection with anyone and everyone of importance in Detroit and Windsor.

After *The Americans* was released in 1974, MacGregor appeared on the *CBS Evening News*, at the Super Bowl, and on the *Today* show. MacGregor was the toast of the town, and Gary the malfunctioning toaster. Theirs was an unlikely friendship, but they had one thing in common—a fierce love of a good prank.

Not long after Gary arrived in Windsor, MacGregor held a party at his Holiday Inn suite overlooking the Detroit River. The place was jammed, shoulder-to-shoulder, leading several of CK's jocks to find space on the balcony, among them Gary, Teddy Bear Richards, and sportscaster Joe Donovan.

"Wow," Gary said, "the river is right there below us."

"Yeah," Teddy Bear said, "three stories straight down."

"You could take this chair here," Donovan said, "and drop it right in the water."

"You could, I guess," The Bear said.

The next thing The Bear and Gary heard was a splash and then a bigger one. Soon, The Bear and Gary joined the game, tossing all the furniture off the balcony and into the river. When the balcony was cleared, they returned to the party in search of more furniture and learned that Byron had stepped out to get more provisions.

"Perfect," Gary said.

Still more furniture went off the balcony, as MacGregor's suite grew ever more spacious. The coffee table disappeared, as well as a table, most of the lamps, and all of the chairs.

When MacGregor returned, he looked around the suite, sat down on the couch—one of the last pieces of furniture not floating in the river—and opened a beer. He didn't say a word. He knew better. He would bide his time. Besides, the place needed new furniture. His only worry was that before he could hatch a worthy scheme, Gary might have punked him again.

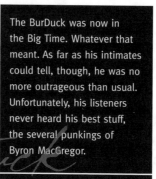

The BurDuck was now in the Big Time. Whatever that meant. As far as his intimates could tell, though, he was no more outrageous than usual. Unfortunately, his listeners never heard his best stuff, the several punkings of Byron MacGregor.

MacGregor hired Jo-Jo Shutty, a former cheerleader, beauty queen, and champion baton twirler, as CKLW's traffic reporter. During rush hours, Shutty, a bubbly Michigan State graduate, climbed aboard the station's helicopter to report on Detroit's notoriously snarled freeway system, which at the time was the second largest in the country.

It was Herb McCord's idea to hire a woman. He wanted a woman's voice on the air to complement the DJs and news reporters, and shortly after Shutty was hired, she and MacGregor began dating.

When Gary learned the relationship was becoming serious—something entirely new for MacGregor—he joined forces with a young area woman and an accommodating Windsor policeman.

Gary coached them, making sure they knew exactly what to do to make the plan unfold correctly, assuring them it was all in good fun.

He then took Herb McCord, instrumental to the caper, into his confidence.

Herb smiled. "I like it," he said. "Where are you gonna be?"

"Home, taking a nap," Gary said. "The best part is being nowhere around when it comes down. Then, no one can blame you."

The next afternoon, MacGregor bustled through the front door of the station on his way to the newsroom. Just as he entered the lobby, a young woman, who appeared to be ready to give birth at any moment, rose with great difficulty from the couch and shouted, "That's him officer! That's the man! Arrest him!"

The officer stood and glared at MacGregor.

"Sir," the officer said, "you will have to come with me. I'm going to have to place you under arrest until we sort this out."

"Wait," MacGregor said, "there has been some misunderstanding. I'm Byron MacGregor—*Byron MacGregor*. I've never seen this young woman in my life."

"That's him," the woman wailed.

"Let's just go to the station and talk this over," the officer said, removing handcuffs from his belt.

"But I swear," MacGregor said.

The woman appeared to be crying—MacGregor close to tears himself—when McCord entered the lobby. He spoke quietly to the officer and then to the young woman, thanked them both, and said he wanted to speak to MacGregor privately.

McCord closed his office door and told MacGregor to take a seat.

"This doesn't look good, Byron," he said, "not good at all. Now I want you to swear to me that you have never made love to that woman."

MacGregor was distraught. He said nothing for a moment.

"Byron, swear to me," McCord said.

"Well," MacGregor said, his famously rich voice cracking slightly, "I can't be sure!"

At that point, McCord believed MacGregor had suffered enough.

"Let's go back to the lobby and talk to them," he said.

MacGregor pulled himself out of the chair and trudged down the hall with McCord. When they arrived in the lobby, the young woman was standing in slender profile, smiling, holding a pillow under her arm. The officer was dangling the handcuffs between his thumb and forefinger.

"Gotcha," the girl said.

The policeman and the girl turned and walked out the door.

MacGregor was speechless. When he realized what had happened, he couldn't help but laugh. Then he went to the Windsor Press Club and had a drink.

Gary Burbank was home napping.

McCord couldn't wait to tell Hennes about Gary's stunt.

"Gary," Hennes said, "is Byron's nightmare."

"Yeah," McCord said, laughing, "and he sure does help keep Byron in the traces."

Once, MacGregor almost got the better of Gary.

The Detroit Tigers had asked MacGregor to perform *The Americans* in Tiger Stadium on Canada Night, when the team honored its Canadian fans. *The Americans* had been written in 1973 by a Canadian journalist just after the U.S. withdrew from Vietnam, amid nationwide divisiveness that was followed by an economic downturn. Its simplistic patriotic boozle was enormously popular with conservatives everywhere. (Later, President Reagan said he liked to listen to it when he felt gloomy.) After the release of the recording and its national success, MacGregor seldom turned down any opportunity for a recitation.

On Canada Night, *The Star Spangled Banner* and *Oh, Canada* would be played then MacGregor would deliver the words, accompanied by the Detroit Symphony playing *America the Beautiful*. It would be played over Tiger Stadium's elaborate public address system with MacGregor hurling his stentorian tones at the baseball fans while standing—where else?—on the pitcher's mound.

In preparation, MacGregor asked Gary to help him by laying down the symphony's recording of *America the Beautiful* on reel-to-reel tape. Gary was quick to oblige.

On the night of the performance, MacGregor wore a tuxedo. To rousing applause, he took his position on the field. He nodded, the music started,

and he began. His voice boomed solemnly into every corner of the stadium. He might have been announcing the Second Coming, or perhaps some more important event.

He extolled the grand nature of Americans whose under-appreciated magnanimity had rebuilt Europe after the war, shored up the beleaguered French franc, and rescued countless victims of earthquakes, floods, and tornadoes. His magnificent oratory was helium with which he inflated himself, then floated splendidly over the crowd.

MacGregor reminded his audience of the Boeing Jumbo Jet and the Lockheed TriStar. He wondered why every international line (except Russia) flew American planes. He wondered why only Americans had put a man on the moon.

Was there a slight tremulous quality to his fine voice when he spoke of America's generosity and openness, then asked the whereabouts of America's friends abroad when she, herself, was in need of friends? (And while he did not count the exact number of smug, self-righteous Canadians, he hinted strongly at their presence.)

A symphonic splendor arose behind him. Between the music and MacGregor's own tonal elegance, he could have been reading the Detroit phone book. There were church bells in his voice, and cannon fire. If a flock of doves had flown from his mouth, no one would have been surprised, least of all MacGregor himself.

There was a brief moment as the final notes of the symphony drifted over the stadium wall. Then the crowd stood, breaking into rapturous applause. MacGregor waved to the crowd and began to walk off the field. Then, something unexpected—the theme music from Warner Brothers' Looney Tunes, and the unmistakable voice of Porky Pig: *Upba-dee, Upba-dee! That all folks.*

The Tiger players laughed and so did some in the crowd. MacGregor was mortified. First, he blamed it on the Tiger staff, but when they explained they'd only played the tape that had been delivered to them, MacGregor knew the real culprit.

Back at his suite and stripping off his tuxedo, he phoned a friend. He had the address in his hand.

"That's right," he said, barking into the phone. "In the middle of the night. I want two tons of horse manure dumped in his driveway. Yeah, two tons! Of course, I know that's a lot and I don't give a damn how much it

costs. He leaves at five. Make sure it's dumped before then."

MacGregor went to bed satisfied that this would be his ultimate victory over Burbank.

The next morning, Gary—always running late—jumped in his Mercury Cougar, hit the gas, and backed out of his garage. The Cougar was immediately mired in a large, damp, dark mountain.

He got out of the car and surveyed the situation. He smiled. My, how he loved that smell—it brought back so many memories. Still, there was no time to tarry. With no shovel at hand, Gary jumped back into the car, raced the engine, and managed to plow his way through MacGregor's mountain.

When he arrived at work—barely on time—the yellow Cougar, his pride and joy, was dappled and dunged.

He began his show as usual, offering no signs that anything was out of the norm. When MacGregor appeared for his first newscast, script in hand, he was smiling. The final item in his newscast: a report from Windsor police that someone had dumped a truckload of horse manure in the driveway at 4250 Riverside Drive.

At CKLW, the old criticisms finally died. He was not only IN the bigtime; he WAS bigtime. Nothing else had changed, though. It was the quality his friends loved him for. No matter what, Gary remained wholly and indisputably Gary.

"Police," he said, "are searching for the scatological scallywags."

Gary said nothing.

"Gary," MacGregor said, "doesn't that address sound familiar? Isn't that *your* house?"

"Hunh? What? Oh, we used to live there but we moved, Byron. I thought you knew that. Who would do such a thing and why? It's a crazy world isn't it?"

MacGregor left the studio gnashing his teeth.

Gary smiled.

Byron is such a great audience, he thought. *Such a big, broad target.*

For Gary, CKLW was like living on a gigantic playground. Every day offered an exciting new exercise in creativity. Being an American living in Canada, on the other hand, was like being the most unpopular and unwanted kid in class. In the mid-1970s, Canada under Prime Minister Pierre Trudeau was experiencing an unprecedented wave of nationalism and outsiders—perceived as taking Canadian jobs—were not warmly received. Instead, they were frequently criticized and largely ignored.

It was an environment that forged an uncommon bond among CK' jocks—who were mostly Americans—and served as a constant source of irritation. It was, to most of them, the only flaw in an otherwise perfect place of employment.

"I didn't think anything about it the first time my bike was stolen off the front porch," Gary complained. "When I got it back, I bought a chain and locked it to the railing. When it was stolen a second time, the cop said something about being American. I said: 'It's a freakin' Honda.' He just looked at me like I was from outer space."

Gary, Cosmic Bob Moody, and Brother Bill Gable were hanging around the station, discussing their grievous imposition upon the Canadians.

"It's like they can look at you and tell you're American," Moody said, "and God forbid you have the least bit of a southern accent."

It was quickly noted, of course, that Moody, duly proud of his Arkansas roots, routinely wore the denim shirt on which his mother had embroidered blazing tributes to the University of Arkansas Razorbacks. Woo, pig. Suey! was not common usage amongst the Canadian citizenry.

"What's wrong with my shirt?" he asked. "Edsel Ford wants one just like it. Mom's making him one, too."

Edsel, they agreed, was surprisingly normal and very cool. "And who would of thought that?" Moody said. "My God, he's heir to the Ford Motor Company and what's he like to do? Hang out with us."

"I remember the first day I got here," Gable said, smiling. "There was a problem with my work permit, so while I was waiting around I went down the street to buy a pack of cigarettes.

"I walk in Mac's Milk and ask for a pack of Winstons. The clerk gives me this look of utter disgust. He says, 'We don't carry Winston.' I said, 'Okay, a pack of Marlboros.' Now, he's looking at me like I am the biggest SOB who ever walked the earth. He says, 'We don't sell Marlboro. We don't sell *American* cigarettes.'

"I just look at the guy and he's truly angry—over a pack of cigarettes. 'So,' I said, 'I guess a six-pack of Budweiser is out of the question.'"

While Du Mauriers and Rothmans were acceptable in a pinch, they were not as smooth as American smokes. Molson and Moosehead couldn't hold a candle to the products of Anheuser-Busch and Miller Brewing Company, and Canadian smoked meat left a lot to be desired when you were longing for a Whopper.

"Unavailable in Canada" was their least favorite phrase and prompted many forays through the Detroit-Windsor tunnel to reach American soil— albeit the sordid variety of Wayne County, Michigan. Even though Detroit was just under a mile away, the trip was seldom simple.

First, there was always the possibility of a traffic jam. At the height of the morning or evening rush, traffic was often stalled for hours at a time.

Then there was customs. Clearing customs in Detroit was generally not a problem; getting back into Canada was an entirely different matter. If you looked American and sounded American, the agents always suspected that contraband of some nature was being spirited back into Canada.

Of course most at CK' had learned to follow Ted "The Bear" Richards's approach to customs. "Be as outrageous as you can possibly be," Richards counseled, "and you will get a free pass every time. It's a dead solid lock."

Gary had serious reservations about this tactic until he witnessed its deployment during a passing with Bear Richards.

"Anything to declare?" the agent said, peering into the car.

"You damn betcha," Richards said with a zealot's glee. "We got four AK-47s, a couple of .45 autos and enough explosives to light up Goyeau Street from one end to the other."

"Oh," the agent said, "it's you. Welcome back to Canada. You may pass."

"See," Richards said, as they passed the checkpoint. "Works every time."

Small things seemed to give The Bear an inordinate amount of pleasure.

Gary, Cosmic Bob, and Len King, who moved from New Orleans to work in MacGregor's news department, found a less incendiary approach to clearing customs, and it was quite by accident.

Gary and Moody longed for all things southern: cooking, accents, attitudes—anything. To make themselves more comfortable they gathered at Gary's home and sang the "blood hymns" from his *Broadman Hymnal*.

When that failed to soothe their ache for the South, they would call directory assistance in Mississippi just to hear the operator's voice drawl: "Nine, nine-five, five-fo-three-nine."

It cheered them no end. Her language was slow and sweet, like syrup rolling down johnnycake. They applauded the operator and praised her.

"Y'all boys call again," she said. "Sorry ya so lonely up thare. Come on home when ya can."

Their chronic complaint was about the food in Canada and the impossibility of getting anything that remotely resembled southern cooking. "You couldn't get a plate of black-eyed peas, collard greens, and fried chicken around here if your life depended on it," Gary groused. "Give me biscuits. Give me gravy and stick those scones or whatever they are up your arse."

This absence of southern delights led to a continual search of the Detroit newspapers for soul kitchens and grocery stores. Gary, Cosmic Bob, and Len were forever scouring the advertisements and quizzing those more familiar with Detroit on where to find their fare of choice.

Generally, they were urged not to explore Detroit's black neighborhoods. True, they might find what they were looking for, but they might well find something else—like a bullet.

"If you are not aware and alert, if you're not vigilant," Hennes said, "then you are not listening and you are not smart. Detroit can be a dangerous place."

So, they pined away, settling for an occasional trip to Kentucky Fried Chicken, until the day Cosmic Bob struck the mother lode.

There it was in the newspaper, in big, black type: *Farm-Raised, Grain-Fed Mississippi Catfish Steaks and Fillets. Get 'Em While They Last!*

"Praise be," Moody said, rushing into the jock's lounge. "Look at this, Gary. We're gonna have ourselves a fish fry, baby. Let's go! We gotta go."

The market was in a particularly ominous section of Detroit but Gary, Cosmic Bob, and Len were not dissuaded by the threatening looks they received; the magnitude of the prize overrode the prospects of a bad end so far from home.

The man behind the counter was enormous.

"And what brings y'all in here?" he said, a tone of mistrust in his voice.

"Catfish," they said, in unison.

"And all the fixin's," Gary said. "We're havin' ourselves a fish fry."

The man behind the counter smiled. "Not from around here are ya?"

"No, not really," Gary said. "Memphis. Mississippi."

"Arkansas," Moody said.

"Just up from New Orleans," Len said.

"Hmmm," the man said, smiling broadly. "Splains just about everything. Well, order up!"

When they arrived at the Canadian border, the customs agent, a stout, no-nonsense officer, peered in the car. "Anything to declare?" he asked.

"Hell, yes," Gary said. "Three dozen farm-fresh Mississippi catfish filets. Two jugs of peanut oil."

"A big ol' bag of stoneground cornmeal," Moody added, "and a five-pound bag of Aunt Jemima Self-Rising Flour."

"Onions, cabbage, fresh tomatoes," King said, "and a jug of buttermilk."

"We didn't forget the cayenne pepper, did we?" Moody said.

"Got it, right here," King said. "And the black pepper and garlic powder."

"Scared me for a minute," Moody said.

"Frying up a mess of catfish, gonna make some hushpuppies and coleslaw," Gary said, unable to hide his glee.

"Catfish?" the agent said, frowning. "Disgusting. Pass. *Please!*"

"Thanks," Gary said.

"Wait," Len said, as they pulled out on Goyeau Street. "We didn't tell him about the sweet tea and RC Cola."

"Drive," Moody said. "I'm starving."

"Got to remember to tell The Bear about this," Gary said. "He'll love it. I was never comfortable with the guns thing."

"Hey," Len said, "why did he call catfish disgusting?"

"Up here," Moody said, "they won't eat them. They think they are nasty bottom-feeders."

"Like us," Gary said.

Most at CK' regarded Gary with respect and a degree of awe. While he was not blessed with great technical skills, he possessed a mad magic that made him as much fun to watch as he was to listen to: the way he closed his eyes and went to that place in his mind where "his people" cavorted back and forth.

"Almost as if he's having himself a religious experience," King said.

Brother Bill Gable marveled at how Gary's facial expressions and

gestures changed with each character's emergence. "It's as if they're more than characters," Gable said, "more like creations, like he can see these people—like they are right there in the studio with him. And then he's surprised by what they said."

"I think," Moody said, "they *are* real—to Gary. He doesn't really know what's going to happen when he opens the mike."

Until Gary's arrival at CKLW, morning drive in Detroit was shared by Dick Purtan at WXYZ and J.P. McCarthy at WJR. Both were veterans of the Detroit market and, while talented in their own right, they owed something of their popularity to longevity. Success in Detroit, as in many markets, was often the result of familiarity—especially in the case of morning drive.

For years, people in Detroit turned to Purtan and McCarthy in the morning for the information they needed: weather,

Living in Canada had its downside. The CK' jocks from the South—with their accents— were truly marked men. The highlight of their stay, though, might have been bringing three dozen catfish and two jugs of peanut oil through customs.

school closings, traffic, the latest news, scores, and the proximity of the latest crime. Purtan and McCarthy were respected, likeable, familiar, trusted; their prominence was all the more remarkable since both WXYZ and WJR steered clear of the most current trends in rock 'n' roll and R&B, opting instead for "Chicken Rock," anything regarded as safe and unlikely to offend. The Doobie Brothers had no place at XYZ or WJR and neither did Al Green.

"McCarthy and Purtan were superstars in Detroit," said radio historian Art Vuolo. "But they were also very straight and along comes this young whack job, Gary Burbank: crazy, nuts—perfectly in synch with the times."

"He's irreverent, a talented 30-year-old iconoclast," said McCord. "He's talking to the people who didn't have a voice. He's taking on everything and everybody, not afraid of anything, and he's doing it with a refreshing honesty and a sense of humor that makes him an immediate hit . . . in sixty days, he's top-of-mind. He's eroded an audience Purtan and McCarthy, who were both extremely good, spent years building."

CKLW's "Morning Mouth" was featured in the *Detroit Free Press*, the *Detroit News*, and the *Cleveland Plain Dealer*. "Gary is easily recognized by his many voice changes and character creations that run from the corny pun to euphemisms, satire, and, well, just about anything that is bad about humor," wrote Bob Duncan and Harvey Zupke. "In all solemnity, the Morning Mouth show is as awful as you'd expect—and hilarious."

Reporters called from Boston, Buffalo, Toronto, and Chicago. Within a year, Gary Burbank was being compared to WNBC's Don Imus, New York's hottest, most outrageous, new radio star. Gary found the comparison annoying.

"We're nothing alike," he told reporters. "Imus attacks. I satirize. There's a big difference in lampooning someone and making them the butt of a joke. My humor is bloodless. It doesn't leave a scar."

In some ways, Gary was uncomfortable with the degree of the attention he received in Detroit. His success, he thought, came from a fortuitous confluence: Rosalie Trombley's play list, a progressive mix of rock and R&B that gave CKLW a large coalition of black and white listeners, an audience he knew and had entertained since his days at WDIA in Memphis; the latitude to experiment presented by Hennes and McCord; the push he felt from the station's other jocks; and, finally, "whatever it is that I do," he said.

Detroit radio was shared turf until Gary arrived. Then it was a land grab. The Morning Mouth took over Morning Drive. He'd never received so much acclaim, either. In his first year, he was named the Major Market Personality of the Year.

In fact, Detroit was a perfect proving ground for Gary and the southern sensibilities that imbued his comedy and delivery. The city grew up around the automotive industry and had drawn thousands from the South in search of work and life beyond cotton fields and coal mines. To a great extent, they were people—both black and white—who never fully left their southern upbringing behind and passed it along to generations who followed. They

knew Deuteronomy Skaggs and Thelma Hooch, "the Breakfast Pig." They embraced Gary Burbank, and he returned their affection.

"He exploded," Hennes said. "He was huge in Detroit and the remarkable thing was that he was so unassuming. Gary was not engaged in being a star. He was engaged in his show. That's it. He loved the job. All the things that came with it—the money, the recognition—meant nothing to him. Gary was still Gary."

When the weather was nice, Gary rode his motorcycle to work. It was a few miles from his house on Riverside to the station, a pleasant ride. At 4:30 or 5 in the morning, traffic was spare and Windsor was peaceful and quiet. Along the way, especially at traffic lights, Gary idled down the engine and did vocal exercises to prepare for the show. His favorite was a particularly loud, long Tarzan yell—always effective at clearing the pipes.

At each light, Gary let loose: Tarzan calling the elephants to help him save Jane and Cheetah from the clutches of jungle miscreants, monkeys scampering through the trees, lions roaring in response to his beckoning call. This practice and the reverie that accompanied it continued until one morning when Gary was pulled over by the Windsor Police.

"What are you *doing*?" one officer said.

"Going to work," Gary said, politely. "Was I speeding?"

"No," the first officer said. "No, but what is that noise you're making?"

"Oh, that," Gary said, smiling. "Voice exercises. I'm in radio."

"But what is that noise?"

"That's Tarzan," Gary said.

"Tarzan?" the first officer said.

"Edgar Rice Burroughs," the second officer said.

"Johnny Weissmuller," Gary said, "the best Tarzan of all, though Lex Barker was pretty good, too."

The first officer was bewildered. "You're the Morning Mouth, aren't you?" he said.

"Yes," Gary said.

"Well, stop with the Tarzan until you get to work. People are trying to sleep and Tarzan is waking them up."

"Sure thing," Gary said.

The second officer tipped his cap. "Weissmuller was the best," he said. "You're pretty good, too."

In 1975, Gary's first full year at CKLW, he was named Major Market Personality of the Year, receiving the award from a field of notables including New York's Dan Ingram and Don Imus; Johnny Lujack and John "Records" Landecker from Chicago, and Robert W. "Boss Daddy" Morgan in Los Angeles. Burbank was the new kid on the biggest street in radio.

It was a huge win for CKLW, Gary Burbank, and Top 40 radio in Middle America, but with the recognition came the certainty that Gary would leave Detroit for radio's highest ground. McCord was convinced Gary was bound for Los Angeles. But there was no evidence Gary was eager to make a move. At CKLW he excelled on one of radio's largest and most powerful stages. It was a professional fulfillment like none he had experienced before. He liked the environment at CK' and he liked the people so much so that on his daughter's birthday everyone from Brother Bill Gable to Jose Llombart came to his house to celebrate with little Tracy.

In a short time, he had freed himself of the gnawing criticism that plagued him at WAKY and WNOE. Finally, he answered that old taunt. He was no longer a big duck in a little pond and it felt good. He was gratified. And, yes, he was happy.

But, once more, he found himself at a familiar and disconcerting crossing.

Carol was not happy in Canada. She didn't like the weather and she didn't like the fact that Gary was out of the house as much as he was. He left for work early in the morning, didn't return until late afternoon, and sometimes there were obligations in the evening. There wasn't much to do in Windsor, the people—outside of their friends at the station—weren't all that friendly and she was uncomfortable venturing into Detroit with Tracy in tow.

She missed her family and friends in Louisville. And with Gary working so much, she needed their support. True, they were fortunate to be making so much money but other things were important, too.

She wanted to go home, at least some place closer to Louisville. She didn't harp on it but her feelings were eminently clear and every time the topic came up, Gary felt like he wanted to run for cover. Time and again, he asked himself the same questions: *Is it always going to be like this? It is always going to be my career versus my family?*

He tried to avoid the topic but even when it was left alone and the discussion turned to silence, the conflict played out in his mind.

Yes, he was happy at CKLW.

Yes, he had proven he could succeed in a major market.

True, he had made a lot of money. Fact was, he didn't even know how much money he had in the bank.

Would Carol be happier if he made more money and stayed in Canada?

No, it was not about money at all. She was lonely. She hated the weather. It bothered her horribly that every time Sean came to visit in Windsor he ended up in fights because kids teased him about his southern accent.

But could he find another job as good as the one he had at CKLW? Would Johnny Randolph have him back at WAKY? *Could* he go home again? What about Chicago, Cincinnati, or Indianapolis?

He didn't know. All he knew was that he was tired of the dispute. All he had ever truly wanted to do was be successful and have a happy, healthy family. That's what he knew.

He avoided the issue for months. Finally, he confided to King and Moody, his closest friends, "my resistance is eroding."

He was at the height of his career and for the first time since he entered radio, he was looking for a new job—and not because he wanted to.

"Things will work out," he said. "They always do."

Chapter nineteen

The last stop

At WHAS in Louisville, he was at his most inventive. Everyone thought so. Everyone but the director, that is. And then Gary was off the air, just like that. 'Look on the bright side,' he said. 'Dead and gone, but with a really great obit.'

For the first time since his days in radio school, Gary

was pursuing a job rather than being pursued. It was an awkward place. He could have picked up the phone, made a call, and in minutes claimed work in New York, Los Angeles, or Chicago. Yet he was calling friends in Louisville, modestly asking questions about what was happening in the market, if anything was available. He was greeted warmly but with surprise.

"You're kidding, right? Why would you want to come back to Louisville?"

Gary said he had his reasons. "You wouldn't understand," he said. "But then again, maybe you would."

In the fall of 1977, there were no openings in Louisville. WAKY and WKLO were feeling the fire from heavily armed FM stations. Jimi Hendrix and Led Zeppelin were chipping away at personality-driven radio. The terrain was changing—vastly and quickly. The audience wanted Clapton, Leon Russell, Stevie Winwood, The Crusaders, and the less they heard from disc jockeys—the better.

"Long term, not looking the best," friends said. "But if I hear of anything, I'll be sure to let you know—count on it. So, how are things at The Big Eight? By the way, congratulations on the award—Major Market Personality of the Year, that's wild. Heard you were heading to LA . . ."

"Uh, no," Gary said. "Trying to get home."

"Oh, sure. I understand."

But no one did. At times, Gary wasn't sure *he* did; he wasn't sure his priorities were in the right place, though something kept pushing him away from the common course of his profession.

He knew what it was. It was the look in Carol's eyes. The knowledge that Tracy would be heading to kindergarten in just a few years. The fear that Sean needed him more than he knew.

Did he want to go to New York, a city he viewed as so crowded that no one had time or room for anything other than personal survival?

Did he want to raise his family in Los Angeles—the soulless City of Angels where image had more weight than anything substantive?

And was Chicago really any different than Detroit?

There was something else, too. He was tired of talking to kids. He wanted to speak to a more sophisticated audience. Could he find that in Louisville, or someplace close to Louisville?

Again, he felt that old disquieting tug.

At CKLW, word leaked that Gary was on the move. No one was surprised. Gary was good and big, ready for the top-story. Good for him.

But as staffers around CK' learned more, they *were* surprised.

Louisville?

Kentucky?

It doesn't make sense.

"He has his reasons," Bob Moody said.

Herb McCord hated the thought of losing Gary and felt that Gary was undermining his own career. "But," he added, "Carol has never been really happy here. She can't stand the weather, the cold. She wants to go

home. She's lucky to have Gary. Most people in his position in this business wouldn't give a move like that the first thought."

On this, they all agreed. Success in radio required a packed bag and a singular frame of mind. Fame came with wounds, and they were not always one's own.

Jeff Douglas was a young, vibrant on-air personality at WHAS in Louisville. He was an easterner whose father was a successful New York businessman. But rather than follow in his father's footsteps, Douglas attended Syracuse University and the prestigious Newhouse School of Communications. His ultimate goal, he confided, was to be "the next Henny Youngman," an aspiration his father found wanting.

On the air, Douglas was smooth, calm, with a hint of summers at Montauk lingering at the edge of his voice.

He was hired at WHAS in the early 1970s, an element in the station's attempt to alter its staid image. Part of the Bingham communications empire along with the *Courier Journal*, the *Louisville Times*, and WHAS-TV, WHAS radio had remained true to Judge Bingham's founding vision, a full service radio station devoted to thorough newscasts, weather reports, farm reports, classical music, and intelligent talk shows such as "Metz Here," featuring the erudite and professorial Milton Metz.

By radio standards, its audience was old. Kids tolerated their parents' loyalty to WHAS for an hour in the morning and an hour in the evening, then quickly turned the dial to more popular stations.

By the late 1960s, Bingham's corporate team determined that it was time for the radio station to become more profitable. Wayne Perkey was hired as the station's first personality, then came Jerry David Melloy, Douglas, and others. Slowly, WHAS entered the fray with the city's top stations.

Douglas earned his stripes on April 3, 1974, when tornados ripped through the Ohio River valley, causing catastrophic destruction. He was on the air when the tornados struck the Louisville area, and he coordinated the first hours of WHAS's around-the-clock award-winning coverage.

As F2's and F4's roared across the city and Jefferson County, into southern Indiana and upriver toward Cincinnati and central Ohio, Douglas was the voice of calm in hours of chaos.

His performance further endeared him to the WHAS family. He purchased a home on the city's near east side. He visited nursing homes,

charming residents with his Henny Youngman routine. All seemed promising for Jeff Douglas, a young man with an easy smile, a beautiful wife, and young daughter.

Then late in 1977, he finished his shift, left the station, went home, and hanged himself.

His friends were devastated, left with grief, guilt, and irreconcilable questions, notably: *What could I have done?* In the days following Douglas's death WHAS staff members took turns filling his afternoon shift. It was duty that only heightened their grief. They could fill the time slot but not their sense of loss. "We can take his chair," Melloy said, "but that's all we're doing. It's just somebody sitting in Jeffy's chair."

With his passing, the energy and work that had been invested in reinventing the station stopped, nearly paralyzed by the unforeseen tragedy.

"It was so unfathomable," Milton Metz said years later. "It was if we all had this yoke around our shoulders. Everywhere we turned there was some reminder of this talented kid we all liked so much . . . we needed something to help get us back on track."

Wayne Perkey had just finished his morning shift when his phone rang. It was Gary Burbank calling from Detroit.

"I'm sorry to call under the present circumstances," he said, "and I'm not really comfortable doing this, but I'm wondering . . ."

Perkey and Gary talked for a good, long while. After the conversation, Perkey hurried to station manager Hugh Barr's office. "I got the guy," he said. "Gary Burbank. He wants to come home."

Barr was incredulous. "Burbank wants to come here? You're kidding."

Perkey was reminded of the words of one of Kentucky's most popular statesmen. "It's like Happy Chandler says, 'I never met a Kentuckian that wasn't coming home.' Let me fill you in . . . . "

Soon, the moving vans were lined up in front of Gary's house on Riverside Drive in Windsor, Canada. Cosmic Bob had been there since early in the morning, helping Gary and Carol pack. In the disarray that comes with any move, Gary talked about going back to Louisville.

Yes, he was taking a step backwards. Yes, there was the pay cut. He wasn't even sure what he had agreed to. The pay cut might be more than $50,000. He didn't care. Besides, WHAS had talked about a television show and providing him with a producer and writers.

"Was any of it in writing?" Moody asked.

"I trust 'em. I know these people. They're good for it."

"You trust too much," Moody said.

Suddenly, Gary thrust his hands into his pants pockets. His face was stilled, as if he had been stopped by some complex problem.

"I don't have any money," he said.

"What?" Moody asked.

"I don't have any money. I need money for the road."

"What are you saying?"

"I'm saying I don't have any money," Gary said. "Carol, where is our money? Do we have any money?"

"In the bank," she said, her voice echoing from another part of the nearly empty house.

"What bank?"

"Transferred," she said. "To Louisville. All taken care of, Gary."

"Do we have cash for the trip?"

"We have cash for the trip," Carol assured.

"You don't know where you did your banking?" Moody asked.

"Uh, no," Gary said.

"Never been to the bank?"

"No. Why?"

"Never cashed a check?"

"No."

"Never made a deposit?"

"No."

"Never inquired about the Canadian/American exchange?"

"What?"

"Never mind," Moody said.

Gary's arrival at WHAS buoyed both the station's spirits and its ratings. Those who had known him during his years at WAKY agreed that this was a different, more mature Gary Burbank, both in performance and personal demeanor. Gary was in his late 30's. His experience at The Big Eight and in New Orleans had elevated his humor, and he seemed genuinely happy to be back in Louisville.

In the first minutes of his first WHAS broadcast, he played "Foggy Mountain Breakdown." As the record concluded with a flourish of banjo

Gary said, "Boy, I know I'm home now, hearing Earl Scruggs on the radio." There was no haste in his delivery. He was comfortable and relaxed. It was almost as if there was a sigh of relief in his voice.

He introduced the Reverend Deuteronomy Skaggs and Pete Moss with Gardening Tips. He chided himself for hitting the wrong buttons and talking over commercials. The phones in the front office rang all afternoon. Gary Burbank was back in Louisville and Louisville was glad to have him.

In character and out of character, he cast himself as a member of his own audience. He had a podium, but he kept it at ground level, and not long after Gary's return to Louisville, WHAS unveiled its new slogan: *We're Serious about Having Fun.*

The *Courier Journal* assigned a feature writer to do a story on Gary. The story was headlined: "WHAS Takes Off Its Tie." Gary took special pleasure in the headline. "I only wear a tie when I'm least expected to," he said, which was true enough. He once showed up to judge a tobacco-spitting contest wearing white tie and tails, and gleaming white slippers.

Metz and Gary, an unlikely duo, became great friends, in part, because of their shared dislike for personal appearances and live reports from the Kentucky State Fair—mandatory for all staff members.

"We were given the onerous task of playing handmaidens to our listeners for hours at a time regardless of their level of intelligence or the banality of the conversation," Metz said.

"Onerous? I like that," Gary said. "See, Milton, that's why I call you 'The Master Broadcaster.' Such command of the language. And that stentorian delivery."

"Stentorian? Splendid, Gary. I know you agree with me because I have seen you shy away from the masses at the fair."

"I'm just not comfortable around crowds of people," Gary said.

"I know," Metz said. "I've seen your methods of escape."

When the crowds grew too large, Gary had two paths of retreat. He might slink out of the WHAS tent and around back where he was obscured from view by trucks and vans. Hidden away, he would gauge the winds and light up. "He liked to smoke these little cigarettes with no writing on them," Metz said. "Gary would return in a far better frame of mind."

If Gary was charged with doing remote reports from the fairgrounds, he often chose another retreat. Engineers from the station transported their equipment to the fairgrounds in large, reinforced cardboard boxes, which

were usually left around the tent. They were approximately three feet deep and five feet wide. Overwhelmed by the crowds, Gary took his microphone and headset, climbed inside the box, and closed the lid. His voice boomed through loudspeakers but he was nowhere to be found. Unless, as Metz pointed out, one followed the cords that led to Gary's hideaway.

From this lowly vantage point, he conducted make-believe interviews with make-believe visitors at the fair: Lizzie and Pearly Gates, sisters from Trimble County, in town for the pie-judging contest; Delmond Sizemore, who had just returned from showing his shoats; and Elwood Scroggins, from Perry County, who just stopped by to say, "Hey."

From the box, Gary used voices that matched the names springing from the recesses of his mind.

"And," Metz said, "what he did from the box was probably far better than any actual interview he or anyone could have obtained at the fair. It was dreadful duty. I wish I could have found it within myself to join him in his retreats."

Instead, Milton Metz—ever gracious—shook hands, made friends, suffered the insufferable—and

> Gary was back in Louisville, a different person. He was more mature, and so was his humor. He invented Snow Sharks, and he covered the state fair while doing interviews from a cardboard box. The interviews? Gary talking to the characters in his head.

smiled when Gary rumbled out of the box, soaked in his own perspiration, entangled in cords.

"Thank God for the box," Gary said.

To that point in his career, Gary's days at WHAS were his most inventive. Perhaps it was a matter of the comfort level he sensed at home. Carol was able to spend time with her family and friends she had known since high school. Gary didn't worry about being away so much.

For the first time in his career, he truly had the space to develop the shtick he'd always hoped to. He drew from the everyday matters of life that inconvenienced, bewildered, or angered his listeners and did so with an apparent ease because he always considered himself one of them.

In January of 1978, the Midwest was relentlessly pounded by a blizzard of unprecedented proportion. Temperatures dropped well below zero. Snow fell for days. The winds reached hurricane level, turning daylight into a white, stinging curtain that immediately froze against any surface in its path. Snowdrifts reached as high as fifteen feet on Louisville's streets. Sections of the Ohio River froze and, where it didn't, chunks of ice caused flooding. Schools and businesses closed. A state of emergency was ordered and the National Guard was deployed.

People were shut in, stir-crazy, faced with power outages, fuel shortages and, most of all, the debilitating effect of their own company and anxieties.

In the midst of it all, Gary was trudging his way to work, fighting the ice on the streets, the muck on his windshield, and the thin tread on his tires. It took all of his concentration, then he saw something peeking out from a huge snowdrift. What was it: a sail, some large triangle frame, some figment of his imagination? What was it?

He couldn't stop. Going forward was hard enough in these conditions. He couldn't risk his small frame in these high winds. *Might end up in Pee Wee Valley*, he thought. But what was it? He drove on, chain-smoking, obsessed with what he had seen or imagined he had seen. Then, it hit him: a dorsal fin. Jaws, he thought. He couldn't wait to get to the station.

In the '70s, three movies had a visceral impact on the country: *The Godfather*, *The Exorcist*, and *Jaws*, Peter Benchley's epic tale of a great white shark that terrorizes a New England beach community.

That day he spent his entire show talking about Snow Sharks, prowling Louisville; Snow Sharks on a feeding frenzy throughout Kentucky, diving from snowdrifts upon innocent citizens trying to shovel their walks. He dug out John Williams's haunting soundtrack, playing it underneath his admonishments about these arctic creatures.

His sense of the absurd struck a chord in a community faced with an unfamiliar and dangerous reality. The WHAS switchboard was flooded with calls, all reporting Snow Shark sightings. The operators swore at Burbank, as they often had occasion to do.

Snow Shark pictures were painted on trucks and barns. The *Courier-Journal* and the *Louisville Times* ran pictorial essays on the phenomena.

Each day, Gary developed the bit further.

Here's what you do if you are approached by a Snow Shark . . .

Always, John Williams's theme and Johnny Thompson's tuba thumping that threatening tone in the background.

"Here's what he did," said Dan O'Day, a long-time friend, comedy writer, and radio consultant. "He created an alternate sense of reality and forced it upon the outside world. That's how real comedy is born. That's where Gary links up with Kovacs, Jonathan Winters and Carson."

Gary poked politicians and kept a watchful eye on popular culture. By 1980, when the television series *Dallas* was gripping households across the country, he recorded "Who Shot J.R." It made the *Billboard* charts and landed Gary a spot on the nationally syndicated *John Davidson Show.* He sang at Opryland with actor Larry Hagman, who played J.R. Ewing on the CBS series. When the Kentucky Derby rolled around, Hagman made a point of finding Gary. It wasn't hard, as he was hanging out with New Orleans band leader Al Hirt, who had encountered Gary during a Derby party and bellowed, "Why the hell did you leave New Orleans?" Another recording, *Music to Listen to Records By*, a collection of Gary's bits, was a WHAS promotion, a regional hit, and the proceeds went to The Crusade for Children.

And offers continued to come from major markets.

"No thanks," he said. "I'm happy here. This is where I am going to stay."

Gary and Carol had just moved into a new home with a big backyard and a pool. It wasn't far from Carol's parents, Nancy and Hank. Everything was fine until a new station manager showed up at WHAS.

Gary was on the air when he had his first face-to-face discussion with him. During a newsbreak, he walked into the studio and sat down at the console across from Gary.

"Hey," Gary said, "how's it going?"

The manager stared at Gary, his eyes wide and unblinking. "You make too much money," he said. Then he got up and walked out of the studio. Gary also found himself on notice for that cardinal radio sin—missing spots. Sometimes he played the same ones over and over. He had not complained when the station failed to deliver on its promises to provide him with a producer. But because of this, he couldn't keep up with all the things he needed to do.

He might win small skirmishes here and there, but he wouldn't win the war. For a time, he managed an uneasy truce.

"Gary had an artist's mistrust for management," Herb McCord said, "and, in some cases, rightfully so. He never believed they had any interest in the creative aspects of radio, and his mistrust was not always misplaced."

"Yes, he missed some spots and he wasn't great about filling out all the reports we had to do," Metz said. "But he made up for it on the air. He was wildly popular but he wasn't appreciated by all."

As for Gary, he was at home, replaying the events that led to his departure from WHAS, wondering if he had been too brash and abrupt.
He went through it again in his head.

He had just finished one of his favorite bits, Eunice and Bernice, the Siamese twins attached at the telephone. The bit ran long and he missed another spot. Then the manager burst into the studio. "You did it again," he said. "We talked about this. We've talked about it over and over. Miss another spot, and I'm going to take action," he said.

At WHAS he branched out. He invented new characters—notably Peed Moss who gave gardening tips—and he made records, too. There was, it seemed, so many people in his head. And his work was finding employment for all of them.

Gary said nothing for a moment. He was fed up. "Okay," Gary said. "I don't want to put you under that kind of pressure or me. Today will be my last day."

And so it was. Just like that.

He sat in the dark, the reality of his actions settling upon him. For the first time in his adult life, he didn't have a job. He paced around the house. He went for a walk. Nothing eased his anxiety.

What the hell am I gonna do? he wondered. *Where the hell can I go?*

He walked and he smoked. He was worried. He was someone who had to work, needed to work.

Gary's absence from WHAS was headline news in Louisville. "One

day Gary Burbank was there, giggling and laughing and clowning it up on the radio and the next he was gone," wrote Tom Dorsey, *Courier Journal* television and radio critic. "Burbank passed from the radio scene without even a parting gasp. The news staggered his fans, who never had a chance to say goodbye . . . It's hard to believe we won't be hearing his wild and crazy routines anymore. Burbank is every bit as talented as Steve Martin — maybe even more . . . when he bolted from the station . . . it left a hole in WHAS's schedule as big as Burbank's talent. He is irreplaceable. Everybody knows that. Somebody else will be heard in the afternoon at 84 on the dial, but nobody will ever replace him."

Look on the bright side, he thought. He was dead to WHAS but he'd gotten himself a fine obit.

In the first days following his departure from WHAS, Gary puttered around the house, read, and spent time with Carol and Tracy. He went to see Sean in Mississippi and the folks back home. Occasionally, he made appearances to promote his 45: "Who Shot J.R.?"

For a time, he enjoyed this new freedom but not for long. As many times as he had banged his head against the desk in frustration over an impending deadline, he missed the rush that accompanied the pressure of performance.

Performance, he understood, was his addiction.

He was restless, no longer comfortable in Louisville. There were too many questions about WHAS: Why did he leave? Was he coming back? What was he going to do?

There were offers to come east or go west, but in deference to Carol's wishes, he reluctantly declined. He fumed with frustration. "I'm not going back to bagging groceries just to stick around Louisville," he said. "I tried that once. They're still cleaning up Hogue & Knott's."

Consequently, he accepted the first reasonable offer that came his way. Taft Broadcasting, based in Cincinnati, was looking for someone to do a two-month stint at its Tampa station, WDAE.

Gary didn't know if he liked Florida or not. He had not spent much time there, but he liked Randy Michaels's voice on the other end of the phone, and he knew how much he missed working.

"Sure," he said. "I'm in."

The weather was wonderful, but the wages were abysmal. To make matters worse, the only people who seemed to know about WDAE were

Tampa's football fans, stout souls who weathered woeful seasons and listened to Buccaneer games on the only station that was willing to hitch its creaky wagon to the team.

After working at The Big Eight and The Cuddly Giant, Gary busied himself spinning records for a station no one listened to. But for some reason—he wasn't quite sure why—he believed in Michaels and thought his stint on an alligator farm in Tampa might lead somewhere.

He sat on the porch of a rented townhouse overlooking the Hillsborough River, the sun coming up like a nectarine through a violet curtain. A soft breeze carried the scent of hibiscus and citrus. People in sculls rowed down the river. He sipped coffee and smoked a cigarette.

This is pretty damned nice, he thought, *but it can't last. Still and all, who in his right mind could argue with that sunrise?*

His name was Joe Scallon. He was programming director at WLW in Cincinnati and he was thinking of making some changes.

"Gary," he said, "what would it take to get you to come to Cincinnati? Of course, you know WLW is a legendary station going back to Powel Crosley."

Gary did know WLW. He remembered the night he first heard the station. It was in Böeblingen, and he and some other GIs were trying to tune in something other than Armed Forces Radio.

"Cincinnati?" someone said. "How the hell is the signal getting all the way over here? And this clear?"

Gary didn't know much about Cincinnati. He had passed through a couple of times. He knew about the Reds, Pete Rose and Johnny Bench, and the Bengals. He knew they once made lots of beer there and he remembered reading that it was called "The Queen City," which always made him laugh.

What he knew most about Cincinnati was its proximity to Louisville.

Maybe, he thought, *this is the perfect compromise.*

"Think it over," Scallon said. "This might be a good place for you."

Part V

Finding home

Chapter Twenty

The good doctor

It was a match made in, well, if not heaven, then some other tourist spa. And it proved to be one of the most successful broadcast pairings since Fibber McGee and Molly. Given the humor of Doc and Gary, though, it might have been more like Gomez and Morticia.

In Cincinnati, two college kids jumped in their car and

headed south across the Ohio River toward Florence, Kentucky. Kevin Wolfe and Eddie Fingers were aspiring radio heads pulling night shifts at WSAI-FM and bent on a career in broadcasting. Fingers was on the rock trail. Wolfe had something else in mind.

"You have to hear this guy Burbank," Wolfe said. "Does all these characters."

"Never heard of him," Fingers said. "Why are we driving to Kentucky?"

"We can get a better signal. He's at WHAS in Louisville."

Minutes later, they pulled into a fast food restaurant, ordered Cokes and fries at the drive-thru window, parked the car, and tuned in the radio.

"Listen," Wolfe said, "he's spoofing the farm director—this guy named Barney Arnold."

Ring!
Gary Burbank: Hello, WHAS.
Arnie Barnold: Hello, Gary, this is Arnie Barnold calling.
GB: Well, it's Arnie Barnold. What can I do for you, Arnie Barnold?
AB: Gary, I just saw a very violent act, and I wanted to ask you something. Last week, did you play a song called "Fly, Robin, Fly?"
GB: Right! I played a song called "Fly, Robin, Fly" and a lady called in, and if this is any kind of comment on today's society, and her child, who was eight years old, thought the record—and this is true, folks—thought the record was about one fly mugging another fly: "Fly, Robin, Fly."
AB: Gary, I hate to tell you, but I believe it's true. Because I just saw a robin get mugged by two pigeons and a blue jay.
GB: Ohhh, come on . . .
AB: And three squirrels say they witnessed the crime but didn't want to get involved.
GB: What?
AB: Yeah, now the chief of police tells me that gangs of violent birds are now the single biggest threat to public safety.
GB: Oh, come on, Arnie!
AB: Yeah, listen: I understand now a bunch of swallows have knocked over the First National Bank.
GB: Arnie . . .
AB: And they've barricaded themselves inside Capistrano, and they say they won't be taken alive.
GB: Oh hey, that's silly . . .
AB: They're holding two cats as hostages.
GB: Holding two cats hostage, huh?
AB: And they've demanded amnesty plus 100,000 pounds of unmarked birdseed.
GB: Unmarked birdseed? Arnie, look . . .
AB: We're terrified out here. In my neighborhood the citizens are terrified of gang fights going on between the canaries and the whippoorwills.
GB: (pause) Arnie, have you been smokin' those 'maters again?

AB: Just one.
GB: I think that was enough.
AB: Oh. Well, it was nice talkin' to ya.
GB: Bye, Arnie.
AB: Bye, Gary.
SFX: Click!

"Great stuff," Wolfe said.

"He's out there," Fingers said.

Wolfe was so taken with Burbank's show that he made it a regular part of his day. He would finish his shift at the station, sleep for a while, and run his daily errands from two until six when Gary was on the air. Often he found himself parked, sitting alone in his car and laughing out loud.

He did more than simply listen to the show. He recorded it. He pored over it as if it were a topographical map, examining the terrain. He made notes about the characters. He wrote lines he thought would work in the show, clipped odd stories from the newspaper, and sent them to Gary. He sent him a handcrafted Christmas card. It was a picture of Earth spinning in space and adorned with garden peas. The caption read: *Peas On Earth.* Wolfe invited Burbank to the screening of his senior film project at Xavier University, a blend of science fiction and satire called *Teletypes from Mars.*

Wolfe's correspondence went unanswered until late 1980 when it appeared his career had stalled. He lost his job at WSAI-FM when the station went from album rock to country. He picked up some weekend work at a small station in Hamilton, Ohio, and continued his writing, wondering all the while if he should consider a more secure profession— maybe insurance or public relations.

Then one day, his telephone rang.

"Is this Kevin?" asked the voice on the other end.

For an instant, there was a flicker of recognition. It sounded like Gary Burbank, but it couldn't be. Burbank had mysteriously disappeared from WHAS. Wolfe had heard he was working somewhere in Florida.

"Yes," Wolfe said.

"Kevin, this is Gary Burbank. I'm coming to work in Cincinnati at WLW. I'm wondering if you would like to do some writing for the show?"

Wolfe chuckled. Had it not been for the voice, he would have judged this as some cruel joke. Gary said he was impressed with the material Wolfe had sent him. "Funny stuff," he said. "I kept your phone number from the invitation to your film project. What was it?"

"*Teletypes From Mars*," Wolfe said.

Gary laughed. "Sorry I didn't make it," he said. "I'm wondering if you could come meet with us in the next few days."

There had been no discussion of money or hours, yet Wolfe had already abandoned his thoughts of life in a coat and tie.

Gary's negotiations with WLW and Cadillac Joe Scallon hinged on one thing—the need for a full-time producer. He needed a skilled editor with a thorough knowledge of the area, a sense of humor, and an appetite for an abnormal amount of work.

He was presented with two candidates—technicians with no genuine interest in comedy. "Neither one of these guys will work," Gary said. "But I might have a guy who will."

Scallon was a businessman who readily admitted he didn't know much about radio—other than what *made* good radio—but he believed Gary could take the station to a level beyond religious programming and farm reports.

"It's your call," he said.

Wolfe was convinced he knew Burbank's taste for material as well as anyone, but he was understandably nervous about meeting him. It was entirely possible, he thought, that the man behind the comedy could be nothing like the person who delivered it.

Burbank was walking around the hotel room in white socks and worn blue jeans. Another man, incredibly relaxed, sat on the couch.

"This is a good friend of mine," Gary said, "Len King. We go way back. He's coming to WLW as the news director."

Wolfe took a seat.

"Mind if we smoke?" Gary asked.

"Not at all," Wolfe said.

Gary lit up, took a drag, and offered the smoke to Wolfe. Wolfe took it gingerly and immediately passed it to King. "I like this guy," Gary said. "You passed the first test. All the more for us."

Days later, Wolfe was seated in an office at WLW's headquarters on Fourth Street. Across the desk was George Cooper, the program director, who seemed distressed. "Gary wants to hire you as his full-time producer," he said, "but I don't have a spot in my budget for a producer."

Wolfe felt himself sinking into disappointment. "What I can do," Cooper said, "is hire you as on-air talent. That is in my budget."

Wolfe walked through the revolving doors onto Fourth Street. Everything was a blur. He was in his 20s. He had just accepted a job paying more money than he could imagine, $26,000 a year, and it was the job he had dreamed about.

The tape box whistled through the air before crashing into the wall. "Son-of-a-bitch," Gary yelled. "Where the hell is that sound effect? They promised me the package of effects would be here by now."

He picked up another box and fired it into the wall. Gary and Kevin had been given two weeks to prepare for their first show. For ten days they had worked hand-in-hand, Kevin prepping Gary on the Cincinnati scene, its politics and various peccadilloes. Kevin sat at the console surrounded by mounds of tape. Papers were strewn about the room. Wastebaskets were overflowing and Gary was on a rampage.

"Gary," Wolfe said, calmly. "We don't go on the air for four days. There's plenty of time. We already have a lot of good stuff here."

The two of them took on the entire city. And they did it in such a manner that even those who found themselves skewered managed to laugh at their own wounds. Most of them, anyway. Doc provided a reading of the place, and then Gary took flight.

"No," Gary barked. "That's it. I'm done. I quit. I'm outta here."

"Wait," Wolfe said, "you're quitting before we even *start*?"

There was no answer, just the door closing behind Gary as he rushed down the hall. He was in one of his explosive moods, not quite sure what he was going to say to George Cooper or how he would say it. He was thinking about this when he passed the studio and saw James Francis Patrick O'Neill behind the microphone doing his show. He admired O'Neill.

My God, Gary thought, *that's 'The Morning Mayor' and he doesn't even know why I'm here.*

He stood for a moment, thinking about how people were suddenly deemed obsolescent and kicked out the door. He never wanted to be in that position.

"George," he said, arriving at Cooper's office, "you haven't told JFPO that I'm here to replace him?"

Cooper said he would get around to it.

"Don't you think you should get around to it soon?" Gary said. "I'm going on the air in a few days. Don't you think you owe him that? The man's a legend here. And where in the hell is that sound effects package you promised me? If you don't get it for me fast, I'm outta here."

"Calm down, Gary. It will be taken care of and I *will* talk to JFPO . . . ."

The production room door opened. Wolfe hadn't moved.

"So where were we?" Gary said quietly.

"We were working on the presidents' piece," Wolfe said. "Ronald Reagan with Nancy in the trailer park in Cheviot, getting away from Camp David for some peace and quiet. But Gerald Ford is outside bouncing chip shots off their trailer.

"I was thinking that we could try something like this," Wolfe went on. "You do a great Jimmy Carter. Let's add him to the mix. Maybe throw in Billy Carter as a bartender working in the background."

"What about Nixon?" Gary said. "Let's add Nixon."

"We can have Carter and Nixon and Ford calling the show from the Old Presidents' Home in Newport . . . ."

Wolfe listened closely as Gary recorded, moving through one voice to another. He captured Carter. His Nixon was impeccable and his Reagan wasn't bad at all. *He doesn't do impressions*, Wolfe thought, *he does caricatures*. Gary was able to find the chord in a voice that made it flawlessly strike the right notes. The result, Wolfe concluded, was a comedic effect somehow more real—and human—than the impeccable voices produced by Rich Little and Frank Gorshin.

But that was one of the things Wolfe liked about Gary. No matter where his mind turned, he was always looking for the human element.

Two days before Gary and Wolfe were to begin their show, James Francis Patrick O'Neill had still not been informed that he was being replaced as WLW's morning man. Gary took things into his own hands. After O'Neill had finished his show, Gary walked into the studio.

"You have no idea why I'm here, do you?" Gary asked.

JFPO said he did not.

"No one has told you, have they?" Gary asked.

"I think I know now," O'Neill said. "I was afraid of this."

"I'm sorry," Gary said.

They walked to George Cooper's office together. There was nothing he loved more than performing on radio, and there was nothing he hated more than the business of radio.

In the spring of 1981, there was one thing left to do before Gary and Kevin took the air. "We have to find you another name," Gary said. "Kevin Wolfe just won't do."

Gary viewed Kevin as an academic. He suggested Professor Wolfe.

"No," Wolfe said. "We've already got 'The Music Professor,' Jim LaBarbara."

"How about 'Doctor?'" Gary mused.

Wolfe smiled. "My dad called me 'Doctor' when I was little," he said. "But then he called everyone 'Doctor.'"

It was the strangest marriage the Queen City had ever seen. By most accounts, though, it was a compatible union and Doc's (bottom) neatness made up for Gary's undomestic side. The truth was, they BOTH thrived on their own brand of disorder.

"Doctor Wolfe," Gary said. "Hmmm, how about Doc Wolfe? Doc Wolfe, Media Urologist?"

"I could predict acid rain and do the station drug tests," Doc said.

Gary loved this kid. He hired him to be his guide and conscience, but given his own mercurial nature, how long could he and Doc see things the same way?

More than thirty years later, Doc would say, "It was never an issue. Most comedy teams succeed until one goes in a different direction. But for a few years before I started with Gary, I had listened intently to what he was doing. There was no going in the wrong direction because I knew where he wanted to go, and we were both going to the same place."

In the first weeks Gary Burbank and Doc Wolfe were on the air, things

v0ices in mY heaD
248

stacked up: complaints, tape boxes in the hall, fan mail, hate mail, and phone messages. Most of the complaints came from the sales department because Gary continued to miss spots—sometimes as many as seven a day—and when any of the sales staff went to the studio or production room to talk to him about it, he threw empty tape boxes at their heads.

"I never hit one of them," Gary said, when confronted by management. "My control is excellent."

While the stacks of fan mail and hate mail equaled out, they bore one striking distinction. The fan mail was generally handwritten, while the hate mail was typewritten and came on company letterheads.

Gary and Doc were stirring the staid Queen City social pot, and its leaders didn't like it. Their message was clear: "We don't do things like that around here."

The response came back equally clear: "We do now."

P.J. Bednarski was among the new wave of journalists who arrived in Cincinnati in the early 1980s. He wore his hair long and his tie loose. The radio and television critic for the *Cincinnati Post* had a devilish wit and an eye for anything new and different—as long as it was good. He was a Cleveland native of Polish descent with a degree from Ohio University and a penchant for ruffling the feathers of various media peacocks.

"You know a lot of people around here are not going to like you," Bednarski said, after a long interview with Gary.

"Why's that?" Gary asked.

"Because this is Cincinnati and Cincinnati likes its own," Bednarksi said. "It has its own little caste system. There's the upper class old money, then there's everybody else. They like it that way and they'll do what they can to maintain their sense of superiority."

"That's ridiculous," Gary said.

"But true," Bednarski said. "This is *conservative* Cincinnati, the smallest big town you'll ever experience. They don't like people who challenge their way of doing things—the way they've *always* done them."

Cincinnati was, after all, the home of Procter & Gamble, General Electric, American Financial, and the Cincinnati Reds, who Bednarski said took as much pride in their clean-cut image as they did in their back-to-back world championships, as if the two were inextricably connected.

Bednarski told Gary about the chasm between the east side of town,

where the wealthy resided, and the West Side, populated heavily by blue-collar Catholics who alternated mass and the corner pub and kept their wealth—more considerable than Hyde Park might have imagined—in their mattresses. Then, too, the ancestors of the eastsiders were often the settlers of the West Side.

"Damn," Gary said. "I'm glad I bought a place in Indiana."

Largely reliant on Doc's reading of the city, Gary ran Bednarski's views of Cincinnati past his sidekick.

"Oh, yeah," Doc said. "Did he tell you about city council passing legislation on how many yard sales you can have in a year?"

"What?" Gary asked.

"There's an ordinance in Hyde Park that dictates when you can put your garbage out."

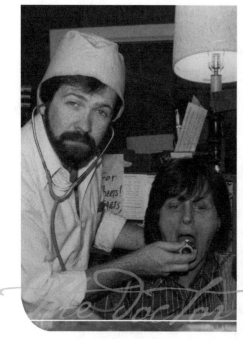

"What?"

"Seriously," Doc said. "In Hyde Park you can't put your garbage out before dark."

"My God," Gary said. "I love this town."

Bednarski's feature story praised Burbank for his irreverence and wit, and he predicted that Burbank's arrival at WLW signaled a welcome—and overdue—change on the local media scene. Where Ruth Lyons, Bob Braun, and *The 50-50 Club* once reigned supreme, and Paul "Baby" Dixon did the Chicken Dance,

> While there was sometimes a doctor-patient relationship between Doc and Gary, it was difficult to tell who was which: they could BOTH wield the scalpel. The good part was that while there might be a wound, it was always a superficial one.

now there was a sassy new sheriff in town.

Burbank lampooned WCPO's Al Schottelkotte, whose nightly newscast set the standard for local television news. Schottelkotte was the grim steward of a newsroom filled with folks who feared his ire—all of whom whispered about their boss's infamous tirades.

Gary and Doc Wolfe gave Cincinnati Al Waddlebody, suggesting that

Al's demeanor—so often terse and dour—was the direct result of whether he won or lost during his daily poker game at Maketewah Country Club. Waddlebody was, they concluded, a perpetual loser.

Schottelkotte was livid. Who was this Burbank and how dare he say such things? Schottelkotte cried slander and libel. Cadillac Joe Scallon, a Boston native, recognized an exposed nerve when he saw one and gave Gary an even greener light.

Frank Weikel was a popular, longtime city-side columnist for the *Cincinnati Enquirer*. Each of his columns included a section entitled "Darts and Flowers," wherein Weikel offered his personal praise and criticism for those he found worthy of attention.

Gary created Weikel-Weikel, noted for his daily banalities and aristocratic manner of speech.

"I want you to stop doing this," Weikel snapped over the phone. "Besides, I don't sound like that when I talk."

"But nobody knows that," Gary said. "And that is the way you sound on my show."

"Isn't it odd," Gary said, turning to Doc, "how those who hold others accountable hate being held to any form of accountability."

At first Cincinnati tittered behind its collective hand. Then it laughed out loud. At least a portion of the city had grown weary of demagoguery.

When the Major League Baseball players' strike hit in the summer of 1981, Burbank and Wolfe voiced their concern for those involved in an industry where the minimum salary was, at the time, $60,000 a year and, consequently, asked their audience to participate in a canned food drive to assist Reds players like Johnny Bench, Dave Concepcion, Ken Griffey, and George Foster who were undoubtedly "living under an overpass near you, sleeping under tattered blankets, and preparing their food with a can of Sterno."

"By the way," Gary wondered, "what was the winner's share back in '76 when the Reds won the series."

"Over $26,000 for every player," Doc said.

"And what was it last year?" Gary asked.

"Nearly $35,000," Doc said.

"Dear me," Gary said, "and that's on top of their salary, right?"

"Yep," Doc said.

"And what's the average salary?"

"About $150,000."

"Hmmm. So anyway folks, be on the lookout for members of the National Guard who will be going door-to-door to secure donations for our players who need your help so very much."

The phone rang in Gary's office.

"Gary, this is Johnny Bench. I wanted to tell you how much I appreciate the canned goods that were delivered at my house today. I can't thank you enough. I was down to my last slice of Wonder Bread."

As the NFL season began, Gary and Doc unveiled "All My Bengals," a daily soap opera focusing on Paul Brown's football team; its coach, Hall of Famer Forrest Gregg; and the players, most of whom Gary crafted to sound like Kingfish on the old *Amos 'n' Andy Show*. The star of "All My Bengals" was Gregg, born and raised in Birthright, Texas, and honed by Vince Lombardi's will in the arctic winters of Green Bay, Wisconsin. Gregg was 6-foot-4, 250 pounds, and he lived by one rule—no bullshit.

"Hey, Gary."

"Yes?"

"This is Forrest Gregg. I just wanted to tell you how much I enjoy 'All My Bengals.' Damn, boy, sometimes I got to pinch myself to make sure it's not me on the radio."

"Glad you like it."

"Sure do," Gregg drawled. "Why don't you come on over to the practice field sometime. Love to meet you and so would some of the players."

"I bet they would," Gary said.

"On second thought," Gregg said, "you might want to just keep on doing what you're doing."

When Gary learned Cincinnati financier Carl Lindner was one of the richest men in the country and refused virtually all media requests outside of *Forbes* and *Fortune*, he created I.B. Ludlow. Bromley, the owner of the Ludlow Bromley Yacht Club and the richest man in the entire world.

Bromley, of course, frequently called the show. "Gary," he bellowed, "this is I (period) B (period) Ludlow (period) Bromley (period, period), the

richest man in the entire universe. You know I was thinking . . . wait, there's that skinflint Carl Lindner trying to sneak into my yacht club again. S'cuse me just a second. Hey, Lindner, why don't you pull one of those shabby old dollar bills outta your pocket and come over here and shine my shoes."

But armed with 50,000 watts and a listening audience that stretched throughout the Midwest and into twenty-eight states, Gary and Doc realized they had to reach beyond Cincinnati for material.

And it wasn't a problem.

Chapter twenty-one

Serious about fun

When Gary's stable of loopy and original characters were unleashed upon an unsuspecting world, no one had any idea of what *mayhem* might ensue. Even Gary. Whatever it was, radio surely had never heard anything like it.

No one was laughing. No one ever laughed. They might as well

have been roofers or bricklayers, laboring over an intricate pattern.

Doc sat silently in front of the console, a stack of papers and faxes before him. Gary paced about the production room, now and then taking a swig from a can of Mountain Dew.

"It doesn't work," he said. "It needs something."

"I know," Doc said. "What if we try . . . ?"

"Damn it," Gary said, interrupting. "He wouldn't say that. It's not true to the character."

"That's what I'm getting at. That's where it's off. Let's step back and look at it this way."

"We're running out of time," Gary said, looking at the clock. "We've only got an hour before the show."

"We've got plenty of time," Doc said. "Let's fix it."

Producers and interns were gathered in the hallway. "How's it going in there?" one asked.

"Gary's ticked off. It's one of those days," someone said. "The pressure is exhausting."

"Yeah, who would have thought comedy was such serious business," another said. "I just hope I don't have to go in there for anything."

"If you do, you might want to wear a helmet."

Then Gary burst into the hall. "Now, that's funny," he said. "See, Doc, you were worried over nothing. Oh, hey guys. What's up?"

"How's it going?" one said.

"All screwed up," Gary said, heading down the hall. "This whole show is gonna suck."

To those on the fringe of Gary's show, the daily preparation was a grim exhibition in mayhem: tapes thrown in frustration; wads of crumpled scripts spilling from waste cans; razor blades and grease pencils feverishly flying; Doc sorting through mounds of newspaper clippings, looking in one book or another for the perfect reference; Gary swearing and scribbling last minute notes in a cursive that only Doc could decipher—and no one laughing. There was rarely a smile until the show was ready to air.

That's when everyone else showed up. Earl Pitts, Deuteronomy Skaggs, and Gilbert Gnarley, all those whom Gary seemed to trust more than he trusted himself. They, of course, were the stars of the show. He was merely their vessel.

Gilbert Gnarley was a confused, eccentric resident of the St. Pia Zadora Golden Buckeye Retirement Community, who on a daily basis made phone calls to everyone from CBS newscaster Ed Bradley to the corporate headquarters of Holiday Inn.

Ring!
Customer service: Holiday Inn.
Gilbert: Yeah, my name is Gilbert Gnarley, G-N-A-R-L-E-Y, and I's

calling in reference to something. I, it's, ah, who do you talk to, to turn yourself in for stealing towels?

CS: Okay, are you calling about a little piece of paper we sent you?

Gilbert: I went to confession and Father Hibiscus said to call and confess and take my punishment.

CS: You really did take towels from the Holiday Inn?

Gilbert: I don't know why he wants me to confess and take my punishment, you know, you're supposed to get off easy at confession. Usually you just have to do three laps around the cloister and dip your head in the water seven times and say a hundred Hail Marys. But no, I gotta take my punishment. I'm being persecuted.

CS: Well, sir, there's really nothing we're going to do for that. We have people that have sent checks on towels that they have taken from Holiday Inn, and we really don't miss them that much.

Gilbert: I do love your hotels. You know it's funny, I'm a traveling salesman on the road, you know . . .

Gilbert was a bumbling Everyman, the good-hearted duffer down the street who sometimes leaves his lunch in the mailbox. His confusion isn't dementia; it's the world's confusion at all its own artifice. There's a bit of Gilbert in each of us.

CS: We certainly appreciate you calling about that, but don't worry about it.

Gilbert: I was thinkin', you know how the library has Amnesty Day for overdue library books? And you can return them at no charge?

CS: Uh-huh.

Gilbert: You can have, like, Amnesty Day and you return your towels with no penalties.

CS: (Laughter) Well, that's a good idea, we'll think about that.

Gilbert: I have hundreds. I have hundreds of towels.

CS: Just don't worry about it.

Gilbert: Oh, I don't know. It does weigh on my mind. How about an Amnesty Day for ashtrays, bed sheets, mattresses, and ice machines?

CS: *Well, just try not to take any more, and we'll understand. Okay?*

Gilbert: *Okay, I won't take any more at all because I feel so good that you talked to me about this. I never took an ice machine, by the way.*

CS: *Well, good. We're glad you didn't take an ice machine.*

Gilbert: *I know a guy who did. I bought it from him.*

CS: *Oh, goodness.*

Gilbert: *See, I . . . if it's from Holiday Inn, it's hard for me to resist. I mean, the paintings on the wall. You have wonderful stationery, by the way.*

CS: *Oh, well, the stationery is complimentary.*

Gilbert: *I must have fifty Gideon Bibles. My whole house is done in the Holiday Inn, uh, mo . . . motif! I sorta look at it as my "Away From Home Home at Home."*

CS: *Well, we certainly understand.*

Gilbert: *You know, people often come to my door and they tell me that it looks like a Holiday Inn! I guess that is 'cause of the sign out front. But I only took one of them. I don't know why they come to my door though, I always keep the "No Vacancy" lit up.*

CS: *Don't worry about it.*

Gilbert: *Okay, maybe it's a sickness or something. I'm a HolidayInniac. (Chuckles).*

CS: *We're glad you stay with us, sir.*

Gilbert: *This is better than having to do laps around the cloister, and sayin' a hundred Hail Marys, and dipping myself in the water seven times. Well, all right, okay, I won't ever do it again.*

CS: *All right, bye-bye.*

Gilbert: *Okay, okay.*

Every "Gilbert" sprang from an idea and the spine of a script, while the success of every "Gilbert" relied on the reaction of the other person on the line and Gary's ability to ad lib.

Ring!

Customer Service: Marketing.

Gilbert: *Yes, my name is Gilbert Gnarley. G-N-A-R-L-E-Y. And I want you to know that you've got a happy consumer on the line.*

CS: *Okay . . .*

Gilbert: *I just want to tell you how much I enjoy your Kentucky Jelly.*

CS: Uh . . . what kind of jelly?

Gilbert: Your jelly.

CS: KY Jelly?

Gilbert: Yes, it's the best stuff. I like the way it comes in a tube, you know. And it's very convenient.

CS: Okay . . .

Gilbert: And other brands like Smucker's, they come in jars, I think . . .

C.S.: I think you've got the wrong company.

Gilbert: If you do any commercials, I'd like to do a personal testimony for you. I even wrote a poem . . .

CS: But, sir, I think you've got the wrong company.

Gilbert: Jam is gritty, apricots are too smelly . . .

CS: Sir? Hello!

Gilbert: I just love my Kentucky Jelly.

CS: But we don't make that type of jelly, sir.

Gilbert: Let me just say one thing, though? The taste is a bit neutral, but it has a nice texture and it spreads so well on toast.

CS: Wait a minute. We don't make that kind of jelly.

Gilbert: Well it says "Kentucky Jelly." Actually it says "KY" . . .

CS: Yeah, but that's not . . . (laughter)

Gilbert: I think you should print calories and fat content on there, too. Do you have a little recipe booklet you could send out?

CS: Okay, hold on for one second. I'm going to transfer you to someone, okay?

Gilbert: Certainly. That's nice. Thank you.

Ring . . . ring . . .

Customer Service 2: How may I help you?

Gilbert: Now, I just talked to that very nice lady who switched me to you. Do you have any recipes?

CS2: Any what?

Gilbert: Any recipes?

CS2: No! Because it's not meant for cooking.

Gilbert: I don't cook it. I just like to put it on a sandwich. But I want to tell you that the serving size I have, I mean, I can go through half a tube in one sandwich. Do you have any recipes or suggestions . . .

CS2: No sir, it's not meant to be eaten.

Gilbert: (Long pause) Hmm, could you repeat that?

CS2: It's not meant to be eaten.

Gilbert: Well, what, pray tell, would one do with jelly if not eat it?

CS2: The KY Jelly is . . . a . . . personal lubricant.

Gilbert: (Long pause) A personal lubricant? Oh . . . you mean when you have to . . . uhhh . . . you have to stick your little dingy-wangy . . . into that . . . hole . . . at the blood pressure machine at the mall?

CS2: (Laughter)

Gilbert: 'Cause, you see, my finger's too fat? It's like . . . I can't get my blood pressure . . . took. But I put this on my sandwich! This is not Kentucky Jelly?

CS2: I'm sorry, you may have the wrong number. Are you referring to KY Jelly?

Gilbert: "K-Y," and then it says "Jelly."

CS2: It's a personal lubricant.

Gilbert: Well doesn't the "KY" stand for "Kentucky?"

CS2: (Long pause) No.

Gilbert: Gasp! What does it stand for?

CS2: It's just some letters that were given to us . . .

Gilbert: I'VE BEEN EATING A PERSONAL BODY LUBRICANT??!!?

CS2: Yes . . . I guess you have.

Gilbert: UUUGGHUAAHHHH!

CS2: There's nothing harmful in it. Could I have your address? One of our medical staff may want to get in touch with you.

Gilbert: Oh, that's okay. I've got my own physician I can see about this.

CS2: All right, I would suggest you do so.

Gilbert: So you suggest I should see a physician about this?

CS2: Well, it's a safe product, but it's not meant to be eaten.

Gilbert: I'll see a safe physician, then. Okay?

CS2: All right.

Gilbert: Okay?

CS2: Thank you.

Gilbert: Okay? Okay.

Gilbert's art lay in his innocence, his craft in his wry stealth; he seldom let anybody get off the phone. Gary's own pleasure in the character rested upon the fact that Gilbert—not the person he phoned—was the butt of the

joke. Gilbert Gnarley was so utterly free of guile that everyone wanted to help him.

Earl Pitts, Uhmerikun, on the other hand, was a cantankerous, hard drinking, gun toting, truck driving, cigar smoking, middle-aged cuss fed up with everything politically correct—all the folderol that softened the country where he was by God born and raised. Every day, in syndication across the country, Earl spoke impoliticly out. When the world turned on smokers, Earl lit up.

Real smokes is fer real men. And I ain't talkin' 'bout them wimpy little plastic tip jobs. I'm talkin' 'bout eight-inch roll monsters, what take 'bout four hours of industrial puffin'.

Earl Pitts was the view from across the aisle. He was from across the tracks, across the river, and just plain cross. He wasn't related to Gilbert Gnarley, but they shared characteristics: Earl, too, was relatively benign. His bark was worse than his bile.

The ingenuity of Burbank's irascible creation lay, of course, within the creator himself. For it was nearly impossible to distinguish where the true intent of the sketch actually lay. Was it a screed against do-good social deputies trying to arrest the earth of tobacco products? Or was it a satire of the smokers themselves, that smelly, raspy-voiced gaggle of folks huddled on the leeward side of buildings, yearning to breathe free no matter what it cost them? Given Burbank, it might have been either—or both. To Burbank, humor was its own reward. Sometimes humor was the *only* reward.

When the world tilted toward coffee salons and delis with a mind-numbing array of options, Earl Pitts, Uhmerikun, demanded a return to simplicity.

You know what makes me sick? You know what makes me so angry I just want to lick a live battery terminal?
Me and my ol' buddy Dub decided to stop in for some chow on our way

to the big gun and knife show. So we walk into one of them yuppie-butt delis, and the waitress asked us what we wanted to eat. We said, what else? Baloney sandwiches. She asks, what kind of bread you want it on? I say, what kind of bread you got?

She said they got rye, dark rye, German rye, rye with caraway seed, pumpernickel, crescent roll, sourdough bread . . . and something called . . . peter bread.

Peter bread?

I mean, who on earth is gonna eat a baloney sandwich on somethin' called . . . peter bread?

I said: Ain't you got no Wonder Bread? You can't make a real man sandwich unless you got Wonder Bread. Bread ain't supposed to look like some sissified French buns. Real bread looks like drywall—WITH CRUST!

Wake up, Uhmerika! If Wonder Bread was good enough to build me a strong beer gut twelve ways, it's good enough to build me a baloney sandwich at some yuppie deli. This country was built on white bread, and don't you forget it!

I'm Earl Pitts Uhmerikun, Pitts Off!

With the proliferation of books and articles on self-improvement and the glut of psychiatrists mending the tattered world's woes, Gary and Doc wondered what happened to common sense. Their answer was Carl Windham, whose solution to every problem—regardless of the complexity or absurdity—was always the same.

Music in:
I am earth,
I am sky.
When we kiss,
Mother Nature turns to smile.
Announcer: It is time once again to consult the wisest man in all the world: Carl Windham. As usual, all phone lines are full, so please do not attempt to call at this time.
We will now take our first caller. Yes, you're on the air . . .
Caller1: Yes, I'm chief of police, and we have riot here in Philippines.
Announcer: I see.
Caller1: They break through our lines and head for Presidential Palace.

All we have to fight with is fire hose.

Announcer: A fire hose? Well, do you have a hydrant nearby?

Caller1: Yes, we have hydrant nearby. We could hook the fire hose up to the hydrant.

Announcer: Carl, we have rioters in the Philippines heading toward the Presidential Palace and they have a fire hose hooked up to a hydrant. What should they do?

Carl: Put some water on 'em.

Caller1: Okay! Thank you! God bless America!

SFX: CLICK.

Announcer: Let's totally change topics now. Let's take a call dealing with . . . ignored ultimatums.

SFX: THUNDER

Caller2: Carl, this is God.

Announcer: Carl, we have a supreme being on the phone. What's the problem, guy?

Caller2: Well, Carl, I've got this planet that's inundated with sin and debauchery. I gave them Ten Commandments. If they obey three, I'm lucky. Except for this one guy named Noah. He's building this ark thing. Basically, I've had it. What can I do to this planet to show my total disgust?

SFX: THUNDER

Carl: Put some water on it.

Caller2: Carl, I'm glad I made you. Bye!

Announcer: Let's take a call about completing novels, and on the phone, you say your name is . . . ?

Caller3: Yes, I'm Ernest Hemingway.

Announcer: How Ernest, may we help you with your novel?

Caller3: I'm writing what I'm going to call The Old Man and the Sea.

Announcer: The Old Man and the Sea? I like it already.

Caller3: And I've got this big fish, this old boat, a foreign kid, and an old man. But something is missing.

Announcer: Ernest Hemingway is having trouble with his book. Carl, what is missing from the book?

Carl: Put some water in it.

Caller3: My God! It does make sense! Carl, the next time you're in the Keys, give me a call!

SFX: CLICK!

Announcer: Wow, I think you've earned some points, Carl. As usual, you've been a bottomless well of wisdom. Thank you for gracing our airwaves today.

Carl: Ain't nothin' but a thang.

Music out:

When we kiss,

Mother Nature turns to smile.

And before each show ended there was usually an appearance by Reverend Deuteronomy Skaggs, whose performance was aided by the voices of the flock that included Leah Burns, Sally Rivera, Heather McIntyre, Duke Sinatra, Roger Naylor, Doc Wolfe, and others.

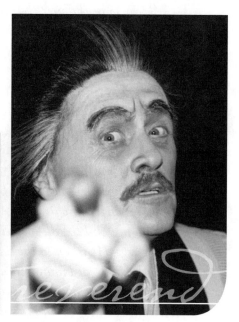

The Reverend Skaggs was Gary's real altar ego. He'd met the stereotype of the radio evangelist in the 1960s when they showed up at his station. And heaven was a clear signal and listening folks still generous with their love offerings.

While Gary had been performing Skaggs since his days at WAKY, the reverend flourished in Cincinnati and largely because of the complement Doc and others brought to bits like "Gospelooza."

Flock: Amalulah!

Skaggs: Welcome to the power hour of bliss! The Reverend Deuteronomy Skaggs and the Little Radio Church of the Right Winged Gospel Truth is on the air.

Chiffon Pie: Prices at the pump have gone sky high, and your spirits are way down low. And with your piddily vacation budget, there's nowhere fit to go. But listen to the Reverend; he's got some dandy news. The spirit-filled summer getaway that will chase away your blues.

Skaggs: Amen! Thank you, Sister Chiffon Pie. Join us, brethren and sisteren, this weekend at the Reverend Deuteronomy Skaggs Gospelooza Tent Revival!

Flock: Amalulah!

Skaggs: Ohhh, they'll be preachin' and singin' and testimony and lots, lots more! Praise the Lord! Give a loud shout of thanks unto Gawwwwwwwwwwwwwwwwwwd for this righteous event, amen.

Skaggs: You know, flock, I was on my knees in prayer, and the Lord, he put a message in my heart. And he said unto me, go to an empty field on the outskirts of the city and set thee up a tent.

'How many cubits?' I asked. And the Lord said 'Skaggs, who knows about cubits anymore? That's Noah stuff. Just make sure it's bigger than anything L.L. Bean's got.'

Flock: Amalulah!

Skaggs: Oh, yes! The tent is up! The t-shirt and food vendors have signed their contracts. And the above ground combination baptismal pool and dunking tank is supposed to arrive today. Hah! We are ready for you, dear hearts!

Flock: Amalulah!

Chiffon Pie: Gospelooza has it all! You'll wanna stay for days! We set ourselves up a campground! And for the kids, we got the Slip N' Slide of Repentance and the St. Francis Pettin' Zoo. Amalulah for the pettin' zoo!

Skaggs: Hearken to the word of Gawwwwwwwwwwwwwwwwwwd from the Book of Hominominies, not your Old Testament, not your New Testament, but your present testament, writ by me. In those days, when it is a hundred degrees in the shade, and yard dawgs will not come out from under the porch, shameless young girls will wear tight halter tops and cut-offs way too short. Satan hath used the summer solstice to tempt and torture us! Gawwwwwwwwwwwwwwwwwwd wilt thwart the Evil One by raising up a servant . . . That'd be me . . . Who shalt shelter and amuse you, and keep your children off the streets. Say Amen!

Flock: Amalulah!

Skaggs: Now friends, don't make me holler, don't make me shout. I want you to come to our Gospelooza Tent Revival and turn your pockets inside out. I want you to eat fudge, drink Coke floats, and witness wet T-shirt Baptismals. I want to see them little green rockets fly from thy pockets and sail under my tent flap now! Amen, flock!

Flock: Amalulah!

"Think about it," said Randy Michaels, who took charge of WLW

in 1983 and is currently chief operating officer of the Tribune Company. "Three and four hours of original comedy every single day. None of it repeated. The best of it was incredible and the worst was still funny. Even on the days when he was off, Gary still made us laugh. When he was on, there was nobody in the country funnier than he was."

Gary was explosive and mercurial; Doc was calm and soft-spoken. While Gary searched for the alchemy of comedy, Doc applied logic and focus to it. Gary seethed with creative energy while Doc recognized the benefits of restraint.

When Doc stacked piles of material about the studio, Gary wanted everything filed away. Gary was chronically late; Doc was true to the clock. For all their differences, they were a perfect fit: Doc played Sancho Panza to Gary's Don Quixote, a blend of logic and fantasy that led to years of companionable success. Battles were settled by compromise, but there were instances when Gary refused to budge.

Doc pushed Gary to repeat bits from the first hour of the show, arguing that listeners who heard it then were most likely not around later to hear it replayed. Gary said he wouldn't compromise any element of the show. Every segment, he said, would have new material.

"It's not compromise," Doc said. "It's just good math. It's realism."

"No, we're not repeating anything," Gary said. "This show has got to be as good as it can possibly be every day."

In the race, Gary only had eyes for the vehicle; Doc watched the race itself.

"Doc was the perfect handler for Gary," Michaels said. "Not only did Doc know how to bring Gary back, but he helped him on a number of levels. Doc was a great music guy, a great voice guy, and he was an unbelievable writer. His 'Senseless Surveys' . . .

Ring!
Hello?
Riley Girt: Hello, you're on the air with Riley Girt and the U.S. Senseless Survey. This is a follow-up to our survey conducted a few years ago, and we'd like to ask you a few questions.
Citizen: (Pause) Yeah . . .
RG: Have you voted in an election since 1966?
Citizen: Uh, you say you're from the Census?

RG: Senseless.

Citizen: Uh, yeah.

RG: Next question: do you believe that the U.S. would be more competitive with Japan if our television cartoons returned to their formerly violent status?

Citizen: I don't see it . . . No, I don't think—well, I don't know what the research says, but, um I wouldn't think so. Not off the top of my head, no.

RG: Next question: would you approve of any of the following more humane methods of execution for death row inmates: being lethally injected in their sleep?

Citizen: (Pause) Um, I . . . I'd need some time to think about that. Um . . .

RG: I understand. What about eating tainted fish as a form of execution as opposed, to say, the electric chair?

Citizen: That's ridiculous.

RG: Lethal drinks, provided that the felon is given a choice of flavors?

Citizen: (Long pause) Are you serious?

RG: Yes, sir.

Citizen: Well I think this is a stupid question. I really do.

RG: No sir, just senseless. Next one: heart over-stimulation and cardiac arrest by letting them get hopped up on PCP and look at really naughty magazines?

Citizen: Um . . . no. I guess I don't go along with that.

RG: How about being allowed to quote 'escape, and rush into the path of an oncoming semi?'

Citizen: This is ridiculous, I . . .

RG: Well, this particular one was suggested by a prisoner himself who said he would get the feeling of freedom for a brief moment before he was hit by a truck, but that would be better than getting a lethal injection in prison and knowing that there was never any chance or any possibility of being free—even for just a moment.

Citizen: Yeah . . . how long is this interview going to go on for?

RG: Just a few more questions, sir, and then we'll be done.

Citizen: Uh-huh . . .

RG: If the emergency ever arose, would you let a qualified proctologist examine your dental work?

Citizen: So, if the emergency ever arose . . . ?

RG: Yes, for instance, say you had a stabbing toothache, and there was a situation where there was not a dentist around, would you let a qualified proctologist examine your dental work?

Citizen: As long as he washed his hands first . . .

RG: And our final question: do you think that Satanism is getting a bad rap merely because of a few quote: 'whackos'?

Citizen: No.

RG: I'm required to read a disclaimer by law, so please bear with me. I'll try and go through this quickly. Any similarity to questions on this survey to queries living or dead is purely coincidental. Any similarity to simulated queries is intentional. Any similarity of the sound 'BLAH' to the previous sound 'BLAH' is factual and cannot be denied. Repeating the 'BLAH' was only necessary to illustrate the point, and not a frivolous 'BLAH' like that one was. A gratis 'BLAH' just occurred in case you hadn't noticed. Thank you very much for your answers here today on the Senseless Survey.

Citizen: Hmm. All right.

RG: Goodbye.

CLICK.

When Gary wasn't preparing for the show or on the air, he was either entertaining his co-workers or driving them crazy. In the early 1980s, Jim LaBarbara's show followed Gary's. LaBarbara was polite and soft-spoken, an enthusiastic advocate of all things Cincinnati. He was also fastidious.

When Gary's show was over, LaBarbara would enter the studio, offering compliments while Doc and Gary busied about clearing away the morning's clutter.

LaBarbara always thanked them for their consideration and Gary always failed to remove one object that LaBarbara regarded with a mixture of disgust and horror—Gary's seat cushion, the traveling cushion: a soiled, dilapidated pillow that had been with him since his days in Jackson, Mississippi.

"Doc," LaBarbara asked, "could you please move that?"

"What?" Doc said. "Oh, Gary's cushion? Sure. It's just a cushion, Jim."

"Has it ever been washed?"

"Hmmm, doesn't appear that it has. There now, it's gone. Have a good show."

"Thank you, Doc."

LaBarbara's reaction only served to inspire Gary, who fully acknowledged that his cushion was rather gamey.

LaBarbara's mailbox in the hallway was directly below Gary's. Each day when Gary arrived at the studio, he gathered his mail, reached into his pocket, and pulled out an old pair of tube socks. He unfurled the socks and tacked them to the mailbox so they hung down in front of LaBarbara's slot.

Then he waited for the plaintive cry from the hall.

"Doc, can you please help me?"

Eventually, and at Doc's urging, Gary stopped antagonizing LaBarbara. "He's such a nice guy," Doc said.

"I know," Gary said, "that's just it."

"Gary drove the engineers and techs crazy," Michaels said. "They loved him on the air, but he was always breaking stuff. A bit wasn't going well, he's slamming stuff against the wall, throwing things around the production room. And they have to fix it.

When news anchor Dan Buckles first appeared on the local scene, the promo photos carried an autograph to his mother: 'Mom, I always shop at Oak Hall for my above-the-waist apparel.' God knows where the rest of it came from.

"One day Gary and Doc are recording and something goes wrong with one of the phones and Gary goes nuts. He's beating the receiver, pieces are flying through the air and he's cussing and yelling.

"One of the guys says something to me about it and I go get him. 'C'mon, I need to talk to you.' He's going crazy: 'Goddammit this. Son-of-a-bitch that. The equipment is crap. How's he supposed to work?'

"I say, 'Hey, I understand. I'll get it fixed.' So he starts to calm down and I say, 'I just need to know one thing—how often you gonna do this?'

"He looks at me and now he's off again. I say, 'No, really, how often you gonna do this?'

"He says, 'What the hell are you talking about? I don't know.'

"I say, 'Well, I need to know. Once, three times, ten times?'"

"He says, 'Why?' and he's all pissed off."

"I look at him and smile and say, 'Cause I need to know how many phones to buy.'"

"And it was over. Just like that. Five minutes later he's back down the hall with Doc turning out something that no one else would do. Yeah, Gary could be temperamental, but most true artists are . . . it's like they say in Kentucky: 'The best horses are the toughest to ride.'"

Ranger Bob was an old cowpoke and host of a children's show that forced fantasy and reality into the same vial and came away with a political statement.

Ranger Bob: Howdy boys and girls and all you little whippersnappers, it's your old pal Ranger Bob, brought to you by Mush.

Music:

When it's hot mush time at breakfast,

When it's time for us to eat.

Ranger Bob: Eat it! Use it to bury your pet gerbil. Just get rid of it so your mommy will have to buy you some more!

Ranger Bob: Well today, whippersnappers, we have a fairy tale for ya!

Kids: Yay!!

Ranger Bob: Now, you all know the story of Snow White, don't ya?

Kids: Yeah!!

Ranger Bob: Well, what do you think happened after the prince awakened Snow White and took her off to his castle uptown?

Little girl: She lived happily ever after?

Ranger Bob: Not quite. You see, Prince Charming was what we call a "rounder." He kissed Snow White and woke her up, but once he'd done that, he was away all the time kissing Sleeping Beauty and other women sleeping around in the kingdom. He sweet-talked Rapunzel into letting him climb up her hair and then seduced Cinderella into letting him slip her the ol' shoe.

Little girl: He's bad! Just like my first daddy was! What happened to Snow White?

Ranger Bob: Well, she'd been abandoned with seven dwarves to feed. She went to the wicked queen to apply for A.P.D.D.

Kids: What?!

Ranger Bob: Apples for Princesses with Dependant Dwarfs.

Little boy: But the queen had tried to kill her!

Ranger Bob: That's the way the government works. The queen had become a democrat. Beauty was not important. She wanted to help Snow White because women should be able to succeed without a charming prince. So the queen started a program called *Affirmative Apples*, which provided free apples to Snow White to make pies for the dwarves. The queen went to the mirror and said, 'Mirror, mirror on the wall, who's the fairest one of all?' and the mirror said, 'My queen, in fairness, you are beyond compare. What is more fair than your apple welfare?'

Ranger Bob was an old cowpoke right out of the nineteenth century. What did Gary know? He never knew what time it was anyway. Ranger Bob's kiddie show was slightly addled, or perhaps Bob was. The content certainly was.

Little girl: And they lived happily ever after?

Ranger Bob: Nope! Snow White kept on getting free apples, and then she claimed disability due to a sleeping sickness caused by the queen's poison apple in the original story.

Kids: Hmmm . . .

Ranger Bob: So, the queen had to provide forest creatures to clean the dwarfs' house and do the laundry. The forest creatures began to complain. They said the queen should get Snow White off welfare. They said Snow White was irresponsible having so many dwarfs on public assistance. The queen began to worry that she might not get re-elected. So she made up a special poison apple. It was made with the heart of a newt. Now you all know that the heart of a newt is so small that Snow White would never find it.

Little boy: Did it kill Snow White?

Ranger Bob: Nope, the government can't be that openly heartless. It was a potion to give Snow White incentive. It would make her want to stop taking free apples from the government. And it worked!

Little boy: But how would she live? How would she feed her dwarfs?

Ranger Bob: Snow White resorted to the only skill she knew: kissing princes.

Kids: Kissing princes?

Ranger Bob: She sent word out to all the charming princes (and not so charming ones) that for fifty shillings she would give 'em a kiss. Then, later on, she wrote a steamy tell-all book and made millions!

Little girl: And they all lived happily ever after?

Ranger Bob: They all lived happily ever after!

Kids: Yay!!

Ranger Bob: Heh, heh! Glad you buckaroos liked that story! Come 'ere, horse. Giddyup! This here's your old pal Ranger Bob sayin', 'This here's your old pal Ranger Bob sayin', adios, muchachos!'

Kids: Adios, Ranger Bob!!

At Riverfront Stadium, Bernie Stowe, the Reds equipment manager, tuned the clubhouse radio to Burbank's show most afternoons. Stowe, who had been with the team since 1946, was a fan, as was Joe Nuxhall, the team's radio broadcaster. Together, Stowe and Nuxhall introduced Gary's show to many of the players.

"You got to listen to this guy," Nuxhall said, a cup of coffee in one hand and a cigarette in the other. "He's nuts."

Slowly at first, the players began to listen, then they laughed, and eventually when Burbank came to the ballpark, they sought him out as they would a movie star who had landed in their midst.

Ron Oester was a hard-nosed, thick-skinned second baseman who grew up in Cincinnati and suffered the combined effects of succeeding Joe Morgan and playing professional baseball in his own hometown.

"Gary," Oester said, "I got to ask you: How do you come up with all this shit? Where does it come from?"

Gary said nothing for a moment. "I don't know," he said. "How do *you* hit a 95-mile-per-hour fastball or a Steve Carlton slider?"

"That's just it," Oester said. "I don't. Not often enough. But you do!"

Chapter Twenty-Two

A promise forTracy

It was a time when everything seemed to be going his way. There was a new contract, awards, acclaim. And a new job offer, as well. And there was the rub: no man suffered more the good *fortune* of a job offer. For in moving on, the family had to move, too.

Gary's popularity and ratings climbed at a dizzying pace, but so

did the workload and the expectations. Doc seldom paused to admire where they had been or how they got there. Gary wouldn't allow it; he was too obsessed with reaching a summit that existed somewhere beyond the next winding slope in his mind.

Each day they came to work earlier and stayed later, tethered to the work. Some days, good material came quickly. When it did, Gary agonized over the ease of the process. On other days, when good material failed to come quickly, he agonized over the difficulty of the process. But every day, it

seemed, they emerged from their angst with new ideas or a new character. Lars Peavey was a product of this arduous comedy workshop and a tribute to one of Gary's favorites: *The Bob and Ray Show.*

MUSIC IN . . .
Lars: Thank you once again to the Bob and Ray Orchestra. Go ahead and take a break here, fellas. Okay?
Music cuts off abruptly . . .
Lars: Okay, thank you. I'm Lars Peavey and this, oddly enough, is the Lars Peavey Show. My guest today is Lazlo Sneedle. Mr. Sneedle, I understand you write reality-based children's books.
Lazlo: That's correct, Lars. I've long felt that children have the capacity to see the world as it really is, and I've dedicated my professional life to that end.
Lars: Could you give us an example of reality-based children's books?
Lazlo: Certainly. My first book, All Dogs Go to Hell, *would be one example.*
Lars: Excuse me, uh, Mr. Sneedle. Isn't that a little . . . strong . . . for children?
Lazlo: No more so than my second book, Strangers Have the Best Candy.
Lars: Uhh . . . Lazlo, I uhh . . . I really think that's a bad idea for a children's book.
Lazlo: Ya think so? Then I suppose you wouldn't like my third book, The Little Sissy Who Couldn't Play Baseball.
Lars: Mr. Sneedle, I think you expect too much from children.
Lazlo: Just trying to help the little bastards get along in the real world, Lars. Which, by the way, is why I wrote Grandpa's Not Asleep, He's Dead.
Lars: I think we've heard enough.
Lazlo: What about my new book, Daddy Drinks Because You Cry.
Lars: What a terrible message for children!
Lazlo: One book I've been toying with is called Where Would You Like To Be Buried? *I think it's a question children need to explore.*
MUSIC UP . . .
Lars: Oh gee, look at the time. The show's almost over.
Lazlo: I brought along a rough draft of a children's TV show I've been working on called The Adventures of Peter Pedophile. *You see, each episode starts with Peter in his apartment . . . Peter is 37 years old, single, weighs 450*

pounds, and has overactive sweat glands that make all his furniture . . .

Lars: Uhh . . . uhh . . . thank you. Join us next time on the Lars Peavey Show when my guest will be Dr. Akmed Blunt, a man who claims he's discovered the lost tomb of Billy Bobankhamun, the gypsy king who was believed to have invented beer. That's next time on the Lars Peavey Show. Until next time, so long everybody!

Music out . . .

Bob Trumpy was in the sports office at WLW with his producer, Doug Kidd, preparing for the evening's show when he suddenly interrupted Kidd. "Wait," he said, "turn the radio up. What the hell is he doing now? I've never heard him do this character before. Listen!"

Trumpy, a four-time Pro Bowl tight end with the Cincinnati Bengals, was one of Joe Scallon's first hires at WLW. After his retirement from professional football in 1977, Trumpy began his radio career at WCKY pioneering "sports talk" in Cincinnati.

He was 6-foot-6, 240 pounds, and his confidence matched his size. He was never in an argument he thought he didn't win. He was handsome, brassy, flamboyant, opinionated, and his voice—

In those heady days at WLW, the station became a kind of cruise ship, always off in uncharted waters and crewed by the wackiest gaggle of hands ever assembled in one place. On the good ship Lollygag, it was always a trip.

thickened by a stream of cigarettes and steaming, black coffee—sounded like it belonged in the tuba section of the Philharmonic. He had many friends and many enemies, and nothing concerned him less than the shifting numbers on either side. He feared no one and respected few, but Burbank and Wolfe—the "two little guys down the hall"—impressed him.

Trumpy knew Burbank had worked in Detroit, Louisville, and Florida; that he was paid well and successful, but assumed at first he was just another radio cowboy passing through.

"Then I started watching him," Trumpy said, "and how closely he and Doc worked together. I've never seen anyone put in so many hours or work so hard for a punch line. In radio, the more successful people are, the less they generally work. If they are going on at 6, they may wander in at 4:30, put their feet up on the desk, read the paper, go on the air and mail it in. Gary and Doc were the complete opposite. The more success they had, the harder they worked."

Like others at the station, Trumpy wondered how long Gary and Doc could maintain their frenetic pace. "Those first few years, it was just Gary and Doc, nobody else," Trumpy said. "They're working all the time, then all these people started showing up, these very bizarre looking people. Gary called them his *writers*. Lord!"

One afternoon, Trumpy encountered a small, quirky man in the hall. His hair was dark and mussed. His pants were too short and his shirt too big. He cleaved to the wall as Trumpy approached.

"May I help you?" Trumpy asked. The small man's eyes darted from side to side.

"May I help you?" Trumpy asked again, a little louder.

"Uh, Burbank. I'm with Burbank," the little man said, before racing down the hall.

Of course, he's with Burbank, Trumpy thought. *Who else?*

The little man in the hall was Kel Crum, one of Gary's most productive writers. What Kel lacked in social and sartorial skills, he made up in sheer brilliance.

"He *was*," Doc said, "Bartleby the Scrivener."

"Kel was off in his own world, and it was far more entertaining than ours," Gary said.

When Crum wasn't lurking about, Bill Tooker was. Tooker was a schoolbus driver from Columbus, Ohio, who looked, Gary thought, very much like Earl Pitts sounded and was equally abrasive in his approach to the world. Word was—though no one knew for sure—that Tooker had been disciplined for handcuffing an unruly child to a seat on his bus, a simple object lesson for others who chose to act up on the ride home.

With each conversation, Gary and Doc learned something new about Tooker.

"You know," he said once, "I used to be a sulky jockey."

"Really?!"

"Yep. Loved to go to the whip."

Tooker always wanted to bring his dog to the studios, but Gary asked him not to. Still, Tooker brought the dog—a floppy, friendly hound.

"So, you brought the dog?" Gary said.

"Yep," Tooker said, as the dog trotted off down the hall, walked into the station manager's office, and promptly relieved itself on the carpet.

"Bill," Gary said, "bring the dog anytime you want."

There was Jim Probasco, a high school band director from Kettering, Ohio, a master of satire. There was Mary Thomas Watts, the leading (if not only) liberal in nearby Clinton County. "Mary Thomas was our Molly Ivins," Gary said. "She was so liberal we had to tone her down and bring her back most of the time. She knew I liked *Designing Women,* the TV show, and that I had a thing for Annie Potts. So for my birthday she presents me with this pair of panties she swore she got from Annie.

"I'm looking at them and I say, 'But Mary Thomas, I don't think these have ever been worn. What good are they?'

"'Imagination, Gary,' she says. 'Imagination!'"

There was an old artistic maxim that suggested a relationship between art and obsession. Gary's obsession put your garden-variety obsession on a back shelf in the basement. In Gary's case, art and obsession were double-first cousins.

There was Damian Dotterweich, the man behind Buzz Fectal and his Dancing Parakeets, and Bill Brohaugh, who earned Gary's respect on a trip to Cumberland Lake when he went waterskiing in his blue jeans in the afternoon and wore the same pants to dinner that night.

These were some of the principal players in what evolved into the BBC, the Broadbank Burbcasting Corporation, a troop of eccentrically talented people who helped maintain the flow that Gary needed and demanded. Without them, he could never have done what he insisted on doing—everything new and fresh.

"And then you got the musicians," Trumpy said. "I guess they were

musicians. They had instruments but they were just as bizarre as the writers."

They were indeed musicians: the Goshorn Brothers of Pure Prairie League were regulars. H-Bomb Ferguson stopped in, as did blues man Sonny Moorman. Singer/songwriter Rufus Thomas, Gary's partner from WDIA in Memphis, came to see him, and one day he looked up and there was his old friend Eddie Braddock, the Memphis record producer: jeans, cowboy boots, aviator sunglasses, leaning up against the door with that sinister smile on his face.

"Any trouble getting in?" Gary asked.

"Nope," Braddock said.

"Why does that not surprise me?"

Regular callers and letter writers were woven into the show. There was Zero, a burned-out hippy who sounded like Tommy Chong at the zenith of herbal inspiration, and Pondicherry Griffin Laynerguyer, whose letters were as intriguing as his pen name. "Gary could find material in an ash can," John Phillips said.

While he seemed too distracted and jittery to listen—as if he was on some chronic caffeine buzz that made it impossible to hear anything beyond the ringing in his ears—he was, in fact, always hearing things, catching nuances in speech that others overlooked.

One fall night, Gary was working with Doc when he happened to hear Trumpy interviewing one of the Bengals players, a large lineman who was as earnest in his message as he was entangled in his language.

Days later, Gary and Doc debuted one of their most popular and longstanding characters, Synonymous Bengal.

> *Ring!*
> Gary: *Hello? You're on the air.*
> Synonymous: *Mr. Burjank, how does this afternoon find you?*
> Gary: *Uh, fine . . .*
> Synonymous: *I happen to be one of the Cincinnati Bengals, and most certainly would like to remain synonymous whereas I don't besmirch my reparation.*
> Gary: *I understand, yes.*
> Synonymous: *I'm calling you on my mobular cellulite helmet phone*

underneath Coach's desk here at Paul Brown Stadium.

Gary: Covertly, huh?

Synonymous: Yeah. Well Mr. Burjank, as you know from the incensed media coverage, there have been some off-the-field attraction with the team.

Gary: Yeah, there have been a few . . .

Synonymous: It is on this topic that I would like to defecate.

Gary: Please do.

Synonymous: First, A.J. Nicholson, who the Bengals drafted in April, was arrested and charged with erroneous buglery after he and a teammate broke into another teammate's humble commode.

Gary: Yes, I read that.

Synonymous: Yeah, and you also recall that Chris Henry was found to be driving while inoculated.

Gary: Yes, I did see that.

Synonymous: Well, he managed to be put on procreation, but I believe he had to agree not to drink and perhaps even attend a meeting of Alcoholics Unanimous.

Gary: I think he did say he would do that, yes.

Synonymous: But then to evaporate his already strenuous situation, Chris has now been accused of supplying alcohol to two convalescent females.

Gary: That's the worst part, I think.

Synonymous: Now Mr. Burjank, I must remind you that both of these men are ignorant until proven guilt-free.

Gary: You're right about that.

Synonymous: From what I can see, the fans and the media are jumping to concussions without knowing the facts. While both players may have been released on their own incompetence, they have to remain silent. But, as a teammate, I cannot hold on to my tongue.

Gary: You can speak all you want. I . . .

Synonymous: In both cases, Mr. Burjank, I am sure there are exterminating circumcisions. And neither Chris nor A.J. should be prostituted simply because they are athletes. They have a right to a fair trial, and be judged by a jury of their queers.

Gary: Yeah, I don't doubt that. I . . .

Synonymous: Mr. Burjank, I would like to ask you and the fans to forget about the teammates' illegal troubles and . . .

Coach (yelling): Synonymous!!!!!

Synonymous: Please accuse me, Mr. Burjank. Coach has called a team meeting so he can inspire us with a stirring melaphaligical story about persistence and courage in the face of adversials. Either that, or he's going to give us some ice cream. Catch you on the flip side!

Gary: Thank you for calling.

Click!

Through all the material and characters, Gary sounded like someone thoroughly enjoying himself. On the air, he never had a bad day. Even if he was ailing—if he had a cold or a cough or a troublesome tooth—that, too, became a part of the show, for nothing, in his mind, was as inescapably funny as the human condition.

That was the soul of all his characters, but none more so than Gilbert Gnarley. While Earl Pitts earned syndication, Gilbert might have been closest to the heart of Gary's comedy.

Ring!

Auto-answer: You have reached Mrs. Butterworth's consumer services. I'm sorry, but all of our lines are busy. Please hold on, and your call will be answered by the next available representative.

Gilbert: Isn't that nice?

Hold music . . .

Gilbert (singing to hold music):

Oh, Mrs. Butterworth,

I love the syrup that you have inside.

Other women have blood and corpuscles and things,

But you have syrup inside.

Syrup inside. Syrup inside.

And I love to pour it out your head. Thank you!

Ring!

Customer Service: How can I help you?

Gilbert: I'm so happy that I'm talking to a gentleman. My name is Gilbert Gnarley. G-N-A-R-L-E-Y. I'd like to pose a very delicate question concerning Mrs. Butterworth syrup.

Customer Service: Okay . . .

Gilbert: What happened to her . . . uh, protuberances?

Customer Service: Excuse me?

Gilbert: Well, Mrs. Butterworth used to have these . . . ummm, protuberances. You know? She used to have two protuberances. And I loved them. Not because they were protuberances, but, you see, they were full of syrup. And now the bottle has changed and I feel like I'm being cheated out of two protuberances of syrup.

Customer Service: Really?!

Gilbert: You're not getting this. Do you understand what I'm saying here?

Customer Service: (Pause) I do understand. I'm not really sure if I want to hear it.

Gilbert: I'm sorry. I've offended you. See, I knew I would. I was trying so hard not to offend you. Did I offend you?

Customer Service: You didn't offend me.

Gilbert: They flattened out the bottle, didn't they?

Customer Service: (Pause) I don't know. I have no idea.

Gilbert: Have you seen the bottle?

Customer Service: I haven't really paid that close attention . . .

Gilbert: Well the bottle used to have . . . you know . . .

Customer Service: I'll tell you what, give me your zip code, and I'll forward your concern to our packaging staff.

Gilbert: Maybe you could make up for the loss of syrup in her protuberances by giving her a larger behind. You know, I like large behinds . . . if they're full of syrup, you know. That's what I meant. Mrs. Butterworth was always so voluptuous, you know. I used to hide her in the cabinet, and when my wife wasn't around, I'd take her out and I'd . . . turn on Jack LaLanne on the TV and pretend that we were doing aerobics together.

Customer Service: (Pause) Okay . . . well, we appreciate your interest in our products and I'll certainly let them know, you know, you're noticing the change.

Gilbert: It was strictly plutonic, though. We were just good friends.

Customer Service: (Pause) Mmmm, hmmm . . .

Gilbert: Let me add sir, that you've been very professional to speak with.

Customer Service: Thank you.

Gilbert: I didn't mean to say anything offensive. I'm not that kind of person.

Customer Service: (Pause) That's okay. You know, we all make observations...

Gilbert: *Can I say one thing, sir?*

Customer Service: *Sure.*

Gilbert: *Without those protuberances, Mrs. Butterworth looks a lot like Aaron Neville in a dress. Doesn't she?*

Customer Service: *I haven't paid that close of attention.*

Gilbert: *She doesn't have that thing on her eye. You know that Aaron Neville thing he's got on his eye.*

Customer Service: *Yeah . . .*

Gilbert: *Now if you were to put that thing on her eye on that bottle, you'd have more syrup. You see what I'm saying here, sir?*

Customer Service: *Uh-huh.*

Gilbert: *It's just a thought.*

Customer Service: *Okay.*

Gilbert: *Okay?*

Customer Service: *Okay.*

Gilbert: *Okay. Okay?*

Customer Service: *Bye.*

Click!

At times, Gilbert got in over his head:

Ring!

976-MATES. This is Miss Frenchy.

Gilbert: *Oh, hi! Miss or Mrs. Frenchy?*

Miss Frenchy: *What is your name?*

Gilbert: *My name is Gilbert Gnarley, G-N-A-R-L-E-Y . . . and, uh . . .*

Miss French: *Gilbert, honey, how would you like me to take your . . .*

Gilbert: *AHHHHHNN-NNOOOOOOO!*

Miss Frenchy: *What do you want to talk about?*

Gilbert: *Boy, this drought's been something hasn't it?*

Miss Frenchy: *Ahhh. Uhhh. Ooooooh. Oh, Gilbert, how's your hot, sweaty . . .*

Gilbert: *SOCKS!! I wear tennis shoes. They are twenty-six years old.*

Miss Frenchy: *Are you hot?*

Gilbert: *No, no, it's been nice down here since last Monday. We had a cold front move through.*

Miss Frenchy: *What do you like to do?*

281

Gilbert: Well, I went horseback riding over the weekend. I had to quit because I ran out of quarters.

Miss Frenchy: I like riding, too.

Gilbert: Oh, yeah. It keeps me in real good shape. We got a nice one in front of K-Mart. It's a scaled down version of a palomino. I like to get on there and pretend I am Roy Rogers. You know Trigger was a palomino.

Miss Frenchy: Ooooooh. Ahhhhhh.Uhhhh. Oooooooh!

Gilbert: You know, you really got to do something about that asthma . . .

Meanwhile, the parade toward Gary's studio continued: the bizarre, the eccentric, and the celebrated—a confluence that sometimes led to the occasional bruised ego.

Miss America arrived at the WLW studios in a limousine with a coterie of handmaidens and publicists. She was tall and slender, a shimmering beauty of a woman who would stop a priest in his tracks. On any other day, she would have been the center of attention, but "The King of the Cowboys," Roy Rogers, was back in his hometown and happened to stop by the station.

While Miss America waited in a corner lounge, Gary, Doc and the crew swirled about Roy. Everybody had a question.

"Is Trigger really stuffed?"

"Where's Bullet, the dog? Don't tell me . . ."

"Did you guys use real guns?"

"I loved Pat Brady! What's he really like . . ."

"How's Dale?"

"How many kids do you have, thirteen, fourteen?"

"Gawd, how did you come up with those Double-R Bars? Best burger in the world . . ."

"The chicken is pretty good, too."

"Wait, where's Miss America?"

"Hmmm, uhhh, I think she left . . ."

"Really? So, Roy, how do you ride and sing and shoot at the same time?"

"Well, Gary . . ."

"Let's sing!"

Driftin' along with the tumblin' tumbleweeds . . .

Everything was coming Gary's way: new and lucrative contracts, a string of Billboard awards, attention from local and national media. He was written up in *Variety*. He was featured on the cover of magazines in Columbus, Ohio; Louisville, Kentucky; and under the headline "The Funniest Man in Ohio," *Ohio Magazine's* Randy McNutt wrote: "The Burbank Zone is a tear in the curtain of sanity . . . for four hours a day an army of the strange appears before your ears."

For the first time in his life, Gary's life seemed to make perfect sense, and when he could hope for no more, he received more—an old, aching wound was finally closed.

It was a quiet night, about a week after Christmas. Gary, Carol and Tracy were preparing for bed when the phone rang. It was Sean, Gary's son, calling from Mississippi. "I was 9 years old," Tracy said. "I remember exactly what I was wearing that night. I was wearing a flowered nightgown and I was sitting on the floor listening. All of a sudden dad yelled, 'You're kidding me! I'll be there as fast as I can.'

"He was so happy. He hung up the phone and said, 'Sean is coming to live with us.' There were tears in his eyes. In fifteen minutes he was on his way to Mississippi. The next day they were back with all of Sean's stuff. Finally, I had my brother, and my dad had his family together. Even as a little girl I could see how much that meant to him."

Tracy had seen Sean three times in her life: once in Canada, when she was 2 and didn't really remember; once more in Louisville during a court proceeding over child support and visitation; and the previous Christmas, when he came to visit for a few days.

Sean never told Tracy how he tired of trailer parks and food stamps. He didn't see the need. "My dad had a good life," Sean said, years later. "I wanted to build one."

Gary was happier than he had ever been, but he was also cursed with the fear that he would awaken one morning and the voices would be gone. Faced with this fear of abandonment, he turned to the only thing he knew. He worked harder, taking advantage of every whisper that came to his ear.

As Gary and Doc accelerated their pace, no character emerged with more clarity than Earl Pitts. The popularity of Earl Pitts lay in the fact that churlish Earl—thanks to Gary's linguistic agility—captured *two* audiences at once. One of them was—broadly speaking—Earl's relatives, all of whom loved him. The other was those who saw Earl as an arresting parody. Odd perhaps, but in their own way they, too, loved him. Even if unwashed Earl

was someone who, in their own manicured lives, they'd never otherwise encounter . . .

Music in (The Marines' Hymn) . . .

You know what makes me sick? You know what makes me so angry I just want to scrape the morning-after hangover stuff off my tongue with a cheese grater?

You ever hear of these things called "Murphy's Laws?" This guy name of Murphy come up with these laws about life. This guy figured that if anything can go wrong, it's gonna go wrong. You know, like a part that breaks down on a car is gonna be the most expensive part, and the part they gotta backorder.

Well, I got me a law, too. I call it "Earl's Law." It goes like this: nobody ever wants to talk to you 'til you're on the toilet. I guarantee you I could go home right now and nobody in my family will say "boo" to me all day. The kids are jabbering with their buddies on the phone, Pearl's watchin' her stories, and come suppertime, everyone of 'em got somewhere to go other than the dinner table. Come nighttime, if they ain't out terrorizin' the neighborhood, they're in their room listenin' to that music – ignorin' me. In the meantime Pearl's gettin' stumped by a Wheel of Fortune *repeat we already seen three times.*

Let's say, though, I grab the sports section and head to the john for a little CNN – the Commode News Network. Bingo! I become the most popular guy in town!

Knock! Knock! Knock! Daddy? Are you in there?

What do you want, Sandra Dee?

Can I have the truck tonight?

Knock! Knock! Knock! Earl? You in there? What do you want, Pearl? Dub's on the phone. You boys goin' bowlin' tonight?

Knock! Knock! Knock! Daddy? You in there? What is it, EJ? Did you see a frog in the toilet before you sat down?

I am not kiddin' you – the only time my family ever talks to me is when I'm in the john. I can guaran-dang-tee you these good-fer-nothin' wallet vultures are gonna miss me when I'm dead. I can see it now: They finally close that coffin lid . . .

Knock! Knock! Knock! Daddy? You in there?

Wake up, Uhmeriker! I say if the good Lord had meant for the bathroom

to be the family gatherin' place, he'd of created more than one seat in there. I think I'm gonna get me a port-a-potty out in the backyard. I'm Earl Pitts Uhmerikun, Pitts Off!

Eventually, Earl was syndicated in more than a hundred markets. There was talk of a national TV pilot. Gary's radio show became a staple of Cincinnati. He won nine regional Emmys for local television shows. He appeared as Earl (looking very much like Bill Tooker), Deuteronomy Skaggs, and Gilbert Gnarley.

"He was wildly popular," Doc Wolfe said. "Everybody wanted a piece of Gary. But unless management was always talking to him or talking about a new contract—no matter how long he had on his current deal—he thought they didn't like him and didn't want him. He was horribly insecure."

Even the best of radio jocks had a bit of vagabond about them. The open mike was always calling. The profession was tough, too: hired today, gone tomorrow. There was one thing that could keep Gary in place, though: a look from the kid.

The promise

Gary and Carol had just purchased a new place in Campbell County, Kentucky, not far from Alexandria. It was a sprawling home secluded by tall oaks and elms with a pool and a tennis court where the kids could play and Gary and Carol could entertain. It was two weeks before school started. Sean was headed for his senior year at Campbell County High School. Tracy was going into fifth grade at Alexandria Elementary. Boxes were strewn about the house. They were still settling in, finding things that had been packed away.

Carol was hurrying Tracy to cheerleading practice when Gary rushed through the door. The look on his face was one she knew all too well.

"I've just been offered a great job," he said. "It's in San Diego! San Diego, *California*!"

He was filled with an exuberance that stemmed from both new opportunity and the gratification that came with being wanted.

"It's great money, *fabulous* money. It's the chance to play the big . . ."

Tracy was ten, going on eleven. She was dressed in her Red Raider cheerleader uniform. When she interrupted, she sounded tired.

"Dad," she said, "Please. I've been to four different schools in five years. If we could stay here, I would like to stay here. I don't want to move anymore. I don't want to leave my friends behind. Not again."

Carol said nothing as Gary and Tracy looked at one another, Gary digesting what he had just heard.

"He had always made time for me and done anything I had asked him to do," Tracy said, nearly thirty years later. "But that night it was like he was seeing me for the first time, *really* hearing me. I could see it in his eyes, him really thinking about what the family had been through for his career. In retrospect, it was the self-absorbed words of a little girl. But he looked at me and said, 'You're right. We'll stay here. I promise.' I was so relieved. I'll never forget that moment."

Gary had threatened to quit many times in many places, but he had never thought about working in a single spot until it was time to walk away from it all. The very idea seemed as distant as the rings of Saturn. Now, it stared him in the face. It was there in his daughter's eyes.

"I promise," he said again. "We'll stay here."

The next day Gary walked into Randy Michael's office. "Randy," he said, "I want to stay here. My family is happy here. Can we work something out?"

"He had about a year left on his contract," Michaels recalled, "and of course I knew how valuable he was to the station. I had long felt you built a station around true talent. There was no replacement for it. I was prepared to give him what he wanted. I said, 'What would you like?' He said, 'I'd like a ten-year contract with a no-cut clause.' I said, 'Done.' I was prepared to give him far more than that. Gary was a horrible businessman, awful in negotiations. But he was motivated by things that don't always motivate others. I was always grateful to Tracy. Without her, we would never have kept him."

Chapter Twenty-Three

Going to the mountain

It had been such a good ride for such a long time that he was surprised to suddenly look up and see where the rest of the *radio dial* had gone. He didn't particularly like where it was all headed, but his head was still full of voices.

Each morning they arose before dawn. They cooked ham

and eggs. They baked biscuits and brewed big pots of coffee and stuffed their backpacks with the leftovers. Then they trudged past the switchbacks and into the Bob Marshall Wilderness. The higher they climbed the less they talked, leaving more of the world behind.

They were on a Montana mountain looking down on Holland Lake, a shimmering 400-acre mirror of all the magnificence that surrounded it: the high blue sky, the clean winds, the towering conifers.

There was snow on the peaks above them. It was September, and soon it would fill the basins.

The higher they climbed the more Gary wanted to dump from his pack. "Dammit," he said, "this is too much like work, and what about that sign back there, the one about grizzly bears? The last thing I want to do is end up in Yogi's picnic basket."

"Gary, you can't just dump stuff on the trail," Len King said. "Look at this place. It's pristine, totally *untouched*. You can't just drop your shit."

"Can't we just go sit on the dock?" Gary asked.

"No," Len said. "C'mon. You're gonna love seeing this. Just a few thousand yards to go."

"What?"

"Come on."

Holland Lake was Len King's discovery. From the first time he saw it, he wanted to share it with his best friends, those he viewed as brothers: Gary and Marty Bass, the principal players in what Marty called "The Traveling Minstrel and Medicine Show." Every time they gathered in the mountains, they laughed and told stories about Louisville and New Orleans. Then, one or the other would say, "The only thing missing is . . ."

"Phyllis Chapman," they said in chorus.

But they had all moved on. Len was working for Ted Turner's new network, CNN. Marty was an established television morning show host in Baltimore, and Gary was one of the most recognized radio personalities in the country.

They went hiking and fishing in the day and at night they built a fire in the fireplace, sitting around and reminiscing, laughing so hard tears came to their eyes: Len talking about how Ted Turner would show up at CNN's office on Techwood in Atlanta wearing a bathrobe and slippers; Gary telling about how he left a three-thousand dollar guitar, a gift from a friend, in the bathroom at a gas station; Marty recalling his cross-country trek from Baltimore to Missoula with a toilet seat as carry-on luggage.

"A real lifesaver," Len said. "The old one in the cabin had a crack in it and every time you sat down it pinched."

"Why didn't you keep it in the box?" Gary asked.

"Where would the fun be in that?" Marty asked. "You should have seen the looks I got."

During the 1990 trip to Montana, Gary was more distracted than usual. When they were hiking, Gary seemed oblivious to the countryside. When they were fishing, he couldn't sit still and muttered to himself. They were on an escarpment in the Missions when Gary broke a cardinal rule and slipped into serious shoptalk.

"Maybe I should go," he said. "If I drive down to Missoula, I can get a flight to Vegas and then to LA. I can still make it. There's still time."

Len was irritated with his friend, but he understood. He sighed. "First of all," he said, "how can you be sitting here in the middle of all this and *even* think about radio? Where would you rather be, here or hanging around in some banquet room with a bunch of radio people?"

Gary said nothing.

"Thought so," Len said. "Relax, Gary. Enjoy this while you can."

"You're right," Gary said. "What the hell. I probably won't win anyway. It's a Marconi after all."

"You will either win or you won't win," Len said. "It doesn't really matter if you are there. If you win, you deserve it. The only thing you miss by not being there is looking at all those people who think *they* should have won. C'mon, let's go."

"Up?" Gary asked.

"Yes," Len said. "Up."

So while Gary was a world away in Montana, sitting around a fire, Larry King won the Marconi Award for Network/Syndicated Personality of the Year. Don Imus was the recipient for Major Market Personality of the Year. The winner of the Large Market Award was Gary Burbank. He found out about it days later, when they were headed home.

"Feel any different?" Len asked.

"No," Gary said. "I mean, it's nice but . . ."

"See, told ya."

The following year, Gary was seated in a San Francisco ballroom wearing an ill-fitting tux. The jacket was too big and the pants were too short. He thought he looked like Kel Crum, his disheveled writer. He was as bored as he knew Kel would have been. He was in a ballroom with hundreds of people, some he knew, most he didn't, and some he recognized from television. The National Association of Broadcasters' Marconi Award ceremony dragged on like a toothache. Gary longed for the mountains. He longed for a drink. It seemed like Dick Clark, the emcee, had been presenting awards for days.

Gary headed for the bar, joining the long queue and paying little attention to those who fell in behind him. He wanted something to numb him from the incessant prattle coming from

No matter what was happening around him, Gary had his own brand of chaos. But it was chaos with a purpose. It was his own great, quirky sense of humor aimed directly at all the racket in the world that was the REAL chaos.

the podium. It seemed each recipient wanted to thank everyone from their long-lost cousins to every executive who had ever deemed them worthy of a job.

"Dear God," someone said loudly. "Can we prolong these festivities any further?"

Gary recognized the voice immediately. It was actor Ed Asner.

"Nice to meet you," Gary said, introducing himself.

"What do you think is going to take longer," Asner asked, "getting to the head of this line or the speech this guy is giving?"

Gary ordered a short whiskey from the bartender, who quickly obliged. As Asner approached, he reached into his pocket and pulled out a wad of bills.

"Are you up for an award?" he asked.

Gary said that he was.

"Congratulations," Asner said, "but do me a favor. If you win, give us a short speech. Please!"

"I promise," Gary said.

Asner turned his attention to the bartender.

"Give me two bottles of Jim Beam," he said, tossing bills on the bar.

"I can't do that, Mr. Asner," the bartender replied.

"Sure you can," Asner said, "and I'll tell you why. Because if you don't, I will not live through this night and you wouldn't want that on your conscience, I'm sure."

Asner received two bottles of Beam, and what seemed like hours later, Gary was on stage receiving his second straight Marconi. Dick Clark, the modern day Dorian Gray, receded from the podium.

Gary looked at the award and the crowd beyond the footlights. Somewhere out there he knew that Ed Asner was pulling at a jug of Kentucky whiskey.

"Thank you," he said and walked off the stage.

Somewhere in the crowd, mixed with the applause, there was a hardy, throaty cry: "Bravo! Jee-zuss Christ! Bra-voooo!!!!!"

Clark, caught short by the brevity of Gary's remarks, rushed back to the microphone, clearing his voice. He offered his best smile. "Thank you, Gary," he said. "We need more speeches like yours."

Gary now had two Marconi Awards. There was no higher recognition in all of radio but it was just as Len said. He felt no different. He was no different, though he had a faint notion that something *was* different—or was about to be.

He thought about making a return trip to the bar or searching through the crowd for Asner, then thought better of it because on stage, at the rostrum, was Paul Harvey.

Gary studied Harvey as he spoke. Harvey's pauses were as long as Gary's acceptance speech. Beyond the pauses, he listened for the notes and pitch. He had been doing a rendition of Harvey for some time, but a new idea came to him: Saul Harvey, Paul's evil twin.

SFX: Radio static tuning out a Paul Harvey broadcast.
Ahhhhhhh!! At long last, I've finally managed to pirate my way into Paul

Harvey's broadcast! Millions of you listeners never knew, but Paul Harvey has an evil twin that he never talks about. Ha ha ha ha, and I'm him!

Hello Americans, I'm Saul Harvey—stand by . . . to get screwed!

Page Two.

Let me reach into my mail bag.

Mrs. Ethel Driekmeier of Boise, Idaho writes:

Dear Saul Harvey,

You sludge bucket! You told me to invest my money in a new Dirt Devil vacuum cleaner. What a rip-off! It doesn't clean anything. It just screams satanic chants at me and spews and then levitates in the air at odd moments. You crook!

Well, Mrs. Driekmeier, nature abhors a vacuum for a good reason. If you are dumb enough to buy a vacuum cleaner named after the Prince of Darkness, then you deserve what you get.

Page Three.

I bet a lot of you out there are listening to me on your wonderful Bose Acoustic Wave Radios that my wussy brother Paul recommends. You haven't lived unless you've tried the new Bose Beelzebub CD Player. And if you order today, you will get a free CD: Michael Bolton singing "Sell Your Soul to Kenny G."

Ha ha ha ha! I'm Saul Harvey, pirate of the airwaves, and I'm coming back soon to sell you a used Yugo. Good day . . . suckers! Ha ha ha ha . . .

SFX: Radio static tuning back to a Paul Harvey broadcast.

Back in Montana in 1991, Gary sat on the dock staring at the lake. Fall wasn't far away. There was a distinct bite in the air and he pulled his jacket closer around his neck. He was 50 years old. He felt good and looked good. Well, for a man of his age and mileage, anyway. He had a wife who loved him, two wonderful children now grown, a nice home, money in the bank, and a few years left on a ten-year, no-cut contract. So what was bothering him and why couldn't he put his finger on it? *Maybe*, he thought, *it's because it is so quiet here? Maybe I need to be distracted to think clearly.*

He tried to return to his book. It was about hunting in Montana, a man and his young son in a stand waiting for elk. The boy—maybe 12 or 13—was impatient and filled with questions.

"Dad," he said, repeatedly, "when are they coming? Are they coming yet?"

Finally, tired of shushing the boy and weary of his fidgeting, the father said, "Son, if we knew when they were coming, they would call it shopping."

That's good, Gary thought. *I like that. Not enough of that around any more.*

For some reason, that's when it hit him. Everything was changing and not necessarily to his liking. And the change was most evident in every facet of entertainment: radio, television, films, music. It was nothing like what occurred in the '50s and '60s when there had been an enormous explosion of creativity. This was an implosion of much that had been gained from those years. Civility had left the building and subtlety was left at the curb. Dialogue had been replaced by diatribe, and the babble was unending.

Where there was once George Carlin, there was now Sam Kinison maniacally bellowing one expletive after another. *M*A*S*H* was gone and *Roseanne* had arrived. Rush Limbaugh was on one end of the dial, and Dr. Laura on the other. Rhythm & Blues and rock had been supplanted by grunge. Nobody was playing B.B. King, everybody was tuned in to Alice In Chains, and the biggest star in radio was shock jock Howard Stern, whose every joke seemed confined to genitalia. In this new world of entertainment, you were either in or out, the Kool-Aid was on tap, and everyone was drinking freely.

What surprised Gary most was that he had either been too focused on his own work or too oblivious to see what was happening all around him. Randy Michaels was a friend, but he was—without apology—a businessman first. Michaels was the John McEnroe of radio: ugly strokes, nasty attitude, beautiful results. He knew music was lost to FM. He didn't think Cincinnati was big enough or ready for an all-news station. Instead, he planned a station—a network, in fact—built on an odd mix of personalities. He fired Jim LaBarbara, "The Music Professor," and slowly weaned WLW from all music.

Michaels and Alan Gardner stepped into LaBarbara's spot. The idea was to elicit reaction. It didn't matter if it was good or bad. *Reaction* was the intended result. If it led to hate mail or headlines, all the better. "There was no one more polarizing than we were," Michaels said, "and by design."

During one show, Michaels's topic was: "Who would you kill? How would you like to do it? And what would you do with the body?"

He hired late night host Bill Cunningham, a trial attorney who was one

part Elmer Gantry and two parts P.T. Barnum, whose evening fare included strippers and prostate exams, surrounded by a stream of conservative political rhetoric.

When Bob Trumpy left WLW for NBC, Cris Collinsworth was hired to replace him. Collinsworth, also a former Bengal, was an easygoing Floridian and a law school graduate. He based his opinions on fact and supported his ideas with persuasive arguments. Soon, he was paired with Andy Furman. Furman grew up in Brooklyn and developed an early eye for the corner shill game. Off the air, there was no finer gentleman. On the air, Furman often turned lunatic. During his days as public relations director at Monticello Racetrack, Furman hosted "Ku Klux Klan Night." Anyone who wore a hood got in free. That promotion—prompted by a news story about the rise in local Klan activity—got Furman fired and made his name. Furman enjoyed placing a burr under the saddle of those who generally enjoyed a smooth ride, and no one intended less harm.

At one point, Michaels hired radio psychic Lynn Gladhill to host overnights. Ms. Gladhill drank wine on the air and uttered obscenities. She told listeners she was doing the show "only in her pantyhose." Months later, and to some surprise—given the path the station was taking—she was fired. It was never clear, however, if she was dismissed because of her dress or her drama.

When critics asked Michaels about all the changes he was making at WLW, he said he was "teaching the grand old lady of radio how to dance."

Gary wasn't sure how he had missed all this. He wondered where he fit in this changing tableau or *if* he fit at all.

As far as Michaels was concerned, Gary fit perfectly. If Gary viewed himself as isolated from everything and everyone else at WLW, he thought, nothing was farther from the truth. "This was a guy who, by his very nature, brought everyone together," he said.

"Gary was an artist, and artists, well, they just see things differently and not always the way they are. That's part of what makes them artists. It was my job to make sure he had what he needed in order to excel, and sometimes that was just talking to him and telling him I appreciated what he did."

Days later, Gary walked into the studio. Doc Wolfe was working on a script.

"Hey, welcome back. How was the trip?"

Gary said nothing.

"Uh-oh," Wolfe said. "You're thinking about quitting again, aren't you?"

"Yeah," Gary said. "It may be time."

Wolfe had weathered many of Gary's dark moments in the past, the threats to quit, the feeling that he was no longer funny. He listened as Gary talked about his concerns. Wolfe said little. He nodded and offered encouragement when he could. He knew Gary well. The best thing to do was to listen. The remedy was work; the cure was the laughter afterward.

"Look around, Doc," Gary said. "Nobody is doing what we are doing. We are surrounded by talk shows. People are angry all the time. Acerbic! Nasty!"

"Yeah," Doc said. "But maybe that's a good thing. We're *different.* People like different. I have this idea . . ."

By morning's end, the show was ready and Gary had put aside his concerns.

(Fade up piano solo from Love Story.)
"She was my angel in white. She hovered above me in nervous anticipation. Upon her command, I opened my mouth. I alone knew of her compulsion. I alone knew of her desires. I sat quietly as she performed her deed. Our eyes met as she told me, 'Okay, rinse and spit!'
"She was my dental hygienist. I was her . . . abscession.
"Absession."
(Drill reels and screams.)
"Ah, the pain of it."

When the tape ended, Gary and Doc looked up at one another and smiled. They were still *on.* They were different and Doc was right. People still *liked* different.

Different was encapsulated by a moment that occurred one evening before the Cincinnati Reds opened spring training. There in Tampa Bay, one of Gary's characters—the terminally cranky Earl Pitts—assumed a life even larger than his radio persona, and in so doing saved a poor sinner from what would have undoubtedly been a crippled future. It was a startling testimony to Earl—and the power of Gary's own feverish imagination.

It was the week in which the Reds hosted "Dream Week," with fans paying a handsome price for the privilege of playing ball with former players, as well as local celebrities such as Gary. For the most part, the participants played poorly during the day, then made up for it by their evening performances in the various watering holes of Tampa Bay.

One evening, Gary and company noticed one of their celebrities huddled in a corner with a statuesque brunette. Suddenly, a commotion arose, the celebrity obscured by the looming presence of two men whose size, dress, manner—and tattoos—announced them as bikers. From where Gary sat, they appeared to be nine feet tall, with shoulders as wide as a rick of wood.

Ol' Earl could step so far over the line that he couldn't find it in his rearview mirror. And over time, he got even edgier. There was a time, though, when reality blurred and Earl saved the life of a media mogul who, himself, stepped across the line.

Gary managed to pry his way into the middle of the confrontation, where the celebrity's star power had dimmed to the wattage of the small light found in refrigerators.

"That's my woman you're hitting on," one biker said, thrusting out an accusatory forefinger the size of a masonry drill.

"Whoa, now," Gary said.

"Is this a friend of yours?" the biker said. "If he is, you best decide how *good* a friend he is, 'cause he's about to get his ass kicked."

Gary considered the question and its potential consequences. Did he really want to be a victim of a beat-down somewhere in Pinellas County? Were he and the Queen City celebrity really *that* close?

Then, inspiration struck. Gary stepped back, hooked his thumbs in his belt loops, looked up at the bikers, and slipped into character: "You know what makes me so angry I could lick a live battery post? Some mamby-pamby, limp-wristed, commie-lovin', fancy pants what slinks into a bar and tries to steal another man's woman . . ."

The bikers looked at Burbank and then one another. "Son-of-a-bitch," one said. "You're him. It's you. You're Earl Pitts!"

"Yep," Gary said. "I'm him."

"Hey, man," one said, "didn't you used to work in Tampa? Here, sit down. Let me buy you a beer. Waitress!"

"None for me, thank you," said the celebrity, slipping away. "Nice to have met you fellas."

"Yes," Gary said, "I worked at WDAE."

"Don't know it," one said.

"The Bucs' station," Gary said.

"Oh, yeah, sure. But we hear Earl down here all the time."

Lynyrd Skynyrd played on the jukebox, something from *Endangered Species*, perhaps. The music mixed with the clatter from the pool table.

"Earl is syndicated," Gary said. "Plays around the country."

"Earl's vindicated?"

"That, too," Gary said.

Gary spent a good part of the evening drinking with the bikers and the brunette. "You know," Gary/Earl confided, "Pearl's got sisters: Ruby, Onyx and Cubic Zirconia, and they is hot! 'Course Earl has this thing for women what with names of precious stones."

"I can't believe we met Earl Pitts, and all on account of that other little guy," one of the bikers said. "Where did he go, anyway?"

"Oh, he left," Gary said. "He's really a good guy."

"Yeah," one biker said. "We all make mistakes. C'mon, we'll roll over to Pass-a-Grille Beach. You look like you ride."

Gary politely declined. Earl did as well. After all, the two of them had arrived together.

The next day at the Reds complex, Gary had a couple of hits and stole a base. Earl Pitts was credited with a save.

Chapter twenty-four

Exit, stage left

The extravagant and fanciful universe Doc and the others helped Gary build had become as real as any local zip code. It was not only inhabited by *themselves* but by an enormous audience of listeners. Still and all, it was more precarious than it sounded.

Gary was nearing the end of another contract and once

more talking about retirement. He had threatened to quit so many times over the years that no one at WLW paid much attention, although he still had the capacity to create a ripple of curiosity.

On December 17, 1999, *Cincinnati Enquirer* radio and television critic John Kiesewetter wrote: "This is it, says Gary Burbank . . . this is *really* going to be it. After years of threatening to retire, Mr. Burbank claims he will quit when his contract expires December 11, 2000.

"'I know I've said this before—and the bosses say, 'Yeah, Gary, sure'—but I seem

more resolute about it this time,'" says Burbank. "'I kind of feel like a comic who has been on stage for eighteen years, and the applause keeps getting less and less.'"

As a small intramural coda to Gary's quasi-announcement, Doc Wolfe had been called to Bill Cunningham's office, where they were discussing the implications of a possible Burbank-free WLW.

"No, I don't think Gary is going to quit either," Cunningham said, peering across his desk at Wolfe. "But the fact is he won't work here forever and I want you to know that when he *does* leave there will no longer be a place for you here."

Cunningham had risen from nighttime talk show host to program director and tact, as Wolfe saw it, was only one of several qualifications he lacked for the position.

"Thank you, Bill," Wolfe said, "for your candor."

"You're welcome," Cunningham said.

Cunningham had merely confirmed what Wolfe had suspected for some time: *his* livelihood was tied closely to *Gary's*. Wolfe loved the guy, but he also realized his protégé was no more predictable than the path of a tornado.

Gary was financially set with one home in Kentucky and another in Florida, while Wolfe had two young sons to raise, a new house on the east side of Cincinnati, and had not seen a raise in some time. Gary had the ability to find work anywhere in the country, while Wolfe had lived in Cincinnati virtually his entire life and had no desire to move.

What exactly *would* he do if Gary quit?

Doc loved his work. He was certain he would never have another job he enjoyed as much. The very idea of doing something else was a painful one. Even his own demented imagination couldn't construct a satisfactory future for himself. But maybe eighteen years was enough. Maybe it was time for something more secure. But the very word *security* itself had such a hollow, dispirited ring to it.

And so Doc began to think about moving on, all the while attempting to persuade himself it was the thing to do. Gary didn't seem to enjoy the work as much as he had in the past. He didn't trust the producers and engineers who cut tape and handled the recorded portions of the show. He seemed distracted by the loss of immediacy that came with the technical advances in editing. He insisted the old way—using razor blades and grease pencils—was more effective. He spent more and more time in Florida, working from his

studio on the Rainbow River near Ocala, and he worried more and more that he wasn't funny any longer.

Gary was approaching his 59th birthday. How long would he continue to work? He couldn't say because he *didn't* know. One might as well ask him how long he was going to live.

Eventually, Doc arrived at a conclusion that seemed—finally—both obvious and overdue: reluctantly, he began the painful search for a new job.

At first, Gary was angry. He couldn't understand why Doc was leaving. *Advertising?* How could Doc leave radio for *advertising?*

Doc sat quietly, offering explanations in the short gaps Gary's outburst provided. Doc had seen Gary like this before: starting a sentence by yelling at someone, by mid-sentence admitting he might be wrong, and ending it with an apology. Doc recognized Gary's reaction for what it was: a mixture of emotions he couldn't express.

It was hard to imagine Gary without Doc. They were joined at the ad-lib. Imagine Kirk without Spock, Penn without Teller, Abbott but no Costello, Tom but no Jerry, Moby without Ahab, Brad Pitt without, well, what's-her-name. Imagine that.

"I'm sorry," Gary said, finally. "I didn't mean to yell. It's just that I have always felt . . ."

"Responsible," Doc said, finishing Gary's thought.

"Exactly," Gary said, "for everybody involved in the show, but you above everyone else. We've been doing this a long time. Everything is going to change. Actually, Doc, I'm happy for you and I'm relieved."

"I know," Doc said. "The show will be fine."

"But it will be *different*," Gary said. "And I don't know that it will ever be as much fun."

In early September of 1999, Doc Wolfe left the BBC.

On October 11th of 2000, Kiesewetter reported that Gary had signed a new contract.

"Never mind, again!" Kiesewetter wrote. "Gary Burbank, who said last year he would retire from WLW in December, has changed his mind.

"Burbank has signed a one-year contract to continue his show through December 2001. 'I'm going to retire after that—for sure,' says Mr. Burbank. Burbank credits Darryl Parks, who replaced Bill Cunningham as program director last year, for bringing stability to the station and changing his mind.

"'Having Mr. Cunningham for a boss 'was sort of like working for Charles Manson. It was like a game of Twister with dynamite,' says Mr. Burbank."

Wolfe's departure left a huge gouge in the creativity of the show, and to worsen matters, Heather "Feather Pickle" McIntyre left just weeks after Doc. Two of Gary's most creative contributors were gone and Gary was despondent. Duke Sinatra replaced Doc as Gary's sidekick. Duke was more topical, geared toward headline news.

"It was headline, punch line; headline, punch line," said Chad Lambert, one of Gary's producers. "Duke *was* a character and he was very funny, but he brought something entirely different to the show. Pretty soon after Doc left, we were doing a lot of reruns of Gary's best stuff, and it made Gary crazy. But he didn't really have a choice because he didn't have the support system he once had."

With each concession, Gary grew more irritable and removed. During the show, Duke noticed that Gary would finish a line and turn to his left—where Sinatra sat—for a response. "Then," Sinatra said, "he would kind of jerk his head to the right, like he was trying to figure out where Doc was."

Duke's own association with the show began as a frequent caller. Gary had given him a job and made him a sidekick. J.D. Riggs was his guitar teacher. Gary hired him as a producer and tagged him "Slim Tempo." He hired Rob "Señor Buddy Whiplash" Ervin to produce. He picked Lambert up as a 26-year-old intern.

They were devoted to Gary, but they were faced with the daunting prospect of replacing Doc while watching Gary's energy slip away. Then, one morning, everything changed. Gary burst into the office, chuckling to himself.

"I got it," he said. "It came to me early this morning. I always think better in the morning. It's the best part of the day: sun coming up, birds chirping, the air is fresh. There's clarity in the morning.

"Here it is," he said. "Game shows."

Everyone in the room looked first at Gary, then at one another. Meanwhile, he paced about the room hurriedly outlining his ideas to the staff—everyone scrambling for pens and legal pads, taking notes, trying to keep up with Gary's mind. Suddenly, his energy was back and theirs was renewed.

They created "Top Six," in which Gary and Duke would read the first six words in the lyric of a song and callers would try to identify the number. "Stump the Band" was another product of Gary's move toward audience involvement. With musicians Larry and Tim Goshorn in the studio, along with Slim Tempo, callers tried to come up with songs Gary and his guests didn't know. Both segments were huge hits and achieved two purposes: like "Sports or Consequences," they consumed large portions of time, and each caller carried the potential for impromptu comedy.

Guests, particularly musicians, became more frequent on Gary's show. Sandy Pinkard and Richard Bowden, comic singer/ songwriters from Nashville, stopped in whenever they had a chance and, given the *unusual* nature of their performance, were always welcome.

It's also difficult to picture staff parties back in the day. After all, what was the show itself but a party by another name? Attending this one— Christmastime, 1998—was Gary, Duke Sinatra, Charity U-Rycki, and Chad Lambert.

Sandy Pinkard and Richard Bowden made their name by altering the lyrics of well-known songs. "Another Somebody Done Somebody Wrong Song" by B.J. Thomas became "Another Done Somebody's Song Wrong." Kris Kristofferson's "Help Me Make it Through the Night" was transformed into "Help Me Make it Through the Yard" and, of course, there was "I'm Driving My Wife Away," Pinkard and Bowden's version of Eddie Rabbitt's "I'm Driving My Life Away."

Sandy and Richard once showed up at WLW with a .410 under-and-over shotgun. "Don't worry," Sandy said. "We ain't aimin' to hurt nobody unless,

of course, there's a need. It's a gift for Gary." Sandy, Richard, and Gary viewed the world through the same twisted prism. Normal didn't interest them in the least.

Without Doc, Gary threw himself deeper into the show, relying less on others to do voice work. It wasn't that he didn't trust others or their talents; he trusted himself more. While Gilbert Gnarley's appearances were less frequent, Earl Pitts, Uhmerikun, gained a new edge.

MUSIC: The Marines' Hymn . . .

You know what makes me sick? You know what makes me so angry I just want to dress up like Colonel Sanders and tease chickens?

This here is a sad day for Earl Pitts, folks. I ain't my normal happy self. Drivin' in to the station today I . . . I hit a dog. I got to admit I have kilt more livin' things with my truck than most men alive. I mean I got so much fur stuck in my radiator grill you could probably knit ya a full-length road kill coat. I've made more than my share of wild animal widders, but I never hit no dog.

I keep playin' the whole thing over in my mind. I keep asking myself, 'Why couldn't it have been a cat?' And it wasn't my fault, neither. He come out of nowhere. If I'da seen him runnin', I could'a swerved or slammed on my brakes. Could'a beeped my horn.

I just heard this 'dunk' and there's a dog with a trunk bumper tattoo spinning on one leg like a ballet dancin' dog behind my truck.

Slammed on my brakes. I pull off the road and—I go runnin' to hep him. But I's too late. Some little sports car smacked that dog, lift him fifteen foot in the air, and throwed him about a half-block down the street.

If there was any chance that dog was stunned when I hit him, there wasn't no chance in hell now. But I . . . I kinda feel responsible ya know. So I go runnin' through them yards. I find this big ol' dog maybe pantin' his last breath alive. He lifts up that big ol' head and looks at me like he's sayin' to me: 'It wadn't your fault, Earl. It wadn't your fault.' And he kinda wagged his tail a little bit. (Earl starts to choke-up.) Well, what was left of it. Then . . . he starts to lick my hand.

(Earl crying, struggling to continue.) And I think to myself then, 'Why couldn't it have at least been a poodle?

Wake up, Uhmerika . . .

MUSIC UP . . .

Some lady comes runnin' out one of them houses screamin': 'Barney! Barney! You kilt my baby.' I say, 'Not me lady. Some other guy hit him. I just seen it . . . Well, it wasn't like Barney was in any shape to call me a liar.

I'm Earl Pitts, Uhmerikun. Pitts Off!

And, along came Tad Gnarley, Gilbert's nephew.

Ring!

Representative: Hi, Motor Sports Entertainment . . . may I help you?

Tad: Is Richard there?

Rep: Richard Petty?

Tad: I know. I know he is too busy to take personal calls but I just had to ask though. (Laughs). I was calling about—you have something called, uh, Driving Time, where you can learn to be a NASCAR driver?

Rep: Yes, basically, it's a driving experience where you get behind the wheel of a Winston Cup car . . .

Tad: Oh my God! You know my hero used to be Calvin Klein but it's all changed. I'm not the man I used to be, I'll tell you. (Laughs) My name is Tad Gnarley—G-N-A-R-L-E-Y. And my uncle, Gilbert, he told me you had a program that would help me realize my dream. I'm currently enrolled in beauty college but that's not my dream any more. I thought it was but that was before I had my four-barreled, fuel-injected epiphany. You know what an epiphany is, don't you?

Rep: Uh . . .

Tad: It's a revelation, an inspiration, a defining moment. I'll tell you, my defining moment occurred watching Winston Cup.

Rep: (Laughs nervously)

Tad: I watched those rumbling, steel Trojan warriors speed around the track and I knew what I had to be . . . and it's a NASCAR driver.

Rep: Unlike other sports, racing—you're just not kicking a ball around. It's expensive equipment, cars and a crew . . .

Tad: Um-hmm. Oooo, it just sounds like fun. You would have your own, like, entourage. But I know what you're thinking. What makes someone like him think he can be a NASCAR driver? I'll tell you. Two words: Jeff Gordon. He is my inspiration. Now, King Richard is my hero but Jeff, he's the one that lights my fire.

Rep: Well, uh, everyone has their own person they look up to . . .

Tad: Sure, but I have a couple of questions before I sign up. First of all, do you happen to know . . . after I become a registered NASCAR driver, uh, how much say would I have about my car?

Rep: What do you mean by that exactly?

Tad: I'm mostly concerned with the color. I'm thinking a hot pink with white trim, nothing overstated, mind you, maybe a little fur around the rear-view mirror, something like that, paisley inserts on the doors panels, and, of course, tinted windows. But that would be it.

Rep: Well, uh, first. Uhhh, basically . . .

Tad: I would like to wear a matching pink jump suit and helmet, of course, with a bright red silk scarf and bone white goggles. Oh, can't you just picture me? Woooo! I'm simply atwitter.

Rep: Uh . . .

Tad: Another thing, are the seats Corinthian leather? Do you know that? I just can't imagine vinyl. Ya know, ewwww!

Rep: It depends on how much money you have to invest . . . Uh.

Tad: How 'bout a CD player? Can I request that? You know I gain my racing strength from Barbara. I'll tell you, nothing gets me juiced up faster than the thought of suiting up, putting the pedal to the metal, and streaking around that giant oval in my pink powder keg as the wind whips my scarf to the soaring sounds of (singing): Memories . . . What the something, something . . .

Rep: You know, nobody gives a novice with no experience, you know, a top car to drive . . .

Tad: I almost forgot. I need a sponsor because they all have sponsors. Who's available?

Rep: That's your own . . .

Tad: Hey, you know if I went with Pepto-Bismol as a sponsor we could stay with the pink motif.

Rep: First thing you should do is definitely attend the racing school, see what's like . . .

Tad: Yeah, but I wanted to call and see if I would be accepted. You understand what I'm saying?

Rep: Yeah, I mean anybody . . .

Tad: Anybody . . .

Rep: You have a driver's license . . .

Tad: You have a don't-ask, don't-tell policy, right?

Rep: Well, anybody . . . if you can drive a car . . .
Tad: And I have a driver's license. Ohhhhhh!
Rep: Uh, if you can drive stick shift . . .
Tad: Ohhh, I love those the best!!!
Rep: (Laughs) Okay.
Tad: I'm crazy about . . . listen, I'm gonna think very hard and I'm going to call you back within two days. I've got two people to talk to about this.
Rep: All right.
Tad: Ooooooooo!!!! Thank you.
Rep: Okay, bye-bye. Uh . . .
Tad: Okay!!! Toodles!
CLICK!!!

Gary had regained his footing when a series of events occurred that did his show no favors.

In November of 2000, George W. Bush was elected president. The nation was gripped by the Florida recount, amid charges that the election had been stolen from Al Gore. During the summer of 2001, Cincinnati was torn by riots after a police officer shot and killed 19-year-old Timothy Thomas during a foot pursuit. Turmoil and strife filled the radio waves. That fall, the 9/11 attacks occurred, followed by war in Afghanistan and Iraq.

Up and down the radio dial it was Osama bin Laden and Saddam Hussein, anthrax attacks and weapons of mass destruction, Rudy Giuliani and Donald Rumsfeld, Rush and O'Reilly, and color-coded security levels. No one wanted to fly and everyone fought the urge to flee. It was us against them, no middle ground.

The nation searched continually for news, and there seemed to be no room for satire or parody. The world wasn't a funny place, and world events turbocharged conservative talk radio, driven by the loudest voice in even the smallest argument.

There's still a place for what I do, Gary thought, *but it's shrinking. I'm outnumbered and surrounded.* Even before 9/11, few were doing the type of show Gary did and virtually no one on the AM dial. Now when he went out, he saw grim faces confronting a dangerous and changing world.

It all made him think of his mother, Dot, and Raymond, the only father he had ever known, both gone. He remembered how he would introduce Raymond to his friends and Raymond would try to persuade them it was

the first time Gary had ever worn shoes, and how he loved Woodstock, the bird in Charles Schultz's *Peanuts* comic strip. He missed his conversations with Ray and all the times he sat and took notes while Ray railed against the world, unwittingly providing Gary material for Earl Pitts.

Shortly after Ray's death, Dot encountered a friend on the street. "I'm sorry you lost your husband," the man said.

"I didn't lose him," Dot said. "I know right where he is and it's a lot easier keeping tabs on him there."

The man laughed and cried so hard she had to put her arms around him.

He remembered the day in Memphis after Dot's funeral, their friends gathered around telling one funny story after another, tears of laughter mixing with those of loss. And David Welch, his childhood friend, saying, "This is just the way Dot would have wanted it."

"Grammy told the best stories," Tracy said.

"Yes, she did, honey," he said. "She sure did."

For all that surrounded him, Gary thought the need for what he did was even stronger than before. In the AM Tower of Babel that radio became after 9/11, Gary was determined to offer a clear voice – more than one, actually. For how long, he didn't know.

MUSIC: The Marines' Hymn . . .
You know what makes me sick? You know what makes me so angry I just wanna make me a coonskin cap with the raccoon still livin'? This is a personalized message goin' out to all you geeky-fied, pantywaist, pencil-necked, fruit baskets out there pretendin' like you're real men.

You know how you can tell these real man wannabes? They don't know how to wear a ball cap. I seen more freaky lookin' ball caps on more pinheads than I care to admit. Frankly, us real men are getting' a little sick of it.

Number one, you got your real man cap curl where you curl the bill. Now here's the news, Columbus: the world is round and so is the bill on a real man's ball cap. So when the guy at the hardware store starts cuttin' the tag off that sucker—'fore it ever goes on your pea-pickin' noggin'—ya gotta grab that puppy and personalize it.

Some men prefer the A-frame. That's when ya pinch that boy 'tween your hands and ya put one nice crease right down the center. Kinda nice when ya out on a rainy day and it's good run-off. Kinda makes yer head look pointy, though.

And some men like the double-edge curl. That's like, uh, putting both sun visors down in your truck windows. Curl down both sides so it almost looks like a box with, uh, ball cap blinders by both your eyeballs. Know what I mean? That's good for factory work and construction work so's nothin' can fly up in ya eyes.

Now men like me, we like the combination of the A-frame and the double-edge curl. Looks like ya got a little dollhouse stickin' off your forehead. Ya got to pull that cap down so low it sits on ya eyebrows.

I'll tell ya a little man secret here. Ya pull your cap down low enough, you can talk to a good lookin' babe starin' straight at her chest and she'll never know it. Not that I ever done that.

But never – I repeat never – think you gonna be no real man if you bend your ball cap into a goober. Know what I'm talkin' about? Hhhuuu!

Wake up, Uhmerika!

MUSIC UP . . .

Real men knows there is only three times ya ever take off your ball cap: during the National Anthem, washin' yer hair, and makin' love to a woman . . . indoors.

I hope this helps.

I'm Earl Pitts, Uhmerikun. Pitts off!

One day, Gary was rifling through his mail when he came across a letter from Dan O'Day in Los Angeles. He had been invited to participate in one of O'Day's comedy seminars. There was a panel that included Gary Owens of *Laugh-In* fame; Nancy Cartwright, the voice of Bart Simpson; and actor Fred Willard, an alumnus of *Second City*, co-founder of the *Ace Trucking Company* comedy group, and a frequent guest on *The Johnny Carson Show*. Gary would be O'Day's special guest, interviewed by O'Day himself.

O'Day had known Gary since the mid-1970s, had written about him in *Radio & Records*, the music industry trade paper, and Gary had been a guest speaker at other O'Day seminars.

"You're the funniest man in America nobody knows about," O'Day said. "Can you come out here?"

The words echoed in Gary's mind: "the funniest man in America nobody knows about."

Now *that's* funny, he thought.

"I'll be there," he said.

Nancy Cartwright was one of the first to speak at O'Day's seminar. She talked about how she had grown up in Dayton, Ohio, scooping ice cream in a drugstore before she found work at a radio station. There, she discovered her gift for voices, which gave her enormous success as one of the nation's most notable comic voice-over talents.

When Gary Owens introduced Gary, he said, his voice booming, "I'm pleased to introduce a man who is probably funnier than any of us in this room—the funniest man in America too few know about—Gary Burbank."

He took the microphone, scanned the faces in the crowd, all waiting to hear someone they didn't know.

"Since most of you don't know me," he said, "let me tell you a little bit about myself. I started here in Hollywood making movies and doing voices for cartoon characters, but I wouldn't let that stop me. I worked hard and before I knew it, I landed a job in Detroit working at a rock 'n' roll radio station.

"But I kept after it and that led me to New Orleans and Louisville, Kentucky, and Jackson, Mississippi; all the way to West Monroe, Louisiana, and eventually, to KLPL in Lake Providence, not far from West Monroe.

"Now," he continued, "I'm in Cincinnati, but I figure if I keep working hard, I can finally realize my ultimate dream of scooping ice cream in Dayton, Ohio."

The crowd howled with laughter.

He followed with some Earl Pitts and gave them a taste of Big Fat Balding Guy with A Cigar in his Mouth and his Pants Half-Zipped. He ad-libbed. Gary didn't want to stop but he had to, and with good cause. A man in the crowd was frantically jumping about, holding up his hand.

"Stop," he pleaded. "You gotta stop. I'm laughing so hard I'm about to pee my pants. I got to go to the bathroom but I don't want to miss anything."

Afterward, all Gary could think about was the reaction he had received. The flight home seemed short. He loved looking down on the changing landscape: the brown mountains, the green plains, the rolling hills of the Midwest. He wanted to jump out of his seat and yell, "Guess what? I'm still funny!"

Instead, he ordered a drink. When the plane landed in Cincinnati, his pockets were filled with cocktail napkins filled with notes and ideas for sketches. He wanted to go to work. He hadn't felt this way in a long time.

Even for those who knew Gary best and worked with him longest, he was a paradox. No one loved radio more, and there was no one who needed more the immediate approval of a radio audience. "I often thought," Doc Wolfe said, "that if we could have found a way to pipe the laughter from the cars and the homes and all the people listening and laughing back into the studio, Gary might have been one of the greatest performers radio had ever seen."

The LA experience provided Gary with a laugh track that he leaned on for years. O'Day asked him back to other seminars, and every time Gary felt that his work was out of touch, he turned to those who were working on the rim of comedy. They were the ones who sustained him, along with people like Len King, Marty Bass, Bob Moody, Bill Gable, Johnny Randolph, Doc Wolfe—who never lost touch—and those who encouraged him everyday:

Duke Sinatra, Chad Lambert, J.D. Riggs, Rob Ervin, and the writers. He needed all of them more than ever before.

He felt buried by an impending future, and while it may not have completely arrived yet, it was too close to be stopped. He could hear the sound of pickaxes in his head, which he imagined as the sound of more debris being piled around him. When he stopped to sort through his feelings, he recognized that this sound was merely the aural sense of how the radio programming that he loved was

Dan O'Day's timing could not have been better. When he called Gary to LA, before an audience of radio producers, Gary made them laugh. Always a validation, Gary thought, making strangers laugh. Your friends are supposed to laugh.

being chipped away. *Of course, it would occur to me as a sound*, he thought ruefully.

The sound was loudest in meetings. How he hated meetings: everyone talking, no one listening, the clock ticking, the sound of pickaxes. Unseen consultants handing down edicts as if they were Papal documents.

There was yet another meeting. The staff had been gathered so that

management could explain the direction the station was taking. The meeting didn't smell like a locker room, but it felt like one, and as far as Gary was concerned, the message must have evolved in some such place. This time, the edict was: "We're going for the lowest common denominator."

"Wait a minute," Gary said. "Did I hear that correctly? 'We're going for the *lowest* common denominator?' Is that so you can understand it?"

The answer was "Yes."

"I'm not changing anything," Gary said.

"Wait, Gary, come back. You don't under . . ."

He understood perfectly: radio was changing, and he didn't want to change with it.

Chapter twenty-five

The drive home

> It was like the sudden rush of well-being that would-be suicides are said to acquire once they've made their decision. In *Gary's* case, it wasn't himself he was dispatching but an entire brigade of voices that had been entertaining a huge audience of listeners.

A quickening—maybe that was the only way to describe it.

Duke saw it in the studio. Doc heard it listening on the radio at home. Chad Lambert recognized it while driving his car. Gary seemed more at ease. It was if he had been released, or just returned from an overdue vacation.

At first, Duke found it puzzling. Then he gave himself up to the notion of the new Gary. *Who cares?* he thought, finally. *It's terrific!*

Gary was broadening his characters, and while management

urged him to simplify his show, he went the other way. Nothing pleased him more than a good fight, especially when he had a worthy cause, and his cause was his work.

"Lay one thought over the other, juxtapose ideas, push the logical against the illogical, and if you're lucky, you get a laugh," Gary said. "If you're fortunate, you get a new thought or a new way of looking at the world around you. And how did you do it? By making people laugh. How great is that?"

Nothing typified the change in Gary more than the development of Howlin' Blind Muddy Slim (your sixty minute jelly belly toe jam man), a character Gary had performed for years. While Earl Pitts was syndicated and no character came closer to the heart of Gary's comedy than Gilbert Gnarley, Howlin' provided Gary with the opportunity to explore music, culture, religion, and, if he chose, The Flintstones, all in one piece. Howlin' performed with musicians such as Sonny Moorman or Larry Goshorn sitting in, which heightened the immediacy of the act.

The character was based on legendary blues performer Jimmy Reed, whom Gary had performed with in Memphis. Howlin' *was* Reed, but he was also every blues player Gary had ever come across in his days as a musician. Howlin' was raw, smooth, uneducated, crafty, self-destructive, and self-possessed. He was on the downside of society and the upside of humanity, and beyond all that, he afforded Gary the chance to play guitar, something he dearly loved to do. With a few lessons here and there, he had become an accomplished guitarist, keeping a promise he made long ago as a serviceman in Germany.

And more than anything else, Howlin' was representative of the inexplicable changes others saw in Gary.

Music in (blues riff):
Howlin: (strumming guitar) Come on round here. Come on. It's all right. You skinny. You got no job, you get skinnier (chuckles, coughs).
I'm sorry. I'm a little late here. I got this buddy down here. He might need some hep down der, too. Uh, he works at Lockjaw Liquors and Daycare. Y'all been over der? You go in and pick up your bottle and leave your kid off, ya know. Anyway, he had go to de back ya know and he told

me, 'Howlin', will you take care of de cash register 'till I get back?' I's tryin't get it open (chuckles).

And I standin' der tryin' to get dis thang open and this woman, she walk up to me and she say, "Scuse me, I'm in a hurry. Could you check me out please?' Heh-heh. So I look her up and down and I say, 'Nice rack.'

Let me git a drink here and then I gonna learn y'all some blues . . . I found this over der. Dis guy is sittin' in the club and he had this big ol'coat look like a Eskimo or something. He was drinking somethin' and he lef a little spider in the bottom of it and it was yak milk. Then I found some absinthe. Then I found some Bay Horse whiskey. Then I found some DeKuyper, that's rum. I think, isn't it? Don't matter, anyway.

Then somebody was drinking some bubble gum schnapps. Then some Dewars went in der. So, yak milk, absinthe, Bay Horse whiskey, DeKuyper, bubblegum schnapps, and Dewars. You know what I call this drink? Yaba-Daba-Do! Heh, heh, heh. Yaba-Daba-Do. One drink and you wearin' a shirt and tie with no pants . . .

Since Gary's early Memphis meet with The King, it was only natural that at some point Gary actually BECOME The King. They might have actually had the same motto, too: 'Ambition is a dream with a V8 engine.' Elvis said that, but Gary could have.

What does not kill us will only make us have to take another dose of stool-softener. I think Nietzsche said that. Yeah, yeah, he said that. He's a bass player I used to know. And uh, Freddy.

You know it's good to have religion. I got it. You got to have that. I ain't gonna sit here and preach to y'all, though. But I was drunk. How I got it I was drunk down in Georgia, ya know, out in the woods, ya know, and I stumble on dis baptismal service. It was by the Withlaccoochee River, which is right down south of Tifton.

And I see dis guy in de wadder and he was wit dis preacher and the preacher say, 'Son, are you ready to find Jesus?' And he say, 'Yes, preacher, I am.' And de preacher he dunked him in de wadder and he pulled him back

up. He say, 'Have you found Jesus?' He say, 'Yes!'

Well, I guess I musta got too close. Stumble down der to de wadder and the preacher grab me. He carried me out there in the wadder and he say, 'Son, are you ready to find Jesus?' I say, 'Yeah, sure.'

He dunk me under that wadder and he pull me back up, and he say, 'Have you found Jesus?' I say, 'Naw, I haven't.'

Then he dunked me again and dis time he held me down a little longer, ya know, and he pulled me back up: 'Have you found Jesus?' I said, 'Uh, no, not yet.'

Then he held me under seemed like a coupla minutes that time. Man, I come up. Gaaaahh! And the preacher say, 'Have you found Jesus now?' And I's gaspin' for air and I say, 'Are you sure this is where he fell in?'

Heh, heh, heh. That happen. That's a true story.

'Course I write a song about it.

(Playing guitar and singing)
They told me to look for Jesus
But I was drawin' a blank
I even got more imbalanced
When I left a scum ring 'round de bank

But I did finally find him
When I die I'll be playin a harp
But I have to admit I have some gnawin' doubts
I keep thinkin' I could have mistook him for a carp

He say, 'You wanna find Jesus?
'You got to swallow your pride'
I say, 'He ain't under dis wadder
He might'a walked to de other side.'
I say, 'If you are lookin' for Jesus
I know where He is without fail
Der's about fifteen thousand of 'em
In the Miami, Florida jail
In the Miami, Florida jail

In the Miami . . . Florida . . . jail

Heh, heh! But I's just jokin' wit ya. I found Him. He's all right with me. He ought to be all right wit y'all, too. I'll tell you right now, I'm just gonna say that right now so I don't get struck by lightning.

Heh, heh! Lightning is my bass player and he's very religious, very religious.

All right, ya'll come back here and I learn you some more blues. This is Howlin' Blind Muddy Slim, your sixty minute jelly belly toe jam man.

While it seemed improbable, Earl Pitts acquired more of an edge and became more of a bigot:

You know what makes me sick? You know what makes me so angry I wanna put about 20,000 volts in my bug zapper?

It's these mamby-pamby, bleedin' heart, wimperin' and moanin', 'No Nuke!' picket sign carryin', Reebok wearin', granola-eatin' ACLU crybabies that don't like the death penalty . . .

"Wake up, Uhmerika!

MUSIC UP: (Washington Post March)

We got a good supply a people on death row an' a real old electric chair. Let's wore it out, and then find a new way to bump off murderers.

I'm Earl Pitts, Uhmerikan! Pitts off!

Gilbert Gnarley, based on Howard McNear's portrayal of Floyd the Barber, Gary's favorite character in *The Andy Griffith Show*, kept in step:

SFX: Ring!

Operator: Sports careers, how may I help you?

Gilbert: Yes, how do you do? My name is Gilbert Gnarley, G-N-A-R-L-E-Y, and I saw your advertisement and I've always wanted a career in sports. And now that I'm a retired eccentric I have time on my hands, you know.

Operator: Ha! Okay.

Gilbert: You know, when I was a youngster, I was pulled out of a fire at Russwood Park by the Public Relations Director for the then-Memphis Chicks, a Double A Southern League team. Delbert Coggins was his name.

Operator: What are you looking to do in the sports industry?

Gilbert: I want to be in public relations, just like Mr. Delbert Coggins. He went on the radio one time, and he said that if the stands were not full for

a game on Saturday night, he would shoot himself in the head on the pitcher's mound.

Operator: Hmm . . .

Gilbert: He called it Hemingway Night, and turned out standing room only. You see, everyone showed up thinking there would be at least one empty seat and they would see Mr. Coggins's brains on the rosin bag.

Operator: Huh.

Gilbert: He was a very hated man, but he knew human nature. He knew people would come.

Operator: Of course.

Gilbert: That inspired me to be a sports public relations guy.

Operator: Okay. What have you done in the past?

Gilbert: I've frittered my life away. I've got some pretty good ideas in the sporting field myself. Would you like to hear one?

Operator: Sure.

Gilbert: How 'bout this: Show Us Your Scar Night. Everyone loves to talk about their scars. It's a people thing.

Operator: It sounds like you're good with people . . .

Gilbert: I'm not sure if we should allow C-sections, though. You'd get a lot of women in there.

Operator: It sounds like you've got your own public relations going there.

Gilbert: How 'bout this: What do you like to eat when you go to the ballpark?

Operator: Hot dogs!

Gilbert: Yeah! How about: Make Your Own Hot Dog Night.

Operator: That's a pretty good idea.

Gilbert: Yeah! You go over to the slaughterhouse, and you buy sacks of stuff from pigs and pass it out to all the patrons coming to the ballpark. People could take their bag of pig stuff, dump it in the top of a sausage making machine, and voila! A hot dog! Interesting and educational.

Operator: Yeah, well, I think our program could help you out a lot, then. You're going to learn about the sports industry and have access to a lot of job openings. It sounds like you're willing to work in the minor leagues.

Gilbert: Minor league, major league—I'll start wherever you want me. I've got plenty of time. All I need is a bus ticket. Every place has Farmer's Night, you know. They have cow-milking contests and kids catching greased pigs.

Operator: Oh yeah.

Gilbert: Well, I think this is no longer a rural country, so how 'bout we have Business Night instead of Farmer's Night? You'd have stapling and filing contests. You could get a bunch of bosses chasing around greased salesmen.

Operator: That's a pretty good idea.

Gilbert: Should I put these ideas on my resume?

Operator: I'd put them on the cover letter.

Gilbert: You know I never like to start a letter off with 'Dear Sir' because it may be a woman that reads it. I prefer to use nicknames if I know who I'm sending a letter to. I have a nickname I use for everybody. I call everybody 'Slim.' So I'll just start the letter off 'Dear Slim.' Women like that, too.

Operator: This program, Gilbert, is $199 for six months or $249 for a year.

Gilbert: Well, that might be out of my price range. Let me think about this and consult my roommate about it. I'll get back to you on this.

Operator: Okay.

Gilbert: Okay.

SFX: CLICK!

In March of 2007, Gary announced that he would retire from radio when his contract expired in December. No one believed him, of course. Why should they? He had been threatening to quit before he ever started at WLW, which had been twenty-seven years before.

"I didn't believe it for months after the announcement," Duke said. "But then it started to soak in. This time, it was real, and it was like he was elevated because he *was* leaving."

Gary sat at a picnic table near the pool behind his home. He sipped a beer, then set the bottle on the table. Nightfall was approaching, and a breeze played in the trees above him. "People come up to me now and say: 'Since announcing your retirement, it's like there's no pressure. You've always been funny, but not *this* funny.'

"Maybe there's some sense of relief now that I realize I won't have to wake up every day and *have* to be funny."

Gary was not one for self-analysis, but he did know one thing: it was time to go. It was, he said, as if he bought a chalet in the Swiss Alps then

awakened one morning in Slovenia. Where there had once been room for entertainment, the airwaves were now filled with rancor and bile, populated by controversy and its creation.

Darkness had fallen, but Gary had not bothered to turn on a light. "I want to keep it high and I want to keep it dry," he said, talking about how he wanted to go out. "What will I do for that last show? I might just call in sick."

Of course, Gary's imminent retirement meant others would be leaving with him.

SFX: Ring!

Gary: Yes, hello?

Synonymous: Mr. Burjank, how does this afternoon find you?

Gary: Synonymous? Oh, hey!

Synonymous: I happen to be one of the Cincinnati Bengals, who most assuredly would like to remain synonymous whereas I don't besmirch my reparation.

Gary: We don't want that. I've never done that . . .

Synonymous: I am calling you from my mobile celluloid helmet phone underneath the Coach's desk at Paul Brown Stadium.

Gary: Yeah, okay.

Synonymous: Well Mr. Burjank, as your listeners can protest, I have been making contraceptions to your program for more years than I care to dismember.

Gary: You have been here a long time, yeah.

Synonymous: Well hopefully, I have prorated valuable incitement for the fans of the Cincinnati Bengals and helped them become more knowledgeable, and even ecclesiastic about the team.

Gary: There have been a few ecclesiastical happenings here.

Synonymous: But now, it's time for me to make an important denouncement.

Gary: You?

Synonymous: Yes, and I want to do it excessively on your program.

Gary: Well, you excessively can do it.

Synonymous: Mr. B, most players would of course call a press confluence to make such procreation, but I have a fear of public speaking and prefer the indelicacy of radio, you understand.

Gary: Indelicacy? Yes, I understand.

Synonymous: Well, I've been enamored by your decision to retire.

Gary: Oh, you have?

Synonymous: And I'm announcing my retirement from football defective at the concussion of this season.

Gary: No kidding? You're going to retire along with me? Wow!

Synonymous: Now I know many fans will be shocked and disarrayed, but I feel the time has come. I don't want to end up being reappropriated to the taxidermy squad next year only to be quietly released mid-seasonly.

Gary: No, nobody does.

Synonymous: But I think I'll hang it up now. I've had a good career, after all. It won't go down in the anal areas of football history, and I will never be embalmed in the Hall of Famousness, but I managed to play for a long time, and I am very fornicated for the opportunism that I was awarded.

Gary: You deserve every moment you've had.

Synonymous: So, I know you're asking what comes next for Synonymous. Some fans may esquire this. Actuality, I am not sure my own self. I may continue my education.

Gary: Really?

Synonymous: I have a bachelor's degree from the college of Farts and Sinuses at my Alma Meter. And perhaps I will go for my Masterful Degree. Conversationally, there's also the probability of stepping into the broadcast booth and being a colorful common denominator.

Gary: You would be great at that, I think.

Synonymous: Yes, I feel I would be gratuitous at this. How iconic would that be, Mr. B? You retiring from broadcasting . . . and me just getting my face wet?

Gary: Um, yeah. Okay . . .

Synonymous: There are ludicrous possibilities for me out there no matter what road I swallow. I feel the world is my oyster cracker, and I am looking forward to my postcoitus career. I do appreciate you letting me defecate on your airwaves over the years and letting me lend my expertise on the subjugation of pro football and the Bengals organization.

Gary: Well thank you Synonymous, it's been . . .

Synonymous: Enjoy your retirement Mr. B, and I will talk to you on down the road. Do keep me Synonymous.

Gary: Always.

Synonymous: I must be off.
Gary: Bye.
SFX: CLICK.

Every sketch held a message, including Gary's obituary delivered by
WLW News Director Jeff "Hondo" Henderson.

*Gary Burbank passed away today due to as-yet-unrevealed causes.
Burbank was known for his clever wit, his pithy remarks, and his biting
satire. Gary was known by his listeners as the man who never spit on a
squirrel.*

*Here's Doc Wolfe, his co-host for eighteen years, being interviewed in the
unemployment line: 'One thing that people always said about Gary was that
he smelled like a hero. He never would say what his cologne was, but it just
seemed to captivate people just like his personality. Hey, move! I'm next!'*

*Burbank's characters were so real they
had taken on a life of their own, with Gilbert
Gnarley even being hunted by creditors who
thought he was
real. His other
hilarious characters
included Eunice
and Bernice,
the Reverend
Deuteronomy
Skaggs, Ranger
Bob, and Carl
Windham. Here's a
clip of a Carl Windham bit: 'Put some water in it.'*

"A brain trust of a dozen writers fed the manic machine that was the BBC," someone wrote. And that, in itself, made it more than likely the strangest corporation the Queen City had never seen. The voices behind the voices, you see.

*Duke Sinatra was given his start by the magnanimous Burbank: 'Yeah,
he was all right. He was a good enough guy. He helped me in my career, a
great friend as well as a boss. But, you know, it's not like I would have kissed
his ass on Fountain Square or anything . . . um, well . . . unless he asked me
to. And if he would have asked me to, I would have done it! God I love that
man!'*

*Gary Burbank will be missed by millions of fans around the world. The
National Guard will be called in for funeral crowd control, as the memorial*

service for Gary Burbank is expected to draw more than the JFK procession.

The coffin will be pulled by a riderless horse, with a backwards microphone in the stirrup.

(Choking up.) I'll miss you, Gary. This is the bereaved Jeff Henderson reporting.

(Long Pause.)

Was that convincing?

Gary maintained his place as the butt of the joke. "You learn as a comedian that when you make yourself grandiose and you win, it's not funny," he said. "It's funnier when you're an idiot."

Of course, Gary wasn't the only one leaving the airwaves. He was taking a lot of others with him. So his characters got together to hold a farewell meeting.

Announcer: Meanwhile, in an office boardroom, the characters of Gary Burbank meet to discuss their fate and their future. Dan Buckles is leading the proceedings . . .

Dan Buckles: Okay, let's all settle down now. Folks, we've all been great and entertaining characters, but it's coming to an end. I don't know what we'll do once Gary Burbank is retired.

Eunice & Bernice: Retarded? Gary Burbank is retarded? We already knew that from talking to him on the air. Why does he keep answering the phone while we're trying to call Rush Limbaugh?

Dan Buckles: No, no, not retarded. He's retiring.

Eunice & Bernice: Ohh . . . retiring. He can't retire!! You know what we always say? We always say a day without Gary Burbank is like plastic vomit without pieces of plastic spam. We always say that.

Dan Buckles: Well, he's calling it quits after the 21st, and I hate to think after that I'm going to be interrupting the Bill Cunningham show. Although, if any show needed to be interrupted . . .

Big Fat: Hello there! I'm a Big Fat Balding Guy with a Stubby Cigar in his Mouth and his Pants Half Zipped . . .

Dan Buckles: We know that.

Big Fat: This retirement thing is serious! Timmy the Termite is so depressed, I saw him mixing himself a Raid cocktail.

Flock: Amalulah!

Reverend Skaggs: Maybe I can get work as a running mate with Mike Huckabee. Although, I might be too secular for him. Hah!

Flock: Amalulah!

Gilbert Gnarley: Uhh, maybe Gary could stay with me at the St. Pia Zadora Golden Buckeye Retirement Community.

Mylan Flatts: Could not!

Gilbert Gnarley: I could even give him this 1-900 number I found where you could listen to Mrs. Butterworth talk naughty.

Dan Buckles: All the characters are being let go except for that scary redneck who smells like Red Man. Uh, Howlin' Blind? I would appreciate it if you would refrain from drinking during the meeting.

Howlin' Blind: I'm just mixin' a little drink I made from the spiders I found in the bottles around here. I found some Bourbon, then I found some Red Bank Wine, then I found some Riesling and some Fat Tire Beer, and I even found a little breath mint. I put 'em all together, you know what I call this drink? I call it Bur-Bank-Re-Tire-Mint.

One drink—you never want to work again. Two drinks—you feel like Pittsin' off. Three drinks—you throw up in round, pear-shaped tones. Maybe I need to add somethin' to soften it up a bit . . .

Carl Windham: Put some water in it!

Howlin' Blind: Thank you, brother!

Ludlow Bromley: Yeah, right on! Heh! Heh!

Eugene: Hah! Hah!

Ludlow Bromley: That's my brother Eugene.

Ranger Bob: I have ta tell ya, whippersnappers, this is a tough time sayin' adios Muchachos for the last time. I guess I'll have to become a horse whisperer. How do you say 'You're fired' in horse lingo?

Dan Buckles: Uh, folks? Let's focus here. Gary Burbank is parting company with us.

Eunice & Bernice: Gary Burbank is farting in front of company?!? That's rude! He should learn to hold it in until the guests leave. Maybe it's a good thing he's leaving, after all.

Dan Buckles: No, I said parting company. When are you going to get hearing aids, girls?

Eunice & Bernice: Herrings with AIDs? We didn't even know fish could get that disease.

Dan Buckles: Enough already! My friends, this is the end of the road for all of us fictional characters.

Synonymous: But wait, Mr. Blackles! Where do fixational characters go after they've served their platypus?

Dan Buckles: Synonymous, I'm afraid that you, I, Gilbert, Tad, Lars, Ludlow, Eugene, Cole Slaw, Ryle Drepper, Paul Harvey, the Maw Harishi Diaper Rashi, Captain Gorgeous, Your Right To Know Supersedes Your Right To Exist, Press the Face of the Nation, Joe da Boss, that Dial an Ethnic Chicken Joke guy, all of you—will follow me to the Great Beyond. Yes, my dear friends, I can see the Pearly Gates opening wide right now as we speak. From far up above us, I can actually hear the voice of an angel calling us! Listen! You can hear the angel, if you listen . . .

Saint CEO: Cough! Cough! Cough! Oh, wow!

On December 21st, 2007, Gary did not call in sick. Instead, he held a three-hour, open door party with festival seating for everyone who had ever been a part—or a friend—of his show. At times, thirty and forty people crowded into a studio designed to comfortably seat ten or twelve. Calls came in from around the country thanking him for the good times. There were reminiscences and jokes. During commercial breaks, the studio had the feel and sound of a New Year's Eve celebration.

At one point, Gary's wife, Carol, struggled through the crowd. "It's not a wake," she said. "It's a party." Tracy, Gary's beloved daughter, thanked everyone and, on demand, offered an adult rendition of the Red Raiders cheer that accompanied every Sports of Consequences: "We don't . . . We don't . . . We don't mess around," and the entire crowd joined in.

Gary never stopped smiling. He was a man thoroughly enjoying the moment.

His son, Sean, called from Louisville. "Thank you, Dad," he said, "for never forgetting where you came from."

During the next commercial break, Gary scanned the crowd. "I didn't think I could," he said, "but I'm gonna make it through the show without crying. Hey, let's get some beer."

Only one tear was shed in the entirety of the show. It came when sports reporter Bill "Seg" Dennison made his last report for the Gary Burbank Show. After his sportscast, Dennison thanked Gary for his friendship and, most of all, his kindness.

There was a quiet, somber moment. "Thank, *you*, Seg."

Gary cleared his throat. "Wow," he said. "We are almost done here. It's almost time for our song."

The song was Gary's last word after all the years that led up to that day. As the clock neared six, he grabbed his guitar and introduced the song: "I Love Everybody."

I love everybody, especially you.
I love everybody, especially you.
So when you get lonesome,
Remember it's true.
I love everybody, especially you.

It wasn't the round pear-shaped
Tones from my mouth.
It wasn't just the barbeque
I brought from the south.
It wasn't the fact
When you called I was kind.
It was the weird leakage
That came from my mind.

I love everybody, especially you.
I love everybody, especially you.
So when you get lonesome,
Remember it's true.
I love everybody, especially you. Duke?

(Duke as Saint CEO)

It wasn't my coughing
That you came to know.
Cough cough cough . . .
It wasn't my pant suits
Or my fuzzy puppy-o.
It's 'cause I was drinkin'
And I was toasting you!

(Gary resumes)

Yeah, Duke loves everybody, especially you.
Duke loves everybody, especially you.
So when you get lonesome,
Remember it's true.
I love everybody, especially you.

It wasn't just Earl Pitts,
Ranger Bob or Big Fat.
And not just Synonymous,
Let me defecate on that.
The real reason you tuned in
And didn't get lost.
I was the only guy on the air
Who wasn't always pissed off.

I love everybody, especially you.
I love everybody, especially you.
So when you get lonesome,
Remember it's true.
I love everybody, especially you . . .

That was the end of the live show. Gary said his farewell after the song: "The BBC would like to thank everyone who listened and participated over the years. We were one hell of a warped think tank. And especially, I want to thank you all for getting it. When the comedy pie came flying at your face, you didn't blink. You took the hit. You tasted the apples inside, and spit out the worms. I couldn't ask for more. So to all of you I wish: *camarón en jugo de ajo.* For Duke Sinatra, Slim Tempo, and Rob Ervin, I'm Gary Burbank. Goodbye."

It was the perfect Burbank salutation: good will, good humor, and *camarón en jugo de ajo* – "shrimp in garlic sauce."

Epilogue

These days, Gary spends as much time as possible at his home in Florida. He fell in love with the river the first time he saw it, and still remembers Sean, just back from the Marine Corps, running up and down the clear waters in a johnboat fishing all day and not getting a single bite. When Gary asked him why he had not caught anything Sean said, "'Cause the water is so clear the fish can see me as easily as I can see them."

There, Gary spends his days with friends. They fish, play some golf, and float down the river. They tell stories and listen to the water slap against the boat. He spends some time in his studio each day writing and recording Earl Pitts segments, which remain in syndication. On many an evening, he and Nathan Witt sit on the dock playing their guitars and writing music. Several CDs are in the works and their band, Blue Run, has stirred audiences with a blend of blues and slammin' Memphis R&B.

He speaks to groups whenever he is asked and generally leaves them aching from laughter. He does love an audience.

Above all else, he spends as much time as he can with the girls, his grandchildren: Sean's daughters, Abigail, Rachel, and Morgan; and Tracy's little ones, Gracie and Claire.

The girls call their grandfather "Mopper," just one of those things that happens with kids, and though Abigail, Rachel, and Morgan have outgrown his stories, each Thursday evening Gary goes to the studio and calls Gracie and Claire and tells them tales from Ankle Valley.

The stories are filled with characters and funny voices. There are plot twists and life lessons. "All the characters live in Ankle Valley," Tracy says. "There's always a 'Fool's Gold Trail' and a 'Real Gold Trail' and the characters have to choose which one to take. The girls love the Ankle Valley stories."

The Ankle Valley stories, of course, come to Gary naturally.

Other voices

"One time we were at the cabin in Montana and he was reading *The Streets of Laredo*, the sequel to *Lonesome Dove*. I said, 'You musta really liked *Lonesome Dove*.' He said, 'Haven't read it yet.' I said, 'Then why are you reading the sequel first?' He said, ''Cause, I wanna know who gets killed in the first book. I don't want to get too attached to them.'

"I've been at the same television station (WBLZ in Baltimore) for over thirty years, and everything I do, everything I know comes from Gary Burbank."

—Marty Bass, television reporter for WJZ in Baltimore and host of Baltimore's number-one rated morning show

"I didn't think anything was good unless it came from LA or New York. I flip on the radio and I hear Gary Burbank. At first, I thought, 'Who is this idiot?' But then I started listening to him. And I couldn't stop listening to him. He was as good or better than anybody I'd ever heard. I'd be going from one meeting to another in LA and someone would get in the car. They'd say, 'Who's this.' I'd tell them and their reaction was always the same. They would look at me like I was nuts. Five minutes later, they were laughing their ass off and wouldn't get out of the car.

"I've often thought if I ever taught a class in comedy writing or sketch writing, I would take Gary's stuff and say, 'Here, this is how it's done, kids.'"

—Ken Levine, writer for *M*A*S*H, Cheers, and The Simpsons,* and radio fan

"You know, of course, that he is visited by the muse in the middle of the night. Yeah, when he's sleeping. He'll be laying there peaceful and all of a sudden just starts talking in voices, several of them. The first time it happened—we were on the road somewhere—I woke up and thought: 'What the hell is going on?' It's dark. I'm thinking somehow three old men had gotten in the room. I look over at the next bed and Gary's just jabbering away—sound asleep. That mind is a scary thing."

—Ken Boniface, MD and friend

"I've worked with a lot of people in radio. There are 'A,' 'B' and 'C' players. Most of us were 'C' players. There are very few 'A' players, just a small smattering—less today than ever. Gary was not only one of the 'A' players, he had something most of them didn't have, a great comic mind and an incredible gift for delivery and timing. The problem with Gary was that he was so good and so funny, you couldn't get your own work done."

—Jarl Mohn, president and CEO of E! Entertainment Television, president and general manager of MTV and VH1, and ex-jock

"The thing about Gary—from a national perspective—was that he was so consistent. Even on his off-days, he was top-level. He never played down. He never resorted to the expected. He was clever, smart, and he wanted you to come along. You either got Gary or you didn't, and if you didn't, it was your loss.

"His comedy was layered. There were tiers: first, second, and third, and that's exactly what most people in radio don't do. Their humor—when you can call it that—is superficial, smash mouth. Gary invited you to think."

—P.J. Bednarski, national television and radio critic

"Anytime I do an air talent seminar, I'll find a reason to play a bit by Gary Burbank. He takes his personal experience, blends it with a point of view, and adds his own perverse creative outlook. What comes out is something no one else would do. It may not be the best in the world, but it is certainly the only thing like it in the world, and often it *is* the best."

—Dan O'Day, author of *Personality Radio*, radio talent coach, and former major market radio personality

"Sure, Gary could have gone to Hollywood or New York. But it was important to him to be where he wanted to be and around the people he wanted to be around. I'm certain a lot of people feel cheated that he didn't go to Hollywood or New York. But that's just us being selfish. He did

things his way. We should all be so wise and resolute."
—Bob Moody, VP/Programming for Regent Communication, Inc. and member of the Country Music Radio Hall of Fame

"Gary's had as interesting a career as anybody out there. Most true creative people are shy and introspective, and Gary is, too, to a certain extent. But when he gets going, it's a sight to behold. He's one of radio's true greats."
—Herb McCord, president and CEO of Granum Communications

"When I think of Gary, I don't think about his success or how talented the man is—none of that. I think of my friend, the best friend a man could have."
—Len King, *faux* brother, former radio/TV executive for CNN

"Thank God for Gary Burbank. Now that Elvis is dead, bless his heart, Gary is the last surviving alien from the crash at Roswell."
—David Welch, schoolyard friend

"Gary Burbank gave so many people so much joy. He entertained millions of people. He gave them moments they will never forget. I loved the time Gary was with us. We were devastated when he left Detroit."
—Jo-Jo MacGregor

"He's my dad. I've been so lucky. I've been laughing all my life."
—Tracy Purser Songer

Bibliography

Brokaw, Tom. *Boom!* New York: Random House, 2007.

Fisher, Marc. *Something In The Air.* New York: Random House, 2007.

Gitlin, Todd. *The Sixties: Years of Hope, Days of Rage.* New York: Bantam Books, 1987.

Guralnick, Peter. *Last Train to Memphis: The Rise of Elvis Presley.* Boston. Little Brown: 1994.

—. *Lost Highway.* New York: Harper Perennial, 1989.

—. *Sweet Soul Music.* New York: Harper Perennial, 1989.

Halberstam, David. *The Fifties.* New York: Fawcett Columbine, 1993.

Nager, Larry. *Memphis Beat.* New York: St. Martin's Press, 1998.

Manchester, William. *The Glory and the Dream.* New York: Bantam Books, 1973.

Thompson, Hunter S., *Kingdom of Fear: Loathsome Secrets of a Star-Crossed Child in the Final Days of the American Century.* New York: Simon and Schuster, 2003.

Other Texts

Arendt, Hannah. *Between Past and Future,* New York: Viking Press, 1961.

Burke, James Lee. *Jesus Out to Sea,* New York: Simon & Schuster, 2007.

—. *The Lost Get-Back-Boogie,* New York: Simon & Schuster, 1986.

Gitlin, Todd. *The Sixties, Years of Hope, Days of Rage,* New York: Bantam Books, 1987.

Goldman, Albert & Schiller, Lawrence, *Lenny Bruce!!,* New York: Random House, 1971.

Junger, Sebastian. *A Death In Belmont. New York:* Harper Perennial, 2007.

Kaufmann, Walter. *The Portable Nietzsche,* New York: The Viking Press, 1954.

Krim, Seymour. *Shake It For the World, Smartass,* New York: Dial Press, Inc., 1970.

Leonard, Elmore. *Tishomingo Blues,* New York: HarperTorch, 2002.

Maynard, Lee. *Crum,* Morgantown: W. Virginia. West Virginia. University Press, 2001.

McMurtry, Larry. *Boone's Lick,* New York: Simon & Schuster, 2000.

—. *Lonesome Dove,* New York: Simon & Schuster, 1985.

—, Larry. *Streets of Laredo,* New York: Simon & Schuster, 1995.

Morris, Willie. *The Last of the Southern Girls (Voices of The South),* Baton Rouge: Louisiana State University Press, 1994.

Niebuhr, H. Richard. *The Responsible Self*, New York: Harper Row, 1963.

O'Conner, Flannery. *The Complete Stories,* New York: Farrar, Straus and Giroux, 1946.

—. *Wise Blood,* New York: Farrar, Straus and Giroux, 1949.

Porter, Katherine Anne. *The Leaning Tower,* New York: Dell, 1934.

Sloan, Bob. *Bearskin to Holly Fork, Stories from Appalachia,* Nicholasville, Kentucky: Wind Publications, 2003.

Welty, Eudora. *The Optimist's Daughter.* New York: Vintage International,1969.

Weston, John. *The Boy Who Sang The Birds,* New York: Charles Scribner's and Sons, 1976.

References

Cincinnati Gentlemen magazine; Cincinnati magazine; Cincinnati Public Library; CKLW (Windsor, Ontario/Detroit, Michigan); Detroit Public Library; Forest Headquarters, Kalispell, Montana; Holland Lake Lodge, Holland Lake, Montana; Hungry Horse/Glacier View, Hungry Horse, Montana; Jackson (Mississippi) Public Library; KUZN (West Monroe, Louisiana); Lolo, Montana, Visitor's Bureau; Louisville Public

Library; Louisville Historical Society; Memphis Chamber of Commerce; Memphis Historical Society; Memphis Public Library; Memphis Public Schools; Missoula, Montana, Visitor's Bureau; New Orleans Public Library; *Ohio magazine;* Spotted Bear Ranger District, Bigfork, Montana; Rock and Roll Hall of Fame and Museum (Cleveland, Ohio); Tally Lake Ranger District, Kalispell, Montana; *The Cincinnati Enquirer; The Cincinnati Post; The Cleveland Plain Dealer; The Columbus Dispatch; The Detroit Free Press; The Detroit News; The Louisville Courier-Journal; The Memphis Commercial Appeal; The New Orleans Times-Picayune; Variety;* WAKY (Louisville, Kentucky); WDIA (Memphis, Tennessee); WLW (Cincinnati, Ohio); WMPS (Memphis, Tennessee); *WHAS (Louisville, Kentucky); and* The National Association of Broadcasters.

Index

Greg Hoard came to Cincinnati in the winter of 1979 as a
member of the *Cincinnati Post* sports department where he was a feature
writer and columnist, joined the *Cincinnati Enquirer* in 1984 as Reds beat writer,
and has been a frequent contributor to *The Sporting News*, *Sports Illustrated*,
Baseball America, and *Baseball Digest*.
He was sports director at WLWT from 1990 through 1993 when he joined
Fox19 as sports director. His fifteen-year career in television perplexed his family
and closest friends. His late uncle, Ted Sebastian,
always said: "Just proves folks will watch about anything on TV."
In December 2004, after the publication of the best-selling *Joe, Rounding Third
and Heading for Home*, Hoard left television and returned to writing.
He is currently editor-in-chief of *Cincinnati Profile* magazine.
A native of the farmland of southern Indiana, Hoard lives on the west side
of Cincinnati with his wife Cindy and their three children:
Johnson, Beaux, and "The Meg."
He is currently completing a book on his personal experiences
with Cincinnati Reds legends.